That Dark Spring

After training as an archaeologist, Susannah Stapleton worked in museums and art galleries before becoming a historical researcher, unravelling mysteries for organisations and individuals. Her debut, *The Adventures of Maud West, Lady Detective*, was shortlisted for the CWA Gold Dagger for Non-Fiction. *That Dark Spring* is her second book. She lives in Shropshire with her husband and cat. When not writing, she enjoys creating literary automata and preparing specimens for her tiny natural history museum.

That Dark Spring

A True Story of Death and Desire in 1920s Provence

SUSANNAH STAPLETON

PICADOR

First published 2025 by Picador

This paperback edition first published 2026 by Picador
an imprint of Pan Macmillan
The Smithson, 6 Briset Street, London EC1M 5NR
EU representative: Macmillan Publishers Ireland Ltd, 1st Floor,
The Liffey Trust Centre, 117-126 Sheriff Street Upper,
Dublin 1 D01 YC43
Associated companies throughout the world

ISBN 978-1-5290-6558-9

Copyright © Susannah Stapleton 2025

The right of Susannah Stapleton to be identified as the
author of this work has been asserted in accordance
with the Copyright, Designs and Patents Act 1988.

The Picture Acknowledgements on pp. 377–8
constitute an extension of this copyright page.

All rights reserved. No part of this publication may be reproduced,
stored in a retrieval system, or transmitted, in any form or by any means
(including, without limitation, electronic, mechanical, photocopying, recording
or otherwise) without the prior written permission of the publisher.

Pan Macmillan does not have any control over, or any responsibility for,
any author or third-party websites (including, without limitation, URLs,
emails and QR codes) referred to in or on this book.

1 3 5 7 9 8 6 4 2

A CIP catalogue record for this book is available from the British Library.

Map artwork by Hemesh Alles

Typeset in Stempel Garamond LT Pro by Palimpsest Book Production Limited,
Falkirk, Stirlingshire
Printed and bound in the UK using 100% Renewable Electricity
by CPI Group (UK) Ltd

This book is sold subject to the condition that it shall not, by way of
trade or otherwise, be lent, hired out, or otherwise circulated without
the publisher's prior consent in any form of binding or cover other than
that in which it is published and without a similar condition including this
condition being imposed on the subsequent purchaser. The publisher does not
authorize the use or reproduction of any part of this book in any manner
for the purpose of training artificial intelligence technologies or systems.
The publisher expressly reserves this book from the Text and Data Mining
exception in accordance with Article 4(3) of the European Union
Digital Single Market Directive 2019/790.

Visit **www.picador.com** to read more about
all our books and to buy them.

For Jim

Contents

	A note from the author	ix
I.	The Ghosts of Les Baux	1
II.	Post Tenebras Lux	79
III.	A Matter of Time	177
IV.	The Eagle's Nest	237
V.	A L'Asard Bautezar!	293
	Appendix: Olive Branson's works	357
	Acknowledgements	361
	Sources	363
	Bibliography	365
	Notes	367
	Picture Acknowledgements	377

To begin at the beginning . . .
a note from the author

This is a work of non-fiction. As far as any account of a lost world can be, it is completely and provably true. All details, large or small, have been taken from the thousands of historical documents collected while researching the exuberant life and curious death of Olive Branson. These include personal diaries, letters and memoirs; police and judicial files; civic records; newspaper accounts; meteorological reports; photographs and artworks. Dialogue has been reconstructed from official documents and press reports. On occasion, the word perhaps, or similar, has been used. These *perhaps*es are based on known and reoccurring events or actions that are more likely than not to have been repeated at the time in question.

With that in mind, I invite you to settle back and join me in the wilds of interwar Provence for a tale that remains as perplexing today as it was in 1929.

Susannah Stapleton

It is not that Les Baux invites or embraces the stranger. It rather dares you to live there. It is France's haunted bedchamber, not only full of ghosts but a ghost itself.

Edith Shackleton Heald, 1929

«*La pierre tombe, l'âme reste.*»
'The stone falls; the soul remains.'

Paul Manivet, Provençal poet

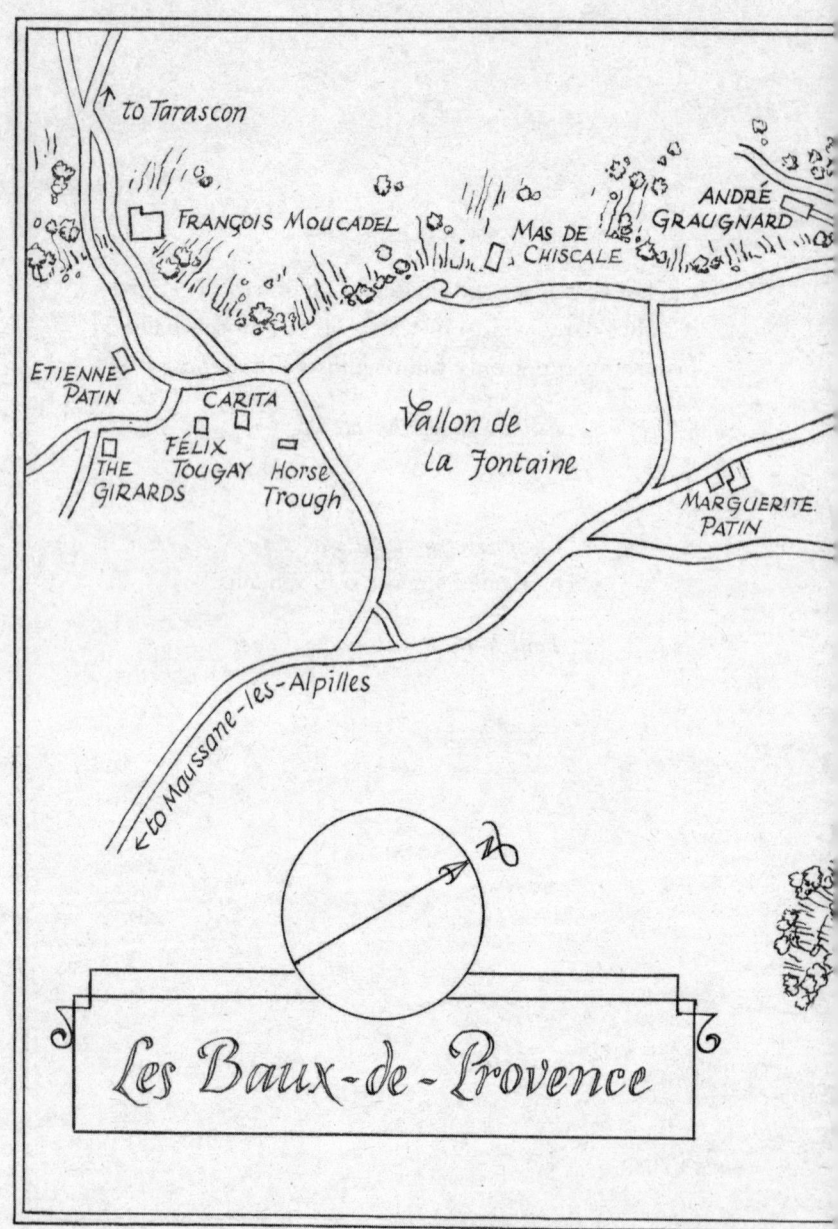

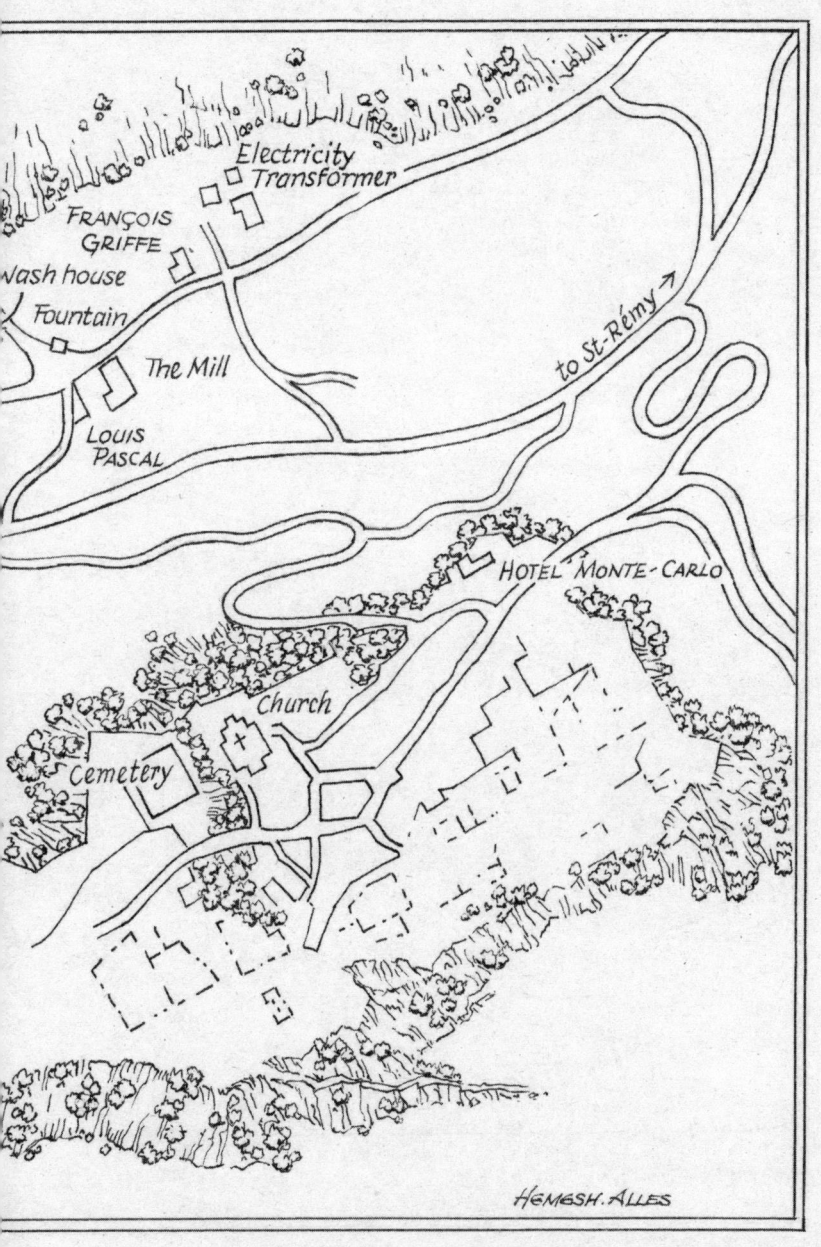

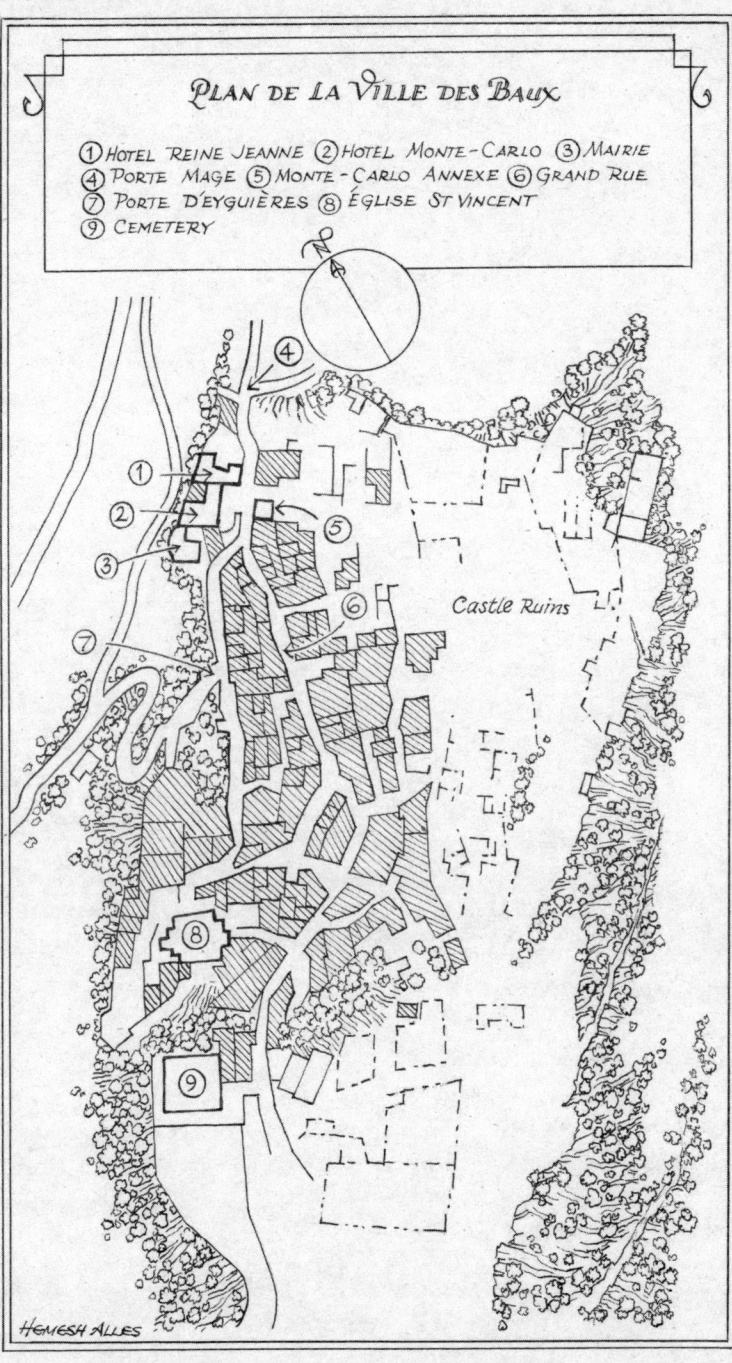

PART I:

THE GHOSTS OF LES BAUX

I

Les Baux-de-Provence, France
Evening, Saturday, 27 April 1929

The Anglaise was dead. It was inconvenient timing, but the villagers kept watch over her body as they would keep watch over any of their dead – at least, they tried.

The first convention to fall by the wayside was that which confined the deceased to his or her own bed until the day of the funeral. As the Anglaise had not died in her own bed, and her farmhouse had been sealed by the authorities, that had not been possible. Instead, they had brought her up to the village on a handcart, intending to lay her out in the little-used mortuary by the cemetery. Just as they were trundling the body along the ramparts, however, having struggled up through the Porte d'Eyguières, young François Pinet called them back and offered a room in the Hotel Monte-Carlo.

The small, family-run hotel was perched at the very edge of the medieval citadel. It had formed the centre of village life for as long as anyone could remember, its cafe and terrace providing the backdrop to endless trivial dramas, and the *grande salle* hosting feasts for every conceivable occasion. That it still did was thanks to the Anglaise herself, whose recent purchase and renovation of the buildings had saved it from being absorbed by the altogether more refined Hotel Reine Jeanne next door.

The bedroom in which they laid out her body held testament to the effort she had expended to rescue the hotel: the fact that the roof was not about to cave in was due to the architect she had engaged to sort out the sagging beams, while the fresh whitewash on the walls was there at her insistence, along with the cheerful blue on the shutters that had been pulled across the window outside. She'd even clambered up a ladder to paint the picture rails herself, in the same manner as she had attacked all the others in the hotel, which is to say somewhat testily, after dismissing the miserable Isnard, who had downed tools on the grounds that picture rails had not been specified in his contract.

No doubt her death had occasioned a few additional details to the room: a chair or two placed near the bed for the watchers, some black crape to cover the mirror, perhaps even a pious cluster of candles. But how far did they take tradition? Did they trouble to leave the window ajar, even though thunderstorms were rumbling across the plain and there had been opportunity aplenty for her soul to escape in the hours since her body had been pulled from the water? Did they maintain a respectful silence, despite all there was to discuss? It wasn't as though the Anglaise had family in the village, or even in France. There was nothing to mandate strict adherence to the rules.

In any event, no such rules applied in the hotel cafe. There, amid glasses of anisette and games of *cheville*,* the villagers would have been able to talk freely about the day's unexpected events. That they discussed the arrival of the gendarmes and the lengthy operation to retrieve the body is a given, but perhaps their tongues also turned to the more general, and perennially interesting, saga of the Anglaise and her ways.

Perhaps they recalled her arrival, how she had blown into Les Baux five years earlier, pale and withdrawn; how they had taken little notice at first as she placed herself quietly around the village,

---

* A local peg game.

settling down with her drawing board underneath the medieval *lanterne des morts* or by the remains of the Saracen's Tower. It was a common enough sight, after all. Artists seemed drawn to the unique melancholy and romance of Les Baux. There could hardly have been a sketchbook in Europe that didn't hold some approximation of the ruined château or a lonely olive tree posing in front of some craggy backdrop. But most left soon enough, defeated by the impossibility of capturing Les Baux's strange essence in graphite or wash.

The Anglaise, on the other hand, once settled into Madame Sous's *hostellerie*, had shown no desire to leave. She'd established a little studio and sent for her ageing greyhound, Spring. Together, woman and dog had soaked up the scent of wild thyme among the ruins and wandered the rocky hills and valleys. Well beyond the first flush of youth, the Anglaise had seemed set on a new beginning. Each day, she had grown browner from the sun and plumper from the meals served in the little courtyard of the Roi René. (Madame Sous and her husband were excellent cooks. One supper of 'tomatoes stuffed with sausage and cooked in olive oil and honey, tart and fragrant with the thyme and marjolaine of the mountain side' had even been immortalized in print by an appreciative American scholar.)[1]

Gradually, she had become part of the scenery. They had got used to the sight of her tall figure striding out towards the vast rocks of the Val d'Enfer, with her sketching kit slung over her shoulder and Spring by her side. Sometimes they'd spot her at night, shuffling along the narrow path to the communal *fumier* with her slop pail, or in the morning, folding herself into Louis Vigne's taxi to explore the backstreets of Tarascon or Arles. Occasionally, Vigne would drive her and Spring the thirty or so kilometres to Avignon to catch the fast train to Paris and on to London. But, over time, her visits home had become less and less frequent, until she was, if not a Baussenc (for she could never be that), then at least a permanent resident of Les Baux.

For all her eccentricities, the Anglaise had seemed to understand the essence of the village and what made it tick. She had taken to wearing wide Arlesian skirts and found herself a fine Camargue hat; she had bought the tumbledown Mas de Chiscale in the valley below and made it into a small but comfortable home.

True, they probably should have told her that the old farmhouse was prone to winter floods; mentioned, perhaps, that the reason it had been left to rot was because the water would cascade down from the hills, surge over the terraces and burst through one door of the kitchen and out the other. The problem was the rock against which the house was built. There was nothing to absorb the rain. Nevertheless, the Anglaise had stuck it out, limpet-like, diverting some of the water into a large cistern and commissioning various useless defences against the remainder, before simply abandoning the old kitchen altogether and squeezing her living quarters into the higher rooms.

She had proved herself to be charitable in nature, eased no doubt by the private income she enjoyed. Her biggest gesture, of course, had been the purchase of the Hotel Monte-Carlo after the death of old Pierre Pinet, thereby not only saving it – and, most importantly, its cafe – from inevitable gentrification, but also sparing the Pinet family's dignity. But there had also been many smaller favours. Just that last Christmas, for example, she had hosted the shepherds' annual lunch, on top of providing her usual sackful of gifts for the schoolchildren; and then there was the palaver of Marthe Patin's lengthy hospital treatment, which she had arranged and paid for despite the raging of Etienne Patin, who'd wanted his wife at home to look after their young daughter.

Yet, the Anglaise had also endured her own share of hardship, of the kind that no amount of money could prevent and which she had borne silently and privately behind the thick walls of Mas de Chiscale. The day's events had been testament enough to that, although there had been signs of her inner disquiet before: the rest cure she had taken with the nuns at Sault, for example, or the time she had lost all her hair (for months, her scalp had been raw beneath her headscarf, with just two silver ringlets that Marie-Thérèse Girard had managed to salvage hanging from her temples like ribbons). Some said it was a nervous disorder left over from the war, others that it was simply her time of life, but no one knew for sure. Whatever the cause, the Anglaise had always tired easily. Sometimes they wouldn't see her for days on end.

As to the arguments and petty feuds, who in Les Baux hadn't felt the heat of her fury at one point or another? The Anglaise had never been one to let things lie. In all likelihood, however, the cafe dwellers of the Hotel Monte-Carlo would have left those tales, along with other more delicate matters, for another day. Surely, even the people of Les Baux knew it was no time to speak ill of the dead?

II

It would be said repeatedly over the following months that, to understand the Baussencs, one first had to know something of their history and the source of their stubborn pride. The name of Les Baux itself was derived from the Provençal *baus*, meaning a rocky spur or precipice. The *baus* in question was a small limestone outcrop that jutted out from the Alpilles – the 'Little Alps' – high above the vast, alluvial plains of the Crau. Whipped though it was by the legendary winds of Provence, this craggy little spot had been inhabited since Neolithic times.

The site was a natural fortress. Its strategic position allowed for defence from all sides and provided a view fifty kilometres south to the azure shores of the Mediterranean. At the western foot of the escarpment lay a narrow, fertile valley with a spring, affording a secure supply of crops and water in times of siege. Antiquarians had unearthed various clues in the vicinity as to Les Baux's distant past: flint blades and stone axes; a Bronze Age burial ground; a Phocaean Greek cemetery; traces of a Ligurian Celtic settlement and the larger camps of their Gallo-Roman successors.

Les Baux's heyday, however, had been in the Middle Ages. By that time the Baux valley had passed into the hands of the Catholic Church and formed part of the Bishopric of Arles (the city lying about fifteen kilometres to the south-west). In the late tenth century, the powerful Archbishop Manasses gave the land to one of his chief administrators, a man by the name of Isnard. It was a gift the archbishop would come to regret. Isnard, a ruthless tactician, constructed a small castle on the Baux plateau and promptly set about seizing more land, aided by a relative called Pons the Elder. The pair's merciless plundering not only saw them excommunicated from the Church, but also set a precedent for the manner in which their fledgling dynasty would continue.

Over the years, Pons' and Isnard's much-feared descendants – the lords of Baux – would justify their bellicosity with a heavy dose of mythmaking. In a linguistic sleight of hand, they would claim lineage from Balthazar (*Bautezar* in Provençal), one of the three wise men of the Bible. After leaving his gift of myrrh with the infant Jesus, or so their story went, Balthazar had continued following the Star of Bethlehem all the way to Provence, where it had stopped once more, directly above the Baux plateau. To proclaim this God-given heritage, the lords of Baux adopted as their emblem a shimmering, sixteen-pointed star, under which banner they took part in the Crusades and waded into the endless power struggles at play in Provence, with the dreaded battle cry of *'A l'asard Bautezar!'* ('To chance, Balthazar!') heralding their arrival.

At its height, the House of Baux controlled nearly eighty towns and villages in the region, including Marseille and Orange. The dynasty was also connected by marriage with noble and royal families throughout Europe, from Monaco to Albania. In the twelfth century, one such connection – and a subsequent disagreement over inheritance rights – led to civil war in Provence, with the House of Baux and its allies taking on the ruling House of Barcelona. The Baussenque Wars did not end well for Les Baux. In 1162, the original castle was destroyed and the surrounding land laid waste.

The lords of Baux, however, refused to be beaten. They built a bigger castle and re-entered the fray. Over the years, as their fortunes waxed and waned, they would periodically adapt their money-making strategies. At least one lord took to piracy, using as his base the port of Cassis; others terrorized the region through banditry and kidnapping, stuffing the castle full of wealthy victims awaiting ransom and tipping those who proved unprofitable over the walls onto the rocks below.

Some modern Baussencs still claimed they could trace their lineage straight back through these robber barons to Pons and Isnard, but a deeper pride came from their cultural heritage and the reputation that the medieval House of Baux had enjoyed as a centre for chivalry and romance.

In the late fourteenth and early fifteenth centuries, Les Baux had exemplified the epitome of a cultured existence. The castle halls, resplendent in tapestries and oriental rugs, played host to sumptuous feasts of wild boar and venison plucked from nearby hunting grounds, and resounded with the great stamping songs and plaintive melodies of the finest troubadours. Outside, the crowds gathered for raucous bullfights and jousts. On quieter days, the noblewomen were said to hold their own form of games: the fabled Courts of Love, in which, armed with guides such as Ovid's *Ars amatoria*, they would gather in their finery to judge matters of the heart.

But the glory days of the House of Baux were numbered. In 1426, in a bedchamber in the castle's north tower, Alix des Baux, the last direct descendent of the dynasty that had enjoyed Balthazar's celestial protection for over 400 years, exhaled her last. With no immediate heir, the title was passed around until it landed on the Count of Provence, otherwise known as Good King René, the erstwhile ruler of Naples. In 1481, Provence itself was inherited by Louis XI of France and incorporated into the

French crown estate. There followed a period of peaceful prosperity for Les Baux, with the castle undergoing restoration and genteel residences being erected in the new Renaissance style.

Yet, behind those elegant facades, more trouble was brewing. The French crown was Catholic, and Les Baux – like much of Provence – had often struggled against papal authority. During the Reformation, it soon developed into a Protestant stronghold. This came to a head during the French Wars of Religion in the late sixteenth century, when the citadel became an outright supporter of rebellions against the crown.

Les Baux's final downfall came during the Thirty Years War. In 1631, Louis XIII, as part of his bid to stamp out further Protestant uprisings, attempted to dissolve the regional parliament at Aix-en-Provence, prompting a revolt led by his brother, the Duke of Orléans. Upon defeat, many of the rebels fled to the trusty fortress of Les Baux. The following summer, the king dispatched his chief minister of state, Cardinal Richelieu, to end the scourge of Les Baux once and for all.

Richelieu's men made camp on a nearby hill and subjected the 'eagle's nest', as the Cardinal called it, to a month-long battery of gunpowder and fury, destroying the castle and almost everything – and everyone – within its walls. By the end of the ordeal, it was said, some survivors willingly took up their pickaxes to help dismantle the last of Les Baux's fortifications.

And so the site had remained ever since. The grandeur of Les Baux was no more. Its mutilated remains began to crumble back into the earth. Silver tufts of sea ragwort sprang up in the cracks of the old city walls, and nettles guarded the base of the cliff. Forlorn reminders of the past lay everywhere: in the haggard, roofless buildings covered with ivy; in the gaping cellars open to the sky; in the sounds of rotten doors creaking and banging in the wind. A particularly poignant relic stood among the remains of one large residence: a bare, mullioned window inscribed with the Calvinist motto *'Post Tenebras Lux'* ('After darkness, light').

It was a humbling sight. Les Baux had once been home to thousands of souls; their footsteps had worn down the threshold of the twelfth-century church and their carriages had left deep grooves in the streets. By the beginning of the nineteenth century, the population had fallen to a light-footed 500. The latest census, taken in 1926, had recorded just 80 in the village itself, with a further 140 on the farms below.

Yet, perhaps old Balthazar was still keeping a watchful eye on his chosen people, for two things prevented Les Baux from sliding entirely into obscurity. The first was relatively benign: the discovery in 1821 of a reddish-purple rock in the vicinity, which proved to be rich in aluminium. It was duly named bauxite, a name that would spread throughout the world as further deposits, and new extraction processes, transformed aluminium from a rare and precious metal to an essential component of everyday life.

The second was either a blessing or a curse, depending on one's point of view. Les Baux's magnificent past, and equally magnificent decay, had been drawing sightseers for over a century. At first, this was just a few hardy Romantics, blown off course from the traditional grand tour, who journeyed over the hills and along rutted tracks to commune with the lords of yesteryear. But, as the roads were improved and the motor car took hold, a visit to the *ville morte* became an essential component of a trip to Provence.

Some had thought the appetite for ruins would diminish following the Great War, that the time-honoured fascination would be overpowered by memories of towns and villages in the north burned and bombed to blackened rubble, of windows blown out like eye sockets, and loved ones similarly annihilated. But that ignored the psychological balm that a place like Les Baux could provide. Broken yet inhabited, it was an unspoken testament to the human spirit, a tale of shattered dreams and ploughing on regardless. It was life at its bittersweet core, writ large in golden, crumbling stone. It put things into perspective.

By the 1920s, summer day-trippers would arrive in small hordes, clambering down from charabancs put on by the Paris–Lyon–Méditerranée railway and other excursion companies. The Baussencs as a whole did their best to ignore this seasonal invasion. A few stepped forward as tour guides, welcoming the opportunity to earn a few extra francs; others set up honesty boxes for jars of olives or the postcards they sold on behalf of printers from Arles and Avignon. Most, however, just erected signs that said *Private!* or *Do not disturb the snails!* and got on with their daily lives. Apart from the two hotels and Madame Sous's *hostellerie*, the amenities on offer remained stubbornly limited to the Pinets' morning *boulangerie*, tucked away down a side street by the main

Les Baux in 1929, showing the rear of the Hotel Monte-Carlo and the town walls.

entrance to the village, and a small tobacconist near the church. Even the cafes – that is, the bar of the Hotel Monte-Carlo and another, more earthy affair, run by Madame Pinet's long-suffering brother – were not entirely welcoming to outsiders.

The Baussenc aversion to hospitality was widely acknowledged. Indeed, in 1926, *Les Tablettes d'Avignon et de Provence*, a weekly magazine devoted to regional tourism, had published a damning assessment of the local psyche, painting a portrait of an embittered and insular population nursing a 300-year-old grudge:

> ... one shouldn't expect to find the enthusiastic and carefree spirit of the Provençal soul here. This semi-literate population is both timid and proud. The Baussencs are not particularly welcoming to tourists ... They listen to the cries of wonder with scepticism. What do they care about the romantic sight of their ruins? They are still tormented by Richelieu's punishment.
>
> This spirit of wild and harsh distrust is evident in relations between individuals. Disputes frequently arise over trivial matters. Two neighbours quarrel about a right of view or a right of way. The incident usually ends up in court ...
>
> This is how life goes on in the old capital of Les Baux. Today, the descendants of that 'race of young eagles, never in bondage'* are ... buried in the rubble of their own town, where memories of the Past erase the Present.[1]

All this could perhaps be attributed to the fact that, save for a few sympathetic incomers and the odd prudent marriage, the population of Les Baux comprised one large family. For hundreds

---

* A quote from the Nobel laureate Frédéric Mistral's epic poem, *Calendau* (1867), referring to Cardinal Richelieu's description of Les Baux as an 'eagle's nest'.

of years, the Graugnards had married the Moucadels who had married the Quenins who had married the Cornilles who had married the Tougays and so on, each person descended in multiple ways from the contrary souls who had refused to leave after Richelieu had done his worst. It was said to have kept the resentment alive in their veins. More fundamentally, however venomous their inter-familial squabbles became, it kept them united against one common enemy: the outside world.

III

It was Joseph Girard who had found the body. A small man in his early thirties, with chestnut hair and blue eyes, Joseph was not a native of Les Baux but the son of a butcher from nearby Saint-Rémy. He had moved to the village in 1922 after marrying Marie-Thérèse, one of the stocky, dark-haired Pinet siblings. The pair now had three daughters, the youngest of whom was just seven months old.

The Girards had been working for the Anglaise for nearly two years by the time of her death, with Joseph taking on the gardening and other heavy work, and Marie-Thérèse the cooking and cleaning. They had also recently taken over the management of the Hotel Monte-Carlo, which the Anglaise had bought from Marie-Thérèse's family.

There are three things worth noting about Joseph Girard. Firstly, he was a kind and industrious soul and had been welcomed in Les Baux despite his status as an *étranger*. Secondly, he lived for his family. He could be lost without them. Early in her last pregnancy, for example, Marie-Thérèse had fallen gravely ill and had been swept off to Saint-Didier for treatment and bed rest. With their daughters Pierrette and Mireille taken in by relatives elsewhere, Joseph had been left alone to fret about whether Marie-Thérèse was being properly cared for, whether she needed clean linen, whether the baby would survive, and so on. Somewhat out of character, he had started to drink heavily. Only a series of stern chats from the Anglaise, whose stock of cognac had begun to suffer, had dragged him back to sobriety.

Thirdly – and, for our immediate purposes, most importantly – Joseph loved to talk. He would talk to anyone: to the farmers in the valley, to his fellow villagers in the streets or in the bar of the Hotel Monte-Carlo – even, in a very un-Baux-like manner, to strangers.

By the time of the trial, some nine months later, Joseph would have recounted the tale of his morbid discovery so many times, both voluntarily and otherwise, that one might have expected him to have perfected its telling. Indeed, that would be the assumption of many of the spectators who travelled to Aix-en-Provence to witness the proceedings. There would even be a small wave of excitement when he was called to the stand.

The case would attract an extraordinary amount of attention for such a parochial affair. This was due not only to the twists and turns the case would take on its way to Aix, but also to a more general fascination with the Anglaise herself and the eerie backwater she had made her home. Olive Branson – for that was her name – certainly made an intriguing victim, not least because not everyone would be satisfied that she was a victim at all. Murder or suicide? That would be the question – still *is* the question – and, in an attempt to answer it, many turned to her colourful past and eccentric spinsterhood for clues.

Joseph, of course, had known the minutiae of Olive Branson's life in Les Baux better than most. It was therefore inevitable that his testimony would be keenly anticipated. As soon as he opened his mouth, however, it would become clear that Joseph's enthusiasm for public speaking was not matched by any noticeable talent. His words – and there were many – would dribble from his tongue in a lifeless drone, with no detail seemingly too small to be inflicted on the airless court. 'Dismal,' the press would note. 'Monotonous verbiage.'[1]

His account of finding the body was a case in point. Those present were well aware that Olive Branson had been found submerged in the water cistern in her garden at two o'clock in the afternoon, yet Joseph chose to begin with his arrival at her house some seven hours earlier.

Olive Branson's photograph on the cover of *Détective* magazine, 16 May 1929.

It had been a fine spring day – a Saturday – when he'd approached Mas de Chiscale at quarter past seven. There had been no immediate signs that anything was amiss: when he whistled for the dogs, they came to the gate, eager as always for their morning walk, and the house was just as Miss Branson always left it before going to bed, with the door to her studio strung open to allow the dogs free rein and the window of the adjoining bedroom off the latch.

Mas de Chiscale, May 1929.

This arrangement of doors and windows had once been a matter of contention between Joseph and the Anglaise: Mas de Chiscale was fairly isolated and he'd worried for her safety. But Olive Branson had been a firm believer in fresh air and was adamant that the dogs provided more than adequate protection. It was hard to argue on that last point. Frida was part Great Dane and part wolf-dog, and her two-year-old pups – Marcel, Tony and

Fly – would become a swirling mass of teeth and hackles if confronted by a stranger. So, yes, the door and window had been open and the dogs had been loose.

Yet, when Joseph had called up – 'Good morning, Mademoiselle!' – there had been no reply. Usually, Miss Branson would be sitting up in bed by the time he arrived, eating her breakfast (two buttered eggs and a *café crème* prepared on her portable oil stove), and would respond with a small shout. But he'd thought little of her silence. As he'd already explained – at some length – she had been out of sorts since her return from England, and he'd assumed she was still asleep. So, after gathering the dogs' leads from the kitchen and collecting the empty milk bottle from the side, Joseph had assembled Frida and the pups and headed out to Carita, the neighbouring farm.

Dogs, eggs, milk bottles... Understandably, Joseph's testimony had a soporific effect in the already stuffy courtroom. Two of the jurors nodded off completely, their lunch sitting heavy in their bellies. Even Juror Six, who had marked himself out as something of an amateur sleuth, started to flag. The president of the court, however, being in no position to let his mind wander, had no choice but to absorb the full, flaccid force of Joseph's interminable account. At one point, he would explode, 'Hurry up and get to the cistern!' and Joseph would reply, 'Monsieur le juge, I'm still a *long* way from the cistern,' and there were hoots of laughter and the president attempted to clear the court, none of which endowed Joseph with the ability – thus far elusive – of getting to the point.

And so, on he ploughed, through the purpose of his visit to the Carita farmyard (to drop off the milk bottle), who he had met along the way (his brother-in-law Louis Vayssière and the farmers Félix Tougay and Louis Graugnard), what they had discussed (the upcoming municipal elections) and his subsequent walk with the dogs (rambling).

It was only after he'd returned at half past eight and released the dogs back into the yard that Joseph had begun to suspect something was wrong. When he approached the studio with a handful of wood to light the fire, he noticed a napkin draped across a planter outside the door. Stepping inside, he saw the remains of Miss Branson's supper still on the table. Her handbag sat by the foot of her chair and, there by the hearth, untouched, were the two pots of water he'd warmed for her evening toilette the night before.

'Hullo, Mademoiselle?' A note of panic had crept into his voice as he edged his head around the bedroom door. The bed had not been slept in, although the clothes Miss Branson had been wearing the previous day were on the chair and her silver wristwatch and rings had been placed on the dresser. It wasn't unknown for her to walk the dogs in her dressing gown or throw on her cape and go sketching in the moonlight if the mood took her, but the dogs had been in the yard and her cape was still on its hook.

It was then that Joseph had noticed that the side drawer of the dressing table was open. The Anglaise had shown him what she kept in that drawer once, and he'd snuck back later for a closer look. The old nickel-plated Orbea Hermanos had been heavy and familiar in his hand; it was the type of revolver they'd used during the war. That morning, though, the drawer had been empty apart from a cardboard box of ammunition. The box, he discovered, was no longer full.

He'd rushed back to Carita to intercept his brother-in-law, Louis Vayssière. Together, they'd done another sweep of the fields with the dogs and scoured every inch of the property: the cellar, the kitchen, the studio and bedroom, the terraces and orchard, even the little privy tucked away under the overhanging rocks next to the cistern.

The cistern? No, they hadn't looked in the cistern itself at that point – or, rather, Joseph had given it a brief glance but had noticed nothing unusual.

A map of Les Baux would be given to the jurors, with important locations and the distances between them marked in red ink. Had they been so inclined, they could have followed Joseph's subsequent journey back to his own house – marked as 200 metres away – to collect his motorcycle, and then the kilometre past vineyards and olive groves and up the steep, winding track to the village and the infamous Hotel Monte-Carlo.

Ever since Miss Branson had bought the hotel from his wife's family, Joseph would explain, they had kept a room at her disposal. She had used it when she couldn't face the walk home – if it was raining heavily, for example, or the mistral was particularly fierce. She had also transferred some of her art equipment there, as working at Mas de Chiscale had become all but impossible with the dogs and her new parrot (an ill-mannered Amazon named Jacquot), not to mention the swallows nesting in the rafters that she indulged by keeping the window open.

But Joseph had found her room empty. The whole hotel was deserted, in fact, except for his niece Madeleine Vayssière, who'd been hovering by the reception desk.

He'd then walked round to the home of Andrée Sous, the antiques dealer, who lived on what passed for Les Baux's *grand rue*. Olive Branson had stayed at Madame Sous's *hostellerie* when she'd first arrived and the two had, for the most part, been friends ever since. Andrée Sous and her husband Jean listened to Joseph's concerns, but knew nothing of Miss Branson's whereabouts. Their only advice – and something he'd already thought of – was to call the taxi driver Louis Vigne in Saint-Rémy: if the Anglaise had left the village for any reason, she would have taken one of his cars.

There was a telephone back at the hotel. After the operator had put Joseph through to the Vigne household, the driver's mother-in-law answered. Yes, indeed, Louis had been called out, Madame Jarmasson said. She didn't know by whom or where they had wanted to go, but they had specifically requested his roadster. Joseph begged her to find out whether that person was the Anglaise and to call him back as a matter of urgency. Leaving Madeleine in charge of the telephone, he got back on his motorbike and returned to the valley to attend to the animals.

The president of the court would interrupt him again as he was launching into yet another diversion, this time regarding the black mare that Olive Branson had planned to sell days before her death (its pitiful origins, its knees, its rehabilitation through daily lungeing, and so on). The court had no desire to hear about horses. Joseph would try again, describing his care of Frida and the pups, but the president was in no mood for a sermon on dog food, either.

The next creatures to appear in Joseph's tale were more to the court's liking: members of the Pinet family. As he would explain, his young brother-in-law's open-top Renault had pulled up outside the gate at about eleven o'clock. François had taken his sisters to Arles on a provisioning trip and was dropping off Marie-Thérèse so she could start her daily chores at Mas de Chiscale.

Rushing to meet them, Joseph brought them up to speed on the morning's events. The older sister, Marguerite Vayssière, stayed in the car, trapped in the dickey seat by assorted baskets and packages, but François and Marie-Thérèse joined him for another round of the house and garden. After ten or fifteen minutes, they agreed that François and his sisters would carry on up to the village, while Joseph took the dogs out for one last search of the valley. They would then all meet back at the hotel, in the hope that Madame Jarmasson had called.

Madame Jarmasson had not called.

Not wanting to wait any longer, Joseph persuaded François to drive him to Saint-Rémy so he could track down Louis Vigne himself. As François's car had been running low on petrol after the trip to Arles, they made a detour south to the pump at Maussane before heading up the long, twisting road to Saint-Rémy.

Twenty minutes later, the Renault drew up outside Louis Vigne's home on the Boulevard Mirabeau. The chauffeur, whose rotund form the court would have the opportunity to appreciate later in the proceedings, had returned from his call and was eating lunch with his family. But he had not seen nor heard from the Anglaise since driving her home from the station at Avignon the previous weekend.

Joseph and François's next stop, at half past twelve, was the gendarmerie on the Boulevard Gambetta. There, they found the head of the barracks, Sergeant Fabre, in the foyer and explained the situation once more. Joseph did most of the talking, as François had a tendency towards muteness when away from his usual haunts. On hearing voices, the young gendarme Roujon had also come down the stairs. Sergeant Fabre suggested that he and Roujon accompany the men back to Les Baux, as soon as he'd eaten his lunch.

As the resources of the Saint-Rémy gendarmerie did not extend to a motor car, Fabre proposed they take the Renault. But François demurred: it was only a three-seater and had weak springs; even if they did all manage to pile in, the old six-horsepower engine would struggle to make the climb up to Les Baux. Besides, he couldn't wait for Fabre to eat, as he had an important errand to run.

Between Fabre's stomach, François's springs and Joseph's anxiety, they had soon reached stalemate. Fortunately, at that point, Louis Vigne turned up and offered to drive the gendarmes in one of his own cars, and François and Joseph returned to Les Baux alone.

Back at the hotel, Joseph had grabbed a quick bite to eat in the kitchen before taking his motorbike back down to Mas de Chiscale. As he passed the public washhouse in the valley, he spotted Félix Tougay rinsing himself down and crunched to a halt, calling out to alert the farmer to the imminent arrival of the gendarmes. He did the same when he passed the road-mender, André Graugnard.

After securing Frida and pacifying the pups with more food, Joseph surveyed the yard and realized there was one place he hadn't looked.

The cistern.

IV

Sergeant Fabre had instructed Louis Vigne to stop discreetly in Les Baux to collect the mayor before heading down to the valley. As he saw it, there was no point calling attention to the matter until they were absolutely sure that the Anglaise was missing. When the car arrived at Mas de Chiscale just after two o'clock, however, Fabre saw that a small group had already gathered at the top of the garden.

Joseph Girard broke away from his friends and rushed towards the car. He was carrying a long branch, torn from a tree.

'We've just found her . . . She's in the cistern.'

Fabre would later state that Girard's throat was tight as he said this and there had been tears in his eyes as he looked down at the branch, struggling for words. 'I just touched the body . . .'

Sergeant Fabre was familiar with Mas de Chiscale. It stood on a steep slope at the edge of the valley. The garden, like the house, was split into three levels. A wide path zigzagged up from the dirt yard and formed three small terraces, each supported by a rough stone wall jutting out from the house. Fruit trees traced the path's route at random intervals.

At the very top, built against the rock, was the cistern: a large trapezoid structure, faced in stone. Everyone in the valley had one like it to collect rainwater, even those lucky enough to have found a reliable spring on their land. Most of the tanks had been in situ for decades, if not centuries, but this one was a recent addition, having been commissioned by the Anglaise shortly after she moved in.

Fabre also recognized the farmers gathered beside it: Ricaud, Vayssière and Tougay, along with the Spanish farmhand Vincent Aracil. No doubt more would arrive in due course. This was, after all, Les Baux, and news travelled fast. He knew these people; he understood the rural frame of mind.

A valley boy himself, Fabre had grown up in a farming family in the Basse-Alpes. The daily grind these men endured, or one very like it, would have been his daily grind, and their reliance on gossip his reliance, had he not glimpsed freedom as a young man while completing his military service in the cavalry. After that, he'd turned his back on the plodding workhorses of the farm and opted instead for a succession of marginally sleeker models by joining the Gendarmerie Nationale. He and his various steeds had trotted their way up the ranks until – just after his forty-fifth birthday, four years earlier – he'd been appointed head of the barracks in Saint-Rémy.

Now, taking charge, Fabre followed the path up to the cistern and ushered the men aside. The Anglaise's dogs were making a racket at the bottom of the yard, so he ordered Joseph Girard to shut them in the cellar.

The cistern was larger than it seemed from the yard. He estimated it was about eight metres wide and jutted out from the rock by about three metres. It was high, too. He wasn't a small man, but the top came up to his nose.

A ladder was resting against the side. After climbing up, Fabre found the tank was almost entirely covered with heavy stone flags. The only part exposed to the elements was a narrow strip at the rear, which caught the rainwater as it ran off the rock. This was covered by a wire mesh set inside a heavy iron grille. One small section of the grille – that nearest the house – was partially raised. On closer inspection, Fabre saw that it could be lifted out altogether, to allow access for maintenance. He placed it to one side and peered into the water. He could just make out a dark mass against the back wall.

Taking the thick branch from Joseph Girard, he lowered it through the opening and felt around. After some manoeuvring, he managed to hook it underneath the mass and heave upwards. A woman's head and torso emerged from the depths. It was pale and rigid, the eyes and mouth closed. In the middle of the forehead, just above the brow, was a clean bullet wound oozing blood.

Fabre let the body sink back down. It was the Anglaise all right. He dispatched Louis Vigne to fetch Dr Cot from Maussane and inform the justice of the peace.

Fabre's immediate problem was one of logistics. How to get the body out of the water? They couldn't simply reach in and pull it out. Although the head and shoulders were almost within reach, the rest was stretched out under the fixed part of the grille. As the rear of the cistern sat beneath a low, rocky overhang, the geometry simply didn't work. Nor could the grille be easily dismantled: the iron girders had been fixed directly into the rock face and also ran underneath the stone flags, which were themselves cemented in place.

The first thing, Fabre decided, was to drain the water. The tank was two thirds full, so it would take some time, but at least they'd have a better view of what they were dealing with. Yet, opening the tap at the far side of the cistern only produced a slow trickle. He called for an axe to sever the pipe. This improved things slightly, but the water still lacked any force.

While they waited, a few of the farmers told Fabre that they'd heard a gunshot the previous evening, just as it was getting dark.

None of them had thought anything of it: gunshots weren't uncommon in a rural valley. Only now did they realize its significance.

Almost everyone agreed that the Anglaise's spirits had seemed low all week. She had just returned from a visit to England, and whatever had happened there appeared to have diminished her. Whenever people had passed the house in recent days and seen her in the garden – stretched out on her deckchair, either dozing or reading a book – she had been unwilling to engage in her usual conversation.

Everything certainly pointed towards suicide, although Fabre preferred to wait until the doctor had examined the body before reaching any firm conclusion. In the meantime, he decided to look inside the house. He called for his gendarme Roujon to join him.

The house had a strange layout. Not as strange as some up in the village, where the homes had been haphazardly carved out of the ruins, but still odd in the way it was stacked up on its steep plot. Its whitewashed facade was fairly sizeable, but Olive Branson had only occupied half the space: just three rooms. The lowest and largest level – once a fine, old kitchen with rooms above – had been put over to rough storage and the occasional hardy guest.

There were three ways in. One blue door – that nearest the cistern – led into her living quarters, while two others on the lower terraces opened into the old and new kitchens respectively. Fabre and Roujon entered at the top of the house, stepping directly into Olive Branson's studio.

As they'd both had occasion to visit the artist while she was alive, they knew what to expect. It was a mess. Apparently, Louis Vayssière had recently moved a cartload of equipment up to a new studio at the Hotel Monte-Carlo for her, but the room was still full to bursting. Every surface was piled with clutter, and what they could see of the floor was filthy, dotted with bird droppings, ink and the odd cigarette end. Dark cobwebs, furred thick with dust, clung to the ceiling joists and crept down from the corners; the unadorned walls were stained with damp. A small, green parrot squawked at the interlopers from his cage.

The right-hand wall was almost entirely taken up by a monumental stone fireplace, its surround black with soot; the other walls were abutted by an assortment of heavy, dark furniture on which had been piled various books and papers, etching plates and drawing boards. Opposite the door, the star-shaped wheel of a large printing press rose up from behind a table, the bed of the machine itself obscured by an old tablecloth. Rags, metallic tubes of ink, and tools of unknown use were strewn nearby.

That Olive Branson had been an unrestrained collector was clear from the mismatched shades of the kerosene lamps dotted around the room and the jumble of objects on the shelves below the large arched window, where Buddhas and African figurines fought for space with bronze animals, decorative pottery and cheap Provençal trinkets. Balanced on the high mantel were three giant blocks of ornate stonework, salvaged from some long-crumbled local monument. The largest – nearly four feet long – depicted Christ and two saints.

Fabre's attention, however, was drawn towards the middle of the room, where a small table covered with a chequered cloth held the remains of Olive Branson's last meal. Looking down, he noted the shrivelled asparagus ends on the side of the plate and the greasy smears where the meat had been, the little dish of butter, the limp, blackened banana skin and the untouched apple. A bottle of wine stood behind the serving dishes, along with a glass containing a few dark, crusty dregs.

To the left of the plate, next to a pair of spectacles, was an open book. Fabre picked it up. It was in English. Of more interest was the soft leather handbag, which stood by the leg of the chair. He emptied it out: various toiletries and a handkerchief; a purse containing 1,739 francs in banknotes and small change; a small, black pocket diary and the Anglaise's identity papers.

The beige *carte d'identité* said Edith May Olive Branson had been born in Madras on 14 August 1884, making her forty-four. The accompanying photograph was a studio portrait, posed with care and professionally finished to give a dewy tone to the skin – a cut above the startled mugshots that gendarmes usually saw. Her papers had been issued just four years earlier, in May 1925, but the intervening years had not been kind. The woman in the photograph looked much younger than the one they knew, with brown hair, not grey, and wearing a flowing silk jacket more suited to a Parisian *salon* than the wilds of Provence.

Olive Branson's identity card.

Fabre told Roujon to gather up the cash and turned his attention to the rest of the house.

A door to the right of the fireplace led across the top of the staircase and into the bedroom. This room was less cluttered than the studio, although hundreds of books were crammed onto the wooden shelves that ran around the room at ceiling height, and there were curios and discarded pieces of jewellery on every surface. Still, it seemed Marie-Thérèse Girard had been allowed in to dust and have a go at the floor: the herringbone pattern of the linoleum was quite visible towards the centre of the room.

There was a tall single bed in the far corner. The last time the gendarmes had been in that room, Olive Branson had been ill and was propped up on the pillows like a dowager duchess, offering a 4,000-franc reward to catch a perpetrator she refused to name, for an incident that had not yet happened. As no crime had ever materialized, the visit was filed away with the other times they'd been summoned to Mas de Chiscale – over wilful damage to some olive trees by her neighbour Moucadel, for example, and a complaint about hunters letting their bullets ricochet off the rocks above the cistern. Such incidents didn't usually fall under the remit of the gendarmerie, but as Les Baux had been without a *garde champêtre* for some time, they'd been duty-bound to respond. On each occasion, they had listened to her concerns and offered support should matters escalate.

Now, Fabre walked over to the bed, moved aside the bolster and pulled back the taut covers. The protective top sheet was covered in dog hair – as were the large floor cushions scattered around the room – but everything else seemed in order.

A large, mahogany-framed armchair in front of the bed had a fur coat draped over one arm and a neat pile of clothes on the other. He inspected the clothes – a pair of white bloomers, some tan riding breeches, a short-sleeved undershirt, a pullover, a woollen waistcoat and a brown velvet corduroy skirt. A pair of yellow shoes lay at the foot of the bed.

Behind the chair, he found the open drawer where Girard said the Anglaise had kept her revolver, and he took out the box of cartridges: 8mm calibre, two missing. Nothing else in the room seemed to have been disturbed.

He returned to the door and made his way down the stone staircase that ran behind the studio hearth and curved around into the kitchen. This was the tidiest room of all. Madame Girard's territory. Non-essentials had been limited to a small memorial photograph of an elderly man, a few religious prints and a plain, rush-seated chair by the hearth. The rest was put over to the usual *batterie de cuisine* and larder items. Three buckets of drinking water had been placed on the floor; pans and colanders hung from a large wooden rack; casseroles and *oulos** were lined up by the fire; and the crockery and glassware were stacked alongside storage pots and tins on the sturdy shelving. Madame Girard had clearly tidied up after preparing the previous night's meal. The only sign of recent activity was a fresh bottle of milk on the side.

Fabre stepped back outside into the spring air.

In time, there would be accusations that Fabre's investigation had been hasty and flawed, a clodhopping fiasco by a provincial fool. That would be unfair. Louis Fabre was no fool and had handled the situation with dignity and compassion. He did nothing wrong, other than, perhaps, lack the creative imagination and resources that a more specialized investigator would have deployed.

Some would also say that Fabre's judgement had been swayed by the fact that Olive Branson was foreign, or a woman, or

---

* Traditional Provençal cooking pots.

unmarried, or simply eccentric. That was harder to disprove – who could know what biases, conscious or otherwise, had guided his thoughts? That said, there was one factor that might have coloured his reading of the scene: that Olive Branson had been an artist.

Fabre was familiar with the ways of artists who flocked to Provence for the clear light and cheap living. He and his men had met enough of them over the years while checking the identity papers of guests at local hotels. He would have known that the drive for creative fulfilment could sometimes make a person seem somewhat unhinged. Most of the time, such artists' eccentricities were harmless enough, but there were some who seemed bent on self-destruction.

The prime example, of course, had been Vincent van Gogh, who had spent just over a year in Saint-Rémy between May 1889 and May 1890, undergoing treatment at the Saint-Paul-de-Mausole asylum following his infamous breakdown in Arles. It had been before Fabre's time, of course, but the Dutchman's shadow still hung over the area. There were those who remembered how he had set up his easel around the town to capture local scenes: busy roadmenders framed by the thick plane trees of the Boulevard Mirabeau, for example, or the golden wheat fields and white-blossomed orchards near the asylum. It had been nearly forty years since Van Gogh had left for Auvers-sur-Oise and his final, fatal breakdown, but the tragic course of events still evinced a mixture of pride, shame and fascination among the local population. In fact, a small museum was due to open in his memory at the asylum that very summer.

But there had also been other artists: less well known, but equally broken. There were theories as to why a spell in Provence might tip a creative soul over the edge (the much-sought-after clarity of light illuminating the darkness within, and so forth), but, whatever the cause, the consequences of an artistic temperament knocked off kilter could be devastating, especially when its owner was far from the solace of home. Fabre himself had borne witness to just such a tragedy three and a half years earlier. It had been another Englishwoman – another Olive, in fact.

He'd still been finding his feet as head of the gendarmerie when Olive Mudie-Cooke had arrived in Saint-Rémy in September 1925. The thirty-five-year-old former war artist had been touring the region with a group of friends and had taken rooms at a local hotel. Fabre had never met Olive Mudie-Cooke – at least not alive – and the case had been so straightforward that he'd had no real need to get a sense of her character. Yet, had he seen examples of her work, such as those hung in the Beaux Arts Gallery in London the year after her death, he would have found her to have been an adventurous soul. The critics had agreed that she'd possessed a rare eye for the spirit of a place, be that the imposing Drakensberg mountains of South Africa, the cool moonlight in Venice, the blistering sun of Spain or the dreary sludge of the Somme.[1] In Saint-Rémy, however, she had only seen darkness.

Her friends had raised the alarm when she'd failed to appear for breakfast one morning. Upon unlocking her room, the hotel staff had found her body, a revolver and a note. The latter had left no doubt that the fatal gunshot had been self-inflicted, and Fabre had been able to close the case quickly and efficiently.

Perhaps, as he stood outside Mas de Chiscale, Fabre's subconscious told him he was dealing with something similar. He hadn't found a note, but the testimony of the villagers certainly suggested that in recent days some unspoken force had been pulling Olive Branson towards darkness.

Dr Cot's car arrived from Maussane at four o'clock. Not long afterwards, Louis Vigne's taxi pulled up with Dominique Muselli, the justice of the peace for Saint-Rémy, and his clerk.

The cistern had been draining for almost an hour by that point, but the water level was still too high to get a clear view of its contents. At Dr Cot's request, the body was raised once more with the branch so he could see the bullet wound. The doctor then instructed Joseph Girard to find a pickaxe to enlarge the drainage hole.

Pierre Cot was a country doctor through and through. His territory included the numerous farms in the hills and valleys surrounding Maussane and Les Baux. Nearly all the men gathered at the cistern had trooped through his consulting room at some point. Some had been young boys when he'd arrived just before the war. Now, most looked older than their years, battered by endless seasons of sun, wind and hard, physical work. (At forty-two himself, Dr Cot was not immune to the effects of ageing, but his signs were more bourgeois: gracefully receding hair and a waist thickened by good food and wine.) He'd patched the men up after accidents, looked after their wives during pregnancy, and seen their sons and daughters through the usual childhood illnesses.

Olive Branson had not been his patient, although she had often sent people his way with ailments they might otherwise have ignored: François Pinet, for example, gaunt and listless with a lingering sinus infection, and Joseph Girard, wide-eyed with worry about an infected finger. She'd even paid the bills of some of the poorer folk. For her own care, however, the Anglaise had favoured her friend Dr Leroy in Saint-Rémy, along with occasional specialists in Marseille. As a result, Dr Cot didn't know her medical history, other than the usual indiscreet gleanings presented to him during his rounds, including the fact, which everybody knew, that the previous summer her nerves had got so bad that Dr Leroy had sent her to stay with the nuns at Sault.

Joseph was making little headway with the pickaxe, so Dr Cot ordered the draining of the cistern to be abandoned and for the body to be removed by whatever means necessary. After some debate, Fabre and the men decided to pivot the Anglaise ninety degrees, so that she lay alongside the right-hand wall of the cistern. There, they would be able to grab her by the wrists and haul her out, clear of the rocky overhang. After much grunting and heaving, with regular warnings from the doctor not to let the body snag on the wire mesh, eventually Olive Branson lay dripping on the stone flags.

She was wearing a pink calico shirt buttoned over a white short-sleeved vest. The shirt only just reached her thighs. Her lower half was naked, apart from a pair of fawn stockings, which were still stretched over her knees despite a lack of garters. Marie-Thérèse Girard arrived at the scene just in time to fetch a blanket.

Crouching down, Dr Cot inspected the wound in her forehead. It was small, less than a centimetre in diameter. Judging by the gunpowder residue that had blackened the surrounding skin, the weapon had been fired at point-blank range.

Turning the body, he could see no bruising or any other signs of struggle, but the limbs had stiffened in a strangely pugilistic manner, with the legs slightly bent and one arm raised higher than the other, as though she had died midway through delivering a left hook. Her left hand was fixed in front of her face like a claw. On closer inspection, it occurred to Dr Cot that this was how the Anglaise had been holding the gun: crouching down in the water, she had steadied the weapon with both hands against her forehead and used her left thumb to pull the trigger. He would need to see the actual revolver, though, to be sure.

Sergeant Fabre was already lying on his stomach by the opening at the rear of the cistern, trying to locate the gun by scraping through the sludge with a long rake. It was past five o'clock by this point and, as predicted, quite a crowd had gathered, with people talking in small groups and watching Fabre and Dr Cot piece together the previous night's tragedy.

Fabre indicated that he'd felt something under the fixed part of the grille, just to the left of where the body had been. He fished it out and dropped it on the flagstones. The crowd saw it was a long revolver, an old wartime model that could hold six rounds. Fabre flipped open the cylinder, revealing that only one round was present, along with an empty casing. The unspent round was identical to the cartridges found in the box by the bed.

Dr Cot emptied the revolver and held it to his own head, experimenting with hand placement and angles until he was satisfied that his assumptions about the suicide were correct. Finally, he took out his fountain pen and some headed notepaper and wrote a signed statement, citing his findings and adding that, even if the self-inflicted bullet wound had not been immediately fatal, Olive Branson would have soon drowned. He handed this to Sergeant Fabre.

One of the later arrivals at Mas de Chiscale that day was Jean Baltus, an artist who lived in Saint-Rémy and had been friends with Olive Branson since she first moved to Provence. He'd been informed of her death by Louis Vigne when the driver had gone to fetch the justice of the peace, and had driven straight to Les Baux, stopping only to send a telegram to his friend's relatives in England.

Baltus was a sensitive man of forty-eight. His neat appearance contained all the trappings of adulthood, not least a trim moustache and a silk cravat, but the timid boy he'd once been still hovered behind his eyes. When he arrived, the operation to remove the body from the water was still underway. Mercifully, he was not asked to help. Instead, Fabre requested that he look through his friend's papers for a suicide note. As he was the only one on the scene both familiar with the house and able to read English, he agreed.

Jean Baltus.

But he found nothing except memories. Their friendship was everywhere in the cluttered rooms. Andrée Sous, in her role as an antiques dealer, had sourced the finer pieces of furniture, but the bulk had come from a second-hand shop Baltus had stumbled across in a slummy suburb of Avignon just after Olive had finished the renovations. He'd given her directions and Louis Vigne had driven her over shortly afterwards. She had been delighted with her haul. When the delivery van arrived, it was crammed with mismatched cupboards and tables – nearly a dozen items in total.

There were also two mirrors, which now hung in her bedroom: one immaculate in a large gold frame and its smaller cousin, spotted with age. The smaller one had especially pleased her; she had always preferred things – and people – with character.

Dr Cot had left by the time Baltus stepped back outside, empty-handed. He was now faced with the distressing sight of the villagers gathered around his friend's body on top of the cistern, attempting to straighten her limbs and unfurl her fingers. He did not stay long.

At half past five, Sergeant Fabre summoned all those who had heard the gunshot to the studio, along with those who had spoken to Olive Branson in the hours before her death. The general agreement was that the shot had rung out at about nine o'clock the previous night and that the Anglaise had been alone at the time. The only people to have seen her all evening had been the Girards and François Pinet: Joseph and Marie-Thérèse had left after serving her supper at seven o'clock, and François had seen her briefly at eight, when he'd dropped off some provisions on his way back from shopping in Maussane.

While Fabre took down these statements in the studio, Roujon oversaw the activity outside. There was some discussion about what to do with the body. It couldn't be left at Mas de Chiscale as the house needed to be formally sealed in case any matters of inheritance arose: Dominique Muselli's clerk had already prepared the linen strips that would be placed across every door and window frame, and was melting the pots of black and red wax for the seals.

No one in the valley particularly wanted a corpse in their house, especially with the funeral arrangements so uncertain. Who knew when the Anglaise's family would arrive from England? Her god-daughters, in particular, would want to pay their respects: they had spent a great deal of time in Les Baux and would be devastated by the news. Eventually, it was decided that the best thing to do was to take the body up to the old mortuary by the cemetery.

Accordingly, Marie-Thérèse Girard fetched the thin top mattress from the bed and placed it on the gravel outside the studio door. While the men lowered the body down from the top of the cistern, she went back inside to choose some bed linen to act as a temporary winding sheet, along with some clean clothes for the burial.

With the body transferred to the mattress, the men carried it down to the lower terrace and dragged it onto a low, single-wheeled handcart. As a makeshift hearse, it wasn't ideal. The flat wooden base was too short for the body to lie down, so they had to strap it in place as best they could. The sheet also kept slipping, exposing Olive Branson's ghostly, punctured face. Perhaps it was when Jacquot the parrot was retrieved from the studio with his cage draped in a scarf that someone thought to place another over the Anglaise's own head. But, with that, they were ready, and a small funereal procession wobbled its way out of the gate, along the lanes and up the steep, stony path to the village, leaving Sergeant Fabre and the officials to finish the formalities at Mas de Chiscale with Joseph and Marie-Thérèse Girard.

V

It is said that ghosts, like the living, vary in temperament. Some are performative by nature, favouring fits of wailing and other affectations; others pace up and down, up and down, tiresome in their eternal neediness. The vast majority, however, just sit, awaiting attention. If they reveal themselves at all, it is through trails of ink and faded photographs, or by whispering from the flyleaves of old, musty books.

In this sense, Mas de Chiscale was heavily haunted. Although Olive Branson had never been a consistent diarist, behind those sealed windows and doors, stuffed in random drawers and stacked along the high shelves in the bedroom, were many notebooks and scraps of paper on which she had preserved her fleeting thoughts. Occasionally, she had even recorded snatches of memoir or committed herself to a travelogue.

This archive, along with the innumerable letters she had written to family and friends over the years, revealed more about her and her life than anyone in Les Baux could ever have imagined. They had little to fear from most of it. In fact, the more curious among them might even have found her papers interesting, containing as they did clues about how she had become the woman they had known.

One green half-quarto notebook, for example, held within its covers a memoir she had started and abandoned seven and a half years earlier, in October 1922. She had been confined to bed at a relative's house in Surrey, struck down by bronchitis and the tail end of the flu, and had been reading Maurice Baring's *The Puppet Show of Memory*, which had been published earlier that year to great acclaim. Baring's autobiography had been crafted without the usual recourse to personal papers and relied solely on memory: 'Memory . . . is the greatest of artists,' Baring had declared. 'It eliminates the unessential, and chooses with careless skill the sights and the sounds and the episodes that are best worth remembering and recording.'[1] In her immobilized state, this approach had appealed to Olive:

Lying in one's bed, not quite flat, because one coughs; not allowed to see people for fear of giving them the Flu, not able to talk to them when one does see them, because one chokes, conduces to a Review of the Past Life – Maurice Baring's 'Puppet Show of Memory' – but that is too discreet. My past life is a succession of pictures – each distinct & complete in itself – the jewelled pictures of the Ink Pool.*

I think the first is light & dust & noise – & being lifted on a black servant's shoulders & held there by him – I loved him very much – while a procession of elephants went by – always from right to left. That must have been in Madras when I was about four and a half. We were back in England, I know, by May and I was five in the August following.

The next thing I remember is a grey day in England – Bedford – and a Funeral procession going from right to left, along Union Street – seen from the passage window next to the Nursery. I was held up to it by my English nurse. It was

---

* An ancient method of divination in which visionary images are revealed on the surface of a dark liquid such as ink.

> my Mother's funeral – but I didn't know. There had been a big party to lunch [including] my old Great Uncle – Uncle Brummel (a descendant of Beau Brummel), a clergyman – but I didn't know at all what it was all about. Uncle Brummel was jolly looking & wore little whiskers. Later on my Aunt & Uncle took me to spend the day with him at the Rectory at Holt & I saw wonderful china & old furniture & a garden full of flowers, and was given jam at tea – made of whole strawberries floating in juice.
>
> I can't remember my Mother at all . . .

The strawberries had been served up in the summer of 1890; her mother had died from ovarian cancer that January. After the funeral, five-year-old Olive had found herself the bewildered new owner of 700 dead butterflies, a large quantity of silverware, and £200. The butterflies were put into storage and Coutts & Co. took care of the riches, but what to do with Olive? Her father was 5,000 miles away in Madras, and India was no place for a motherless child.

Fortunately, no bleak foster home awaited Olive, as was the fate of many children of the Raj. Instead, she remained with her paternal uncle and aunt in Bedford – and what a joyful place their large, red brick house in Lansdowne Road proved to be.

James Branson and his wife Mary had five spirited children, ranging in age from eleven to nineteen, all of whom adored their little cousin. The youngest – Fred, who had been born in Calcutta like most of his siblings – was more than happy to relinquish his role as baby of the family. Next came gentle May: in stillness as beautiful and serene as a porcelain doll, but whose appetite for horsing around with her brothers had not entirely diminished with her transition to longer skirts. William, at fifteen, was all limbs and hormones, and was navigating a discreet path to fulfilment through the study of poetry and young men at Bedford Grammar. As for seventeen-year-old Jim, the polo pony destined to deliver a hefty kick to his head had not yet been born, so he had yet to begin evangelizing about the benefits of eating grass.* Instead, he would shortly be joining his older brother George at Trinity College, Cambridge, where they would throw their all into rugger, rowing and *res gestae* in preparation for the legal careers that were seemingly the birthright of all Branson men. (Their father had been a judge of the Calcutta High Court and now practised as a barrister at Middle Temple; Olive's father was a prominent solicitor in Madras.)

Another shimmer in the Ink Pool: Olive, slightly older now, kneeling in front of an early summer border, a shy smile on her lips. This is how she took her place in the family photograph album: in her white dress and black stockings, her long, mousy hair never quite submitting to neatness. There she is on the lawn, clutching an army of dolls, a rabbit, the family Jack Russell; there she is hoisted aloft on Jim's shoulder as her cousins fool around for the camera. But, also, there are the sickly shadows cast in sepia below uncertain eyes; the wan complexion; the spent figure lost in a novel, in a conservatory shaded by palms.

Olive had never been strong. Her aunt's diary recorded the anxieties of this in rising and falling numbers: 'Olive not quite well . . . Olive's temperature 101 . . . Olive's temperature 98.5 . . . Olive's temperature 103.5. Sent for Dr Berry . . .'

---

* His personal preference was to forage from golf greens. See, for example, J. R. B. Branson's appearances on British Pathé and BBC radio during the Second World War, as well as his ration-busting pamphlet *Grass For All* (*c.*1939).

Olive with her cousin William and dolls.

The Branson family and friends in Bedford. Olive is held aloft by her cousin Jim. To their right are James and Mary Branson; to their immediate left are Fred and May.

That's not to say that Aunt Mary was an anxious woman. Far from it. A stout, fleshy figure with sparkling eyes and a ready smile, she came from solid Norfolk farming stock and was responsible for much of the carefree yet pragmatic spirit of the Branson household.

Mary had been twenty-five when she met James Branson, then a young lawyer from Calcutta, at a friend's wedding in Norfolk. It had been love at first sight. Within days, and after much desperate negotiation with her father, the pair were engaged on the understanding that they would wait at least a year before marrying. James had duly returned to India alone. Six months later, Mary packed a bag and joined him: they wed as soon as she arrived in Calcutta and had remained devoted ever since.

That devotion aside, like many Raj wives, bored and corset-bound in the sweltering heat, Mary looked forward to the day she and her husband would return to England. She also knew that such a move would not be without its challenges, especially for their children: James Branson's mother had been Parsee, her Zoroastrian ancestors having fled their native Persia during the Middle Ages to escape persecution. This Indo-Persian heritage was evident in the features of all James and Mary's children (as it would be, later, in Olive's), and the couple were acutely aware that the British professional classes had words for such wilful mixing of Anglo-Saxon blood, few of which were employed as mere physical descriptors.

Whether consciously or not, Mary opted to send her children into battle with armour capable of deflecting the discrimination they would inevitably face. That armour was self-confidence. Accordingly, the Branson siblings were encouraged to embrace all aspects of themselves and pursue their own idiosyncratic interests with pride. William's poetry, for example, would be celebrated equally alongside his burgeoning medical career, while Jim's nosebag of grass cuttings would be accommodated on high days and holidays with the minimum of fuss.

This campaign to foster individuality and confidence was so effective that Olive's cousin May only discovered that she was not considered white at the age of twenty-two. Newly married, she had been on board a ship to India with her husband, Arthur fforde. She was accompanying a singer on the piano one evening, when she heard another passenger remark, 'That little Coffee and Cream girl can play, can't she? – wonderful accompanist.'

Her husband had been amazed when she'd reported this to him: 'But surely you knew?'[2]

She had not. Her self-image shaken, May offered to have the marriage annulled and to return to England alone. Arthur, of course, refused.

Aunt Mary's approach to child-rearing had, on the whole, been a resounding success. Of her own children, George would become Sir George, a High Court judge; Jim, for all his eccentricities, would run a successful polo stud in Hampshire; William would become a senior doctor at St Barts; and Fred would become a partner in a firm of City solicitors. May's marriage, meanwhile, would be a happy one and would deliver her four spirited children of her own.

When it came to Olive, Aunt Mary's confidence campaign had started with animals. Olive had always loved animals, from the elephants and monkeys in India to the Jack Russells in Bedford. She was therefore treated to regular trips to London Zoo. For her thirteenth birthday, Mary and James had given her a pair of colourful lovebirds.

There were also books – many, many books – their pages capable of transporting a sickly child into lands of fantastic splendour. The theatre, too, had captivated her. She and William had taken in everything from *Alice in Wonderland* to *Julius Caesar*, with enlivening blasts of Gilbert and Sullivan in between.

Shining above all else, however, had been Olive's talent for art. Her innate ability had been clear from an early age and only grew as she matured. As her friend and the future president of the Royal Academy, Sir Alfred (AJ) Munnings, would later recall: '. . . she was, I would say, one of the few people possessing the great gift to draw . . . She could draw anything. A wizard with the pencil . . .'[3]

In the autumn of 1897, when Olive was thirteen, the Bransons left Bedford for Watford, where central London was just a short train ride away. Mary took Olive to the capital's art galleries and, in time, sought out a suitable tutor to open up a path to the Slade or similar. The woman she chose was a cousin and assistant of the social realist painter Sir Hubert von Herkomer, whose art school in Bushey formed the centre of Hertfordshire's artistic community. Olive began her lessons with Bertha Herkomer in April 1901, at the age of sixteen.

It was, however, a short-lived arrangement. Just a year later, James Branson, an undiagnosed diabetic, fell gravely ill and died. With young Fred having followed in his brothers' footsteps to Cambridge, the heartbroken Mary decided widowhood called for a fresh start. She set about creating a new home for herself and Olive, with room for all her adult children and grandchildren, in London itself. By chance, the property she found in Bloomsbury – a large corner house at 59 Gordon Square – would also prove to be the perfect base for Olive's true immersion in the London art scene.

The grand Georgian houses in Gordon Square had been designed with opulence in mind, but Bloomsbury as a whole had never quite taken off with the smart set. It had always struggled to find its identity, with many of its residences put over to boarding houses and student digs. The Bransons had been in their new home for little over a year, however, when a seed was planted in Gordon Square that would put Bloomsbury on the map forever.

The seed took the form of a group of newly orphaned siblings, who moved into number 46 in early 1904. Adrian, Thoby, Vanessa and Virginia Stephen were all in their twenties and eager to escape their stifling Victorian upbringing. Vanessa was studying art at the Slade, Virginia was a writer, and Thoby and Adrian were both at Cambridge.

In 1905, the siblings started to host gatherings for Thoby's university friends. Their liberated discussions on Thursday evenings, which ran long into the night, fuelled by coffee, whisky, buns and tobacco, soon attracted other intellectual and artistic types. Over time, their visitors would include the poet W. B. Yeats, the artists Clive Bell, Duncan Grant and Roger Fry, the writer Lytton Strachey and the novelist E. M. Forster, forming the nebula of what would become the Bloomsbury Group. As Virginia would later write, under her married name Virginia Woolf: 'These Thursday evening parties were, as far as I am concerned, the germ from which sprang all that has since come to be called . . . by the name of Bloomsbury.'[4]

Olive, at nineteen, was too young, and perhaps too shy, to be included in her neighbours' gatherings; even Virginia had sometimes hidden in the bushes to watch her brother's friends arrive. But Olive would have encountered the Stephens and their guests on the curving paths of the square's informal garden and would have felt a shift in Bloomsbury's atmosphere as more and more young bohemians flocked to the area. She had also begun to find her own way into the kind of circles that the Bloomsbury Group would come to epitomize.

Olive had been studying at Frank Calderon's School of Animal

Painting in Baker Street for eighteen months by the time of the Stephens' arrival. A lively establishment spread over five floors, the school attracted students from across Europe and the New World with its thorough instruction in animal anatomy and life drawing, as well as its sizeable menagerie of subjects. Horses of every variety formed a greater part of the curriculum, being posed daily in the large ground-floor studio. The upstairs spaces offered dogs of all sizes, from miniature lapdogs to Russian wolfhounds, in addition to casts and anatomical models of more exotic species, such as monkeys and armadillos, prepared by a member of the Royal Zoological Society.

Olive was in her element, exploring her twin loves of animals and art while making friends of a similar bent. Her work had also caught the eye of Frank Calderon himself, earning her a scholarship. She had a clear gift for animal painting, imbuing her subjects with a calm vitality, their haunches plump with life and their eyes brimming with soul. But she had a growing desire to explore human subjects in equal depth. In October 1905, therefore, she left Baker Street for an art school based at the Rossetti Studios in Flood Street, Chelsea.

The Chelsea Art School was a new venture run by two brilliant young Irishmen: the society portrait painter William Orpen and his wild friend Augustus John. Both had studied at the Slade in the 1890s and had called upon their contemporaries, both male and female, to help provide instruction to a new generation of artists. John Singer Sargent had been recruited to oversee the school's associated sketching club.

Their advertisements made it clear that the school's ethos was fundamentally different from that of most art schools in London at the time. Orpen and John took a holistic view of the artist-in-training, declaring that they would stimulate their students' individualism and expression by 'systematic discouragement of the cheap and meretricious, and hearty promotion of the most real and single-minded view of life, nature and art . . .'[5]

As it happened, the students only benefited from their principals' stimulating presence once a week, the pair having set up the school more as a debt-reduction exercise than through any great desire to teach. But when the duo did appear, they inspected their students' work closely. Again, despite her natural reserve, Olive stood out: during her second term, William Orpen marked three of her anatomy diagrams 'excellent'.[6]

The Chelsea Art School proved short-lived – it closed in 1907 – but the education Olive received there, both in terms of artistic skill and bohemian mores, would stay with her throughout her life. The ideas of personal authenticity and creative honesty were especially resonant and inspired her to seek more from her study of the human form than any life-drawing class could provide. In particular, her instincts drew her towards bodies in motion.

Here, Aunt Mary swung into action once more, accompanying her niece to wrestling matches where animated models in minimal clothing could be found in abundance. Soon, Olive was also stalking London's circuses and music halls. Alongside her sketches of wrestlers and acrobats, she jotted down thoughts not dissimilar to those that must have passed through her cousin Jim's mind when appraising a polo pony:

> *Johnny Summers . . . at the Holborn Empire, March 13, 1909, where he sparred three one minute rounds with his partner. He would be <u>delightful</u> to draw – very fair with light hair that catches a gold glint, & clean complexion – looking well washed & healthy – & very young, with a jolly open face – thoroughly English – neither long nor round . . . He has a very powerful neck – on which his head is well set, very powerful shoulders & strong arms – going down to nice neat waist – he is well built*

& muscular – very light & quick on his feet – & he looks a thoroughly good tempered, delightful soul.

Pencil sketch of circus performers by Olive Branson.

Cousin Jim, however, had never invited a horse back to his studio. Olive picked up models wherever she could, either writing to their managers to enquire about private sittings or approaching them in person. The athletes and performers, whose bodies provided their precarious livelihoods, were used to such requests from artists and were usually happy to oblige for some extra cash.

As a bonus, these sittings were free of the coy constraints that even the Chelsea Art School had imposed on female students. '. . . [W]ould it be in tights or without?' one male trapeze artist had asked in a letter she'd kept from 1911.[7]

All the while, Olive had maintained contact with the School of Animal Painting. Each year, she would join past and present students – mostly young women – as they tumbled into the Essex countryside for Frank Calderon's open-air summer school at Robjohns Farm near Finchingfield. There, under the chaperonage of Mrs Calderon, they would don their painting smocks and set up their easels and parasols amid the straw and manure for six weeks of farm animals and freedom.

Olive at the Calderon Summer School.

It was in Essex that Olive first met AJ Munnings, then an up-and-coming equestrian artist, who had stopped by to visit a friend. As Munnings would later recall in his memoirs, 'She was the best student at Finchingfield, and stood miles apart from the rest. The kindest and sweetest person. The others called her mother.'

Olive's preferred name at that time, however, was simply 'OB'. It had begun when her friends, emulating the men they knew, had ditched their first names and experimented with calling each other by their surnames – Branson, Wolfe, Clay, etc.* Eventually, Olive had dropped her surname, too, resulting in the nickname that would endure for the rest of her life and, in time, be inscribed on her tombstone.

It was a time of exploration in other ways, too. She and her friends travelled to the ateliers of Paris, while long trips down to Cornwall on Munnings' advice brought the newly fledged OB into contact with the Newlyn artists, who included Laura and Harold Knight and a young Dod Procter. She lodged at Penzer House with 'Granny' Beer (the circle's favourite eccentric landlady), visited the Knights for tea at their cottage in St Buryan and took figure painting classes with Stanhope Forbes. Back in London, she rented her first solo studio in Robert Street,** Holborn, and started to experiment in printmaking.

Yet, for all her friends, talent and adventurous spirit, Olive struggled to define her place in the world. Drawing was the only part of her that seemed immutable, but even that came with a gnawing sense of inadequacy: '. . . [I]t seemed to me the only

---

* Her inner circle had included the artists Edith Grace Wheatley (née Wolfe), E. Margaret Holman, Maud Hogarth Clay and Wyn George, among others.
** Now Kirk Street.

thing I could do. I knew I couldn't do the things that all [my cousins'] young women friends could – I used to feel the most awful outsider . . .'[8] Furthermore, she would be periodically plagued by doubt about her abilities, leaving her unable to work and in despair at the disconnect between other people's views of her and her own self-perception. 'There is nothing so spirit breaking as not knowing whether you are a genius – or only fit to clean out saucepans . . .'[9]

Her friends despaired, too. As Munnings said of some prints she had sent him: 'I think those etchings are so good that I am annoyed with you for not thinking enough of them. Why that Cornish coast thing is wonderful. Thank heavens you're working. You ought to do great things – if you don't, then the fault will be yours.'[10]

This last comment, despite being written with the best of intentions, was perhaps not the most tactful thing to say to a young woman afraid that she was, indeed, profoundly at fault and lacking in some regard.

Two scraps of paper squirrelled away in Mas de Chiscale from this time hinted at some ways Olive had attempted to quell such fears. The first was a letter she had received during her early twenties, from Rathgar near Dublin, in exchange for a one-shilling postal order and a sample of her handwriting. The writer, who called herself 'Idalia', had provided a complete breakdown of Olive's character, tempering the news that 'you cannot be said to have the artistic faculty much developed' with more positive insights into Olive's intellectual capabilities, before concluding, 'You possess masculine independence & breadth of character, though womanly enough *au fond*. Somewhat sensitive, very sympathetic, tender & true.'[11]

The second was a thick piece of cartridge paper which, when unfolded in years to come, would invariably elicit a small gasp from its viewer. There, in a startling reminder of what had been lost, was Olive's youthful handprint stamped in red ochre paint, the colour of dried blood. Her fingers, long and slender, were splayed out for eternity above a palm carefully placed to record all the creases and furrows of a life foretold.

These forays into graphology and palm reading had brought no answers, of course. But, even setting aside the usual uncertainty of youth, they were understandable. Olive had been receiving mixed messages about who she was and where she belonged since she was five years old. Yes, she may have found safe and loving harbour with her fellow Bransons after her mother's death, but her place in the family had always come with modifiers. She was 'Cousin Olive' to their simple 'William' or 'George', and Aunt Mary had been exactly that and not 'Mother'. Moreover, while she had lived the life of an orphan, albeit one coddled and adored, she had never been entirely orphaned. Her father had always hovered on the edges of her existence, an affectionate and dutiful correspondent, yet one separated by the kind of distance that could render a person more a concept than a reality.

Nevertheless, she had received constant reminders of his absence. The Raj loomed large in the Branson household, her father and Uncle James being just two of ten siblings born in Madras with ties to England. London was littered with ancient aunts issuing invitations for tea and reminiscence, while Aunt Mary's drawing room witnessed a constant stream of visitors on furlough, each bringing news of some obscure relative or old family friend. Even some of Olive's cousins had returned to the country of their birth: both Jim and Fred had worked in Madras after Cambridge, while May had spent almost a decade near Delhi with her husband and young family. As a result, Aunt Mary had followed the shipping news as others might follow the weather, tracking vessels across the ocean via Gibraltar, Port Said and the Suez Canal as they ferried friends and relatives back and forth. Few of Aunt Mary's ships had delivered Reddy Branson, however. Indeed, Olive had only seen her father four times since leaving India.

On his last visit, when Olive was fifteen, Reddy had not arrived alone. By his side had been his new wife Grace, a tall, dark-haired and somewhat humourless woman of thirty. The couple had been married for two years by that time and had also brought someone else for Olive to meet. The baby, almost impossibly chubby against Grace's narrow hip, had been given Olive's unused Christian name – Edith, or Edie – in memory of her late mother.

Reddy, Grace and Edie had stayed for eight weeks, and that was the last Olive saw of her father. Three years later, at the age of forty-six, he died from tuberculosis, his heart giving out in the house on Mount Road, Madras, where Olive had been born.*

The turning point for Olive's self-confidence came on a family holiday in September 1909. The Bransons' annual jaunt was a campaign of almost military proportions, overseen by their commander-in-chief, Aunt Mary. Its objective was a month of fresh air, good food and laughter. Detailed mess lists in the back of Mary's giant leather-bound journals ensured that the correct

---

* Olive did develop a strained relationship with her stepmother on the latter's return to Britain. Grace Branson would become a militant suffragette and was imprisoned twice, in 1912 and 1913. On both occasions, she went on hunger strike and was subjected to brutal force-feeding. As she'd had a heart defect from birth, this raised serious concerns for her life, which were amplified by her fellow Holloway prisoner, Sylvia Pankhurst. How much Grace's condition contributed to the passing of the Cat and Mouse Act in April 1913, however, is impossible to say.

quantities of provisions and staff were shipped to her chosen destination in good time.

That year, the family had rented Mill Court, a twelve-bedroom country house set in over two hundred acres near Alton in Hampshire. Olive had just turned twenty-five. Some days, while her cousins and their friends went fishing or played tennis on the lawns, she took her sketching kit to explore the estate. She introduced herself to the tenant farmers and played with their dogs. Following a stream one day, she found the derelict fulling mill that had given the house its name and climbed inside to capture all its fascinating details: the rough-hewn oak uprights, the abandoned bundles of roving, and the froth and churn of the water as it came through the sluice gate. One of the etchings she subsequently produced would mark her debut at the Royal Academy's Summer Exhibition the following June.

But her real, life-changing discovery had occurred in a neighbouring field. There, Olive had stumbled across hundreds of brightly coloured caravans gathered around a large white bell tent. The site was mostly deserted, with only a few tethered horses grazing by open fires and the occasional figure quietly attending to domestic chores. Most of the nine hundred or so occupants, she would learn, had been busy in the fields since dawn, harvesting the hops for which the area was famous. As for the bell tent, that was manned by missionaries ready to dispense the gospel through bribes of tea and magic-lantern shows when the 'hoppers' returned.

Over the following weeks, she took to venturing into the camp in the evenings when it burst into life. During the day, she visited the hop gardens to sketch the women and children as they filled giant woven baskets with clusters of flowers destined for breweries around the country. She made lifelong friends that autumn, particularly among the large Stevens family.

The annual hop-picking became a permanent fixture in Olive's diary. This was not just for the sketching opportunities, although she did exhibit a number of portraits of her friends over the next ten years, from eight-year-old Freedom James to fifty-seven-year-old Comfort Stevens.* More than that, like many a bohemian before her, she had fallen in love with Romany culture and its deep sense of community.

In 1910, she came away from Alton with a greyhound puppy, whom she named Spring. Before long, she was hiring wagons to roam the countryside each spring and summer, first with Mark Stevens for protection and then with a young boxer called Jack Gorman. In 1911, she followed Swallow's Circus to Ireland for a three-month tour full of camaraderie and adventure.

At the hop-picking two years later, Olive handed twenty pounds to her friend Margaret Stevens in exchange for an old caravan complete with all its fixtures. With its rumbling yellow wheels and chipped traditional decor, she finally had a home-from-home that spoke to her soul. By forging a bond with those far more displaced than she could ever be, she had found the confidence to live life on her own terms.

---

* Comfort Stevens and her family also modelled for Sir Alfred Munnings' renowned Romany paintings, after being introduced by Olive in 1913.

VI

When dawn broke in Les Baux the next morning, it was the turn of the living again. Despite the cloudy weather, the village was braced for a larger number of visitors than usual that Sunday: on top of the customary day trippers requiring teas and lunches, both hotels had taken sizeable group bookings that demanded special attention.

For its part, the Monte-Carlo was hosting a large party from Arles, who had hired the *grande salle* for a private function. The plans for this – a banquet followed by dancing – had been underway for weeks: a jazz band had been booked and François had been dashing around organizing the food since Friday.

Olive Branson had been due to oversee the proceedings and endow them with her willowy, well-bred charm, a fact which had led to some deliberation during the night as to whether the party should go ahead at all. On the one hand, it seemed disrespectful with her lying in state in the annexe; on the other, they had all viewed the Arles booking as a sign that her plans to rejuvenate the hotel's fortunes were coming to fruition. Wouldn't it be equally disrespectful to discard that early fruit? In the end, it had been decided that it was simply too late to cancel. Instead, the *patronne* herself would have to move.

At nine o'clock, therefore, Joseph walked round to the adjoining *mairie* to inform the mayor of their intentions. A coffin was duly commandeered and Olive was transported back along the ramparts, past the church and into the small mortuary, where she could rest undisturbed when the revelry got underway.

Next door, at the Hotel Reine Jeanne, the news of the Anglaise's death had been met with a certain degree of ambivalence. While deeply regretted, there was no denying that it was also a significant development in the war between the two hotels that had been raging for nearly twenty years. The other side's loss of a general, especially one as competent as the Anglaise, could not be ignored.

The rivalry dated back to 1911, when a series of property transfers had resulted in the large, derelict building next door to the Hotel Monte-Carlo falling into the hands of a young Marseillais named Raoul Dumas. On seeing Les Baux's popularity with tourists and the far-from-luxurious accommodation available at the Monte-Carlo ('Tolerable for those who can rough it . . .' had been one guidebook's summary[1]), the twenty-one-year-old Dumas had decided to offer visitors a more refined alternative.

He was helped in this by his uncle Louis Échenard, an experienced hotelier who had managed some of the finest hotels in Europe. Under Échenard's direction, the building had been renovated, the cellars stocked and the pillows plumped. By promoting the Reine Jeanne's spectacular views and upmarket restaurant, Dumas had soon attracted a discerning, international clientele.

The two hotels formed an L-shape, hugging two sides of the small Place Fortin, but there had been no real need for a feud. Even during the war, Les Baux had been popular enough to support two hotels, and each attracted its own type of traveller. The eight-bedroom Monte-Carlo continued to host those willing to rough it, and retained rights over much of the Place

Fortin, where the Pinets had installed some cafe tables and a small hatch for ordering teas. In turn, the Reine Jeanne offered those with greater means the choice of twenty rooms, many with private bathrooms, and deferential attention to their every need.

Entrance to the Hotel Monte-Carlo on the Place Fortin.

Yet, Pierre Pinet had struggled with his loss of status as *le grand hôtelier* of Les Baux. Every ounce of praise bestowed on the Reine Jeanne festered in his mind. His first legal complaint – a petty grievance barely worth the court's time – had been lodged not long after the arrival of the Reine Jeanne's first guests. Dumas, who was quick to adopt the Baussenc attitude to neighbourly relations, had responded in kind. Most of their subsequent disputes centred on the soliciting of customers and rights of way over the Place Fortin: trivial matters that, nonetheless, had kept many a lawyer in cognac and Gitanes over the years.

Occasionally, however, one or the other would be pushed too far and the village would be treated to moments of delicious drama. The most recent of these had occurred in the summer of 1926, with the Great Turning Out – an event which had also cemented Olive's allegiance to the Pinet family.

The future of the Monte-Carlo had been uncertain for a while. Pierre Pinet had been getting increasingly frail as the years went by. Of his five children, only François – the youngest at twenty-two – was in a position to take over the hotel, but the pair had never seen eye to eye on how it should be run. Dumas had long been offering to take the hotel off Pinet's hands, and that spring, during a moment of frustration with François, Pinet accepted his offer. By the time the old man came to his senses and realized he had no desire to live out his remaining years in a state of surrender to some upstart from Marseille, the papers for the sale had been drawn up and Dumas had paid the deposit.

Dumas was furious when Pinet refused to sign. Somehow, he'd managed to take possession of the Monte-Carlo's keys anyway and, amid much excitement in the village, turned all the furniture out onto the street. This outrage was met with a counter-attack by Pinet's lawyers, with the result that, six weeks later, the keys were returned and the furniture restored. Everything had returned to normal, except Dumas was down 15,000 francs in reparations and legal fees.

Olive had followed the saga with glee, while also quietly supporting the put-upon François in his clashes with his father during her visits to the hotel for lunch.

> *All very well here – & humming with scandals! I saw François alone yesterday – & had a most satisfactory talk – he won't say one word, beyond politeness – if his family is about.*[2]

Dumas's inevitable countersuit to force through the sale was still making its way through the courts when Pierre Pinet died the following January. François took the helm and, for all his modernizing ideas, continued his father's legacy by picking apart every underhand move or perceived slight emanating from the Reine Jeanne.

Madame Pinet, François Pinet and Madeleine Vayssière outside the Hotel Monte-Carlo.

And, in this respect, Dumas did not disappoint. In March 1928, for example, *Les Tablettes d'Avignon et de Provence* had published a letter written by the great Auguste Escoffier, in which the famous chef waxed lyrical about a meal he had enjoyed at the Reine Jeanne.[3] So taken was he with the menu that, after working his way through eight courses of Provence's finest winter fare, he had somehow managed to prise himself from his chair to visit the kitchen and note down some recipes.*

In his haste to spread word of this gourmets' paradise, Escoffier had forgotten to mention that he used to work with the owner's uncle, Louis Échenard, at the Savoy Hotel in London. He certainly omitted the fact that he, Échenard and the Savoy's then manager César Ritz had all been sacked for fraud before regrouping to set up Ritz's own chain of hotels.

The old scandal was no secret in Les Baux, however, and hidden nepotism was just the type of thing to make the Pinets' new ally seethe with fury and indignation. When events led to her purchasing the Monte-Carlo later in the year, it was no surprise to anyone that the Anglaise elected to keep the old feud alive. She relished it, in fact. At the time of her death, she had four outstanding disputes awaiting their day in court.

That Sunday morning, however, the two hotels kept their peace, if only because they were too busy to do otherwise. Like the Monte-Carlo, the Reine Jeanne was expecting a large group from Arles. The distinguished members of the Escolo Mistralenco d'Arles had been making regular pilgrimages to Les Baux for decades. Dumas had poached their custom from the Pinets some

---

* Red mullet with truffles, a pumpkin gratin, pan-fried thrushes and a banana flambé.

years earlier and their ongoing high opinion of the Reine Jeanne was a matter of some import for the hotelier, feeding as it did a wellspring of pride that transcended any notions of commercial or personal rivalry.

The Escolo Mistralenco's name paid homage to their late patron and founder, the Nobel laureate Frédéric Mistral. Mistral was something of a god in rural Provence, and nowhere more so than in Les Baux. Even those who had not picked up a book since their schooldays could recite chunks of his verse and feel it resonate with their own hopes and desires.

The firebrand poet, with his white pointed beard and wide-brimmed hat, had borne a striking resemblance to the American showman Buffalo Bill (a.k.a. William Cody) and had shared the same talent for reviving interest in a dying culture. In Cody's case, this had been the Wild West of his bison-hunting days, which he recreated in his spectacular touring shows. For Mistral, it was the dignity of Old Provence.*

Mistral was born in 1830, into a wealthy farming family in Maillane, a village ten kilometres north of Les Baux across the Alpilles. His childhood had been one of idyllic, barefoot exploration and country wisdom dispensed in the fields in his native Provençal. After leaving Maillane (to attend boarding school in Avignon, earn a bachelor's degree in Nîmes and study law in Aix), however, he had found that the language that seemed so natural to him was in danger of dying out. Indeed, by the mid-nineteenth century, Provençal had become primarily a spoken language, the region's children having been taught in French ever since the

---

* The two men's lives had, in fact, coincided in 1905, when Mistral attended Cody's *Wild West* show during its tour of the Midi. He had subsequently adopted one of the showman's pet dogs, who was said to have mistaken the poet for his original master.

Revolution, when linguistic diversity was identified as a threat to the concept of a united people of France. Provençal had only remained truly alive in the most sparsely populated areas, such as Maillane and Les Baux.

In 1854, together with a group of friends who would call themselves the Félibrige, the young Mistral had resolved to right this wrong. As he would later explain in his memoirs, the group aimed to 'raise and revivify' the Provençal spirit and resurrect the dying language by 'illuminating it with the divine flame of poetry.'[4] *

This choice of medium was not coincidental: Provençal was a variant of Occitan, the melodic and expressive language of the medieval troubadours who had toured the region's castles. The ability to compose verse had long been a badge of honour in Provence. Taking on the primacy of French literature, however, would not be easy.

For his own part, Mistral would devote twenty years of his life to compiling and improving *Lou Tresor dóu Felibrige*, the ground-breaking dictionary he created between 1878 and 1886 that sought to standardize spellings and unite the various Occitan dialects so that they might become stronger through use. His real breakthrough, however, had come in 1859 with the publication of his epic poem, *Mirèio*. Presented in a dual Provençal–French edition to demonstrate the beauty of the language, the work had taken Paris by storm: on publication, it received more press coverage than Flaubert's contemporaneous *Madame Bovary*.[5] The

---

* A similar drive to protect regional identities against the rise of nation states could be seen throughout Europe at this time: for example, in the *Eisteddfodau* of Wales, the *Volksfeste* of Bavaria and the activities of the Catalan *Renaixença*, all of which were either inaugurated or revived during the nineteenth century.

critics called it a masterpiece; it even won over some of the *immortels* of the Académie Française.

On the surface, *Mirèio* – or *Mireille* in French – was a sentimental tale of star-crossed lovers: the tragic story of the wealthy titular heroine and a poor basket-weaver named Vincèn. At its heart, however, the poem celebrated the people and traditions of rural Provence. Mistral was hailed as a new Virgil: a true poet of the soil. Indeed, in the opening lines of *Mirèio*, he proclaimed, 'We sing for you alone, O shepherds and people of the farms!' His language was simple but alive, and his narratives were shaped by the landscapes and legends of the Midi – or, rather, by that small part of it he had known and explored since childhood.

Mistral's personal Provence – the part that was, for him, still true to itself – extended up to Avignon in the north, to Nîmes in the west, eastwards across the Crau, and the fifty or so kilometres down the river Rhône through Arles and the Camargue to the sea. His parents' farm in Maillane stood near the top of this territory.

'As far back as I can remember,' he wrote in his memoirs, 'I see before me, towards the south, a barrier of mountains, whose slopes, rocks and gorges stand out in the distance with more or less clarity according to the morning or evening light. It is the chain of the Alpilles, engirdled with olive-trees like a wall of classic ruins, a veritable belvedere of bygone glory and legend.'[6]

For Mistral, the Alpilles were his country's watchmen. By extension, Les Baux, jutting out on its precarious little rock, was the guardian of them all. He often travelled to the village to contemplate the view from its summit. '*Di Baus fariéu ma capitalo!*' he wrote in *Miréio*: 'I will make Les Baux my capital! . . . I will rebuild our old, ruined castle and add a turret which, with its white tip, shall reach the stars!'[7]

The village and castle had also formed an essential part of one of his later works, another epic romance entitled *Calendau* (1867). This time, the doomed couple comprised a young anchovy fisherman from Cassis and the last princess of the House of Baux. In the opening canto, the fictional princess recounts the story of her ancestry, telling of Balthazar and the wandering star, the crusades, the battles, the troubadours and the feasts, and finally the rubble and the silence. Set in the eighteenth century, just before the Revolution, *Calendau* was seen as an allegory for Provence itself – its past, present and potential future – and Mistral had placed Les Baux at its heart.

The successes of *Mirèio*, *Calendau* and the *Tresor* dictionary, along with the work of Mistral's fellow Félibrige poets, had drawn other writers, linguists and historians to the movement. These *félibriennes* unearthed forgotten manuscripts, researched lost religious rites and found ancient songs still alive in the farms and villages. New literary journals sprang up alongside festivals of Provençal poetry and music, and a folk museum opened in Arles, the latter funded largely by the prize money Mistral received when he was awarded the Nobel Prize for Literature in 1904. With a new regional anthem – *La Coupo Santo* ('The Holy Cup') – to round off any festivities, rural Provence had been roused into a state of ardent pride. The Félibrige's plan to deploy the divine flame of poetry for political ends had been a success.

In turn, the people of Les Baux revered the Félibrige, grateful perhaps for being seen as they saw themselves. The inaugural entry in the guest book of the Hotel Monte-Carlo was in Frédéric Mistral's own hand, and his signature was etched into the stone beside the carved oak door of the church. When he died in the spring of 1914, many Baussencs made the pilgrimage to Maillane to pay their respects.

Les Baux's main monument to the great poet, however, lay above the village, among the castle ruins. Three years earlier, the whole village had turned out – Olive Branson included – for the unveiling of a plaque in his honour. The drummers and farandole dancers had come from Maussane to lead the procession; songs were sung, poems recited and, following a series of elaborate speeches by visiting dignitaries, the marble plaque was revealed. Engraved below the old Baussenc battle cry of '*A l'asard Bautezar!*' were lines from Mistral's *Calendau* and the words: 'To the glory of the immortal poet of Provence, in memory of the powerful princes of Les Baux . . .'

All of which is to say that it was important to Raoul Dumas that the Escolo Mistralenco enjoy their visit to Les Baux that Sunday. It started well enough, with the group slipping into the twelfth-century church for Mass. The service was conducted in Provençal by the Abbé Cheilan, whose prayers echoed pleasingly through the vaulted nave. Afterwards, members of the society treated the congregation to an informal choral concert, including a poem by Mistral newly set to music by the former head of the Arles conservatoire. Lunch at the Reine Jeanne was also a success, with its Escoffier-approved menu and the opportunity to view the tasteful display of traditional arts and crafts in the foyer.

The Escolo's day was only marred when they went for a stroll around the village. This coincided with the end of the banquet at the Monte-Carlo and the start of the dancing. As the group wandered the streets to absorb the atmosphere of their founder's beloved capital, the jazz band struck up its first chords. This soon became a wailing, joyous frenzy that whirled the Monte-Carlo's guests around the floor of the *grande salle* and escaped into the air, its syncopated rhythm all but drowning out the solid beat of the tambour that dwelt in the Escolo's more conservative hearts.

Naturally, there were complaints, and these fell to Dumas to address. Although he refrained from attacking the Pinets immediately or directly, he did not stay silent. Instead, he satisfied himself with an anonymous barb in the pages of the *Croix de Provence* the following week, about the 'queer effect' that their choice of 'negro music' had produced in the 'harmoniously artistic setting of Les Baux.'[8]

And here was Les Baux in a nutshell: an ancient citadel in a modern world, caught in a giant tug of war that pulled it towards the future through necessity and back into the past by desire. Without doubt, the visitors who had been lured to Les Baux by the folk revival sought romance alongside the makeshift stalls of clay figurines and postcards, and demanded authenticity as they took a pastis in the Place Fortin. They liked to see Friquet the donkey eating at a manger that still bore the markings of the Renaissance fireplace it had once been; they liked to know that, behind the weather-beaten doors and crumbling walls, the ancient families persisted. To catch sight of a genuine Baussenc darting into a concealed courtyard was to glimpse a shadow of simpler times.

If these visitors nursed an overly romantic view of the past, it was not without some truth in interwar Les Baux, whose ancient streets, devoid of commerce or other modern distractions, could bring one closer to the ideal Provence than anywhere else. Picking one's way through the cobbles, it was easy to imagine the young maidens from *Mirèio* skipping out to help with the silk harvest, or to follow the mournful gaze of *Calendau*'s love-struck princess across the plain.

True, the silkworms may have died out and the young maidens become more knowing, but the Baussenc year still unfolded according to ancient rhythms. Those who toiled in the valleys – that is, the majority of the population – were covered in the same red dust as their ancestors before them, and the shepherds still wore the same heavy, chestnut cloaks when heading for the hills. As for the songbooks that came out after dinner, their use was not a revivalist pretension but the continuation of a centuries-old tradition. Likewise, the farmers had a talent for easing inherited stories and snatches of verse into conversation as smoothly as they knocked back the fruit of their vines.

But, of course, people also liked jazz and decent plumbing and recently bathed waiters, and all this had served to drag Les Baux towards the present day. Yes, old Elisa Quenin may have sat black-skirted outside her house, wearing a traditional Arlesian headdress and shawl, ready to regale passers-by with tales of medieval adventure or her own personal memories of Frédéric Mistral, but twenty-five-year-old François Pinet was just as likely to saunter out of the Hotel Monte-Carlo in a sports jacket and flannels, looking for all the world as if he had just stepped off the Blue Train from Paris.

Modernity was encroaching upon the eagle's nest, and, ironically, it was the very thing that Mistral and the Félibrige had desired – a wider appreciation of Provençal culture – that had invited it in.

VII

That night, after the last cars had made their way down from the Porte Mage and retreated into the dark hills, the villagers settled to sleep. For most, any residual sorrow about the death of the Anglaise drifted away on the breeze, leaving only a haze of gratitude for soft beds, sound minds and life going on. But, for some, a sense of unease pressed down in the darkness, demanding attention.

Joseph Girard had a physical memory to contend with, the lingering sensation of poking the branch into the water and hitting something soft and immoveable, of casting around, trying to make out the shape through the reflections on the surface, of that gut-wrenching moment when realization hit. But there was also something else.

He had been so certain at first that his employer had died by her own hand. All the details pointed to that conclusion: the missing revolver, her bag resting undisturbed against the chair, her low mood since returning from England. Yet . . . why the water cistern, of all places? And how on earth did she get in there? These questions hadn't seemed to bother Sergeant Fabre, but Joseph had thought at the time – and would tell the police in due course – that you'd have to be an acrobat to get through the opening in that grille. Miss Branson had certainly kept herself active, walking in the hills and riding out on her skittish black mare, but she was no contortionist.

There was also Dr Cot's assumption that his employer had been left-handed. The doctor had said as much, and his theory of her final moments relied on the fact that she had pulled the trigger with her left thumb. But Joseph had only ever seen her write and draw with her right hand.

One might ask why he hadn't pressed these matters at the time – with Fabre or Cot or the justice of the peace, or anyone else who could intervene. In his defence – which was something he would need as events progressed – he'd been deeply distraught and there had been so many people milling around. And now it seemed too late. Sergeant Fabre had closed the case, the mayor had signed the death certificate, and Olive Branson's body would be buried and left to the worms. There was, he thought, nothing to be done.

Over the hills in Saint-Rémy, Jean Baltus was also plagued by doubt. True, he was a ruminator by nature – neurotic, some might say – but certain details of the previous day's events didn't sit well with him. A lull in friendship, caused by busy lives and absorbing work, meant that the last time he'd seen Olive had been in mid-March, when he'd cycled over for afternoon tea at Mas de Chiscale. They'd talked of inconsequential things: the latest escapades of Frida and the pups, the gossip from Les Baux. There had been nothing to suggest that his friend was descending into mental malaise.

Being prone to fretful thoughts himself, he would have known such things could change quickly, but Baltus was unconvinced that anything had. As an artist of nearly thirty years' standing, he was trained to take in every detail, and there had been plenty of detail to absorb in those awful scenes by the cistern. All those who'd seen the body must have been struggling to banish the same vision of Olive's hand clenched and raised in front of her ghostly face. But no one seemed to have interpreted it quite as he did.

To Fabre and Dr Cot, the position of her arms was a sign that she had used both hands to steady the revolver against her forehead as she pulled the trigger. But, to Baltus, it was a posture of defence, of horror even; a shadow of violence frozen in time.

Furthermore, although it was not a space with which he was overly familiar, something had felt awry about Olive's bedroom when he'd gone inside to search for a note. His friend had been 'mess personified', as he would tell the authorities once his thoughts had settled, yet her clothes had been folded neatly on the chair next to her bed and the linoleum had struck him as unusually clean. These were disturbing anomalies, as he would put it, in a house 'of dust and disorder.'

Olive had never been too concerned about domestic matters. Baltus, who himself tended towards obsessive neatness in all things but art, had learned as much early in their friendship. It was February 1924 when Olive, newly arrived in Provence, had invited him to see her studio. It was a fine day, so Baltus had taken the opportunity to do some sketching beforehand and cycled over just after lunch. A small, isolated tower caught his eye not far from Les Baux and he had left the road and pushed his bicycle over the rough terrain to investigate. Finding it to be a dovecote, he spent a few happy hours creating what turned out to be a disappointing sepia (by his own judgement, it had lacked emphasis and the composition was all wrong), before heading on in the fading light to Les Baux.

Olive was living up in the village at the time, in a little rented house attached to Madame Sous's *hostellerie*. Like many buildings in Les Baux, it was curiously disjointed, with the room she was using as a studio extending above the neighbouring tobacconist.

It was also a bit run-down and none too clean, but their spirits had been high as she gave him a tour. After peering through the gloom at the yellow-painted kitchen (primarily in use as a log store; she rarely cooked) and out of the window to the castle, they had come to the spare room. Olive had insisted it was handsome by daylight, with its whitewashed walls, red-tiled floor and little hatch through to her studio. But, by the light of a solitary candle, it had possessed an absurd, dungeon-like quality.

'Ha! *La chambre du crime au cinéma!*' he had cried, rushing forward and stabbing the bed with an imaginary knife. 'The crime room from a film!'[1]

She had laughed and offered him tea. Baltus loved the ritual of *le thé*, as he loved all things English. Since meeting Olive, he had acquired a tweed walking hat and, through her relatives in London, a British army tunic which he used as a painting smock. He had been particularly delighted with the pockets.

After tea, Olive had shown him her works in progress. The detail was exquisite. Barely a fissure of rock in the Val d'Enfer or pockmark in the old town walls had escaped her notice. He knew the scenes well. They shared the same landscape, after all, and, neither being native to the area, they each saw it with an outsider's eye. But where Baltus saw form, Olive saw line. Her vision was expressed in fine greys and blacks against the off-white weave of paper, his through a palette of muted colours that sat voluptuously upon canvas. Her intricate outcrops became his lilac-tinged slabs, her delicate trees his bold spires.

Over the years, they must have found plenty to discuss and admire in each other's work, not least how she arrived at detail from an environment of chaos and he at impressionism from a life of compulsive order: it was as though each of them was drawn to equilibrium by some unseen force. That first evening, however, they had simply gone out for dinner, followed by what would become their habit of a moonlit stroll around the castle ruins, where the silver stones cast stark shadows on the earth. He'd then cycled the six miles home, as he would do repeatedly over the years, with only the rhythmic rattle of his bicycle breaking the cold, clear silence.

By all accounts (that is to say, by each other's accounts, recorded in letters and diaries over the following days), it had been a magical evening and an excellent start to their friendship. And now, as any good friend should, Baltus intended to raise his concerns about Olive's death with her cousin when he arrived from London. For the time being, however, he was at the mercy of his roving, anxious mind. Stabbing the bed, for example? *Mon Dieu.*

PART II:

POST TENEBRAS LUX

I

The angular and bespectacled Englishman who arrived in Saint-Rémy on Monday was not strictly speaking Olive's cousin, but rather a cousin by marriage, having been married to May Branson for thirty years. Like the Bransons, Arthur fforde was a product of the Raj. He'd been in England on furlough from the Indian civil service when he'd started courting May. Olive had been in short skirts back then, but the pair had quickly formed a special bond. She had been a bookish child, and he was a published author, having whiled away the lonely evenings in Poona writing novellas with titles such as *The Sign of the Snake* and *The Maid and the Idol*, to be sold at Indian railway stations alongside cheap editions of Rudyard Kipling. She'd looked up to him, and her eager, sweet nature had brought out his paternal side. He'd helped choose her first bicycle and taken her to see *Charley's Aunt*.

After Arthur had swept May off to India, he and Olive wrote to each other regularly. Olive was an entertaining correspondent. Her deepest confidences were saved for May, but she was always quick to write with the latest goings-on in her increasingly eventful life. By the time Arthur's ill health had forced the ffordes to return to England in 1907 with three young children in tow, Olive – or OB, as she had become – was fully ensconced in bohemian London. Her true roaming days were yet to come, with her gilded caravan and traveller friends, but Arthur had found in the twenty-three-year-old all the foundations for the adventure-filled days that lay ahead: most notably, her growing disregard for convention and her energetic pursuit of an authentic life.

Her career had also started to take off. In 1910, when she received her first acceptance into the Royal Academy's Summer Exhibition with her etching of the old fulling mill, Arthur had written to her, saying, 'I . . . hope that it is just the first step on the ladder of fame, dear girl. Robert Street will be famous one day and No. 5 will have a medallion on it with an inscription "O.B.'s first studio 1908–19xx."'

That ladder was certainly within sight. Critics had been singling her out during group exhibitions with the Calderon Art Society and the Society of Women Artists, and publishers had requested samples of her drawings. Yet, still, Olive doubted herself. Arthur encouraged her to be more confident and bring more of her personality into her work. 'Let us have something with action, life, devilment or such like in it,' he'd urged.[1]

Olive's devilish streak, and her talent for describing the adventures and mishaps that came with it, had always delighted Arthur and May, although that never stopped them from worrying about her. In recent years, May in particular had fretted about her living alone in the backwaters of Provence, especially when she started to get entwined in local feuds. But Olive had batted those concerns away:

> <u>BAD WOMAN</u>. *You must not worry – Imperative. Worry NOT.*
> <u>Defense Absolu</u> *de se faire du Mauvais Sang (our 'Barbarian's French') because there is no need – All goes well – Say to yourself slowly, every night when dropping off to sleep 'Every Day, and in Every Way it takes all sorts to fill this world – & <u>her</u> sort like to get value for life – in a bright sun – & would rather*

be <u>dead</u> than live in England' – !!!!!! <u>Perfectly</u> True – nothing could be truer – I have had enough – & more than enough of England!!! and the damp & the fog – & the slush – and the moral blight – !!! & it amuses me to be a Petty Mediaeval Baron here![2]

Olive's letters had always contained a certain brio.

Arthur had wasted no time in travelling to France after receiving Jean Baltus's telegram on Saturday evening. He left first thing on Sunday, accompanied – at her insistence – by his eldest daughter, Kay. Olive had been Kay's godmother, and the twenty-four-year-old had absorbed much of her spirit, having spent many happy months in Les Baux. Her sister Phyll had spent even more time there, but, like their mother, was too distraught to make the journey.*

When their train arrived at Avignon on Monday morning, they were met by Louis Vigne, who filled them in on the devastating events of the weekend on the drive back to Saint-Rémy. After dropping their luggage at the Hotel de Provence, Louis took them to pick up Jean Baltus and Olive's doctor and friend, Edgar Leroy, before heading out to Les Baux.

By the time the group arrived in the valley at two o'clock, it had begun to rain and Mas de Chiscale greeted them in silence, lifeless under the heavy sky. No dogs came scrambling towards the gate, no cheerful 'Hullo!' rang out from the studio. There was just the lone figure of Olive's solicitor, who had offered to meet them and explain the details of the gendarmes' investigation.

---

* Of the other fforde siblings, sixteen-year-old Bet was too young to travel to Les Baux, and Arthur junior, at twenty-eight, had his own family responsibilities.

The house held so much history, especially for Kay. She and Phyll had first visited in April 1926, when she was twenty-one and Phyll eighteen. They had stayed in the room above the abandoned kitchen, which Olive had kitted out in rudimentary fashion with old beds and a tin bath. Comfort, however, had not been their priority. Although officially the sisters were there to improve their French, their real purpose was to experience Cousin Olive in the wild and bring the chaotic glory of her letters to life.

They had not been disappointed. Kay had lost count of the miles they'd since travelled in search of adventure, with 'fat grunting Louis' at the wheel, or the hours spent discussing the shapes of a creative life with Olive's artist friends.[3] One day they might be watching the thunderous rounding up of the bulls on the Crau, the next cheering an impromptu performance on the harmonium by the engraver Louis Jou ('even if he did miss a good many of the notes & in moments of great stress forget to pedal . . .'[4]), or listening to Jean Baltus – 'Johnny B' – talk endlessly about his beloved Miss Schloop (a hopeless romance, if ever there was one). Phyll had even taken up stone carving with the help of a local mason.

Olive had always taken her role as their godmother seriously: teas and treats when they were younger; adventure and advice as they entered adulthood. She introduced them to a different way of being. Once, in March 1925, when Kay was halfway through her degree in medieval and modern languages at Newnham College, Cambridge, she asked for Olive's help in weighing up future career options. Should she go for something safe and conventional, such as teaching, or pursue the creativity she craved? Olive had replied:

[Your mother] has discussed many plans with me – & I find it so difficult to be helpful. For most of them, I'd rather be dead

if I had to endure such a life – but as she says, 'You have a different character.' I don't think I could ever Schoolmistress, but of course I see the practical advantages – when they are pointed out to me. But all the same, I couldn't bear it!

... The hard part, I think, is that the people who have never practised an art to excel in it have <u>no idea</u> what a hard master any art is – it takes the best – & what it leaves isn't worth much! & they have no idea of the strength of will needed to keep yourself at it when you are discouraged – & things go wrong – or the heart searchings – which one mostly has to keep to oneself, unless by good luck there is someone at hand, who understands.

However, I think it is worth it. One knows the conditions – there must be no doubt at all about them! & I think it is better to wrestle with an art one loves than to make it a hobby & do something more material which conventionally gives a more comfortable life. But, for goodness' sake – Do as you want & not as you're told to do – if you don't want to.[5]

After graduating, Kay had followed her advice, and was now wrestling her way through her first year at the Royal Academy of Dramatic Arts.

She had last been in Les Baux for three weeks at the beginning of the year. The RADA term was in full flow, but she'd been having trouble with her voice – it had weakened to non-existence – and her throat specialist had ordered complete mental and physical rest. If she had to play the role of an invalid, she'd reasoned, she might as well do so in Provence. Phyll, after all, had been there since December, having a whale of a time.

It was perishingly cold when Kay arrived in mid-January. Les Baux was experiencing exceptionally severe weather – so severe that Olive and Phyll had been snowed in for a week over the

New Year. It had since thawed, but the water in the dogs' cauldron in the studio still froze solid on some days. Kay had therefore stayed at the hotel, where Joseph had brought her meals in bed, stoked the fire and made regular appearances with a kettle to refill her hot-water bottle. For the first week, she had done nothing but sleep.

She hadn't been alone in her lethargy. After a Christmas full of revelry, the atmosphere in Les Baux was subdued. The flu was everywhere, but a more existential malaise also hung over the village: the freezing weather had wreaked havoc on the tender buds of the vines, meaning the autumnal grape harvest would be compromised, if not completely ruined. Difficult times lay ahead. Even the annual *fête patronale* to honour Saint Vincent, with its two nights of dancing at the *mairie*, had only briefly shifted the mood.

Meanwhile, Phyll had been out riding Olive's new mare every day and going dancing in Saint-Rémy. Olive, too, seemed full of her usual joie de vivre. For her, life was full of potential. The hotel renovations were picking up steam, so she'd been meeting weekly with her architect and marshalling the stone masons, carpenters and painters into some semblance of order. She'd also organized a small dinner for François Pinet's twenty-fifth birthday, complete with Heidsieck champagne, and bought herself a parrot after falling in love with the one she'd given to Phyll for Christmas. The newcomer, Jacquot, had been bought on a whim and, in Olive's words, was 'very Pot House in his manners' compared with Phyll's more urbane Jou Jou.[6] This, however, had only added to the unruly spirit of Mas de Chiscale the sisters had come to love.

By the end of January, Kay was sufficiently recovered to join Olive and Phyll on a short trip to the Alps. Squeezing into Louis's car with François and his friend Adrien Sautel, they drove the

210 kilometres to the small mountain town of Embrun to stay at a hotel the young men were thinking of buying. They also made a brief foray to the Italian border via the ski resort of Briançon, where François had been stationed during his military service.

A week later, Kay's parents collected her on their way home from visiting her grandfather in Grasse. Phyll and Jou Jou were to stay in Les Baux for another fortnight. Before the sisters parted, however, they made plans to explore the Spanish frontier with Olive later in the year. Now, that would never happen.

It continued to rain as Monsieur Martin-Caille, the solicitor, introduced himself and led the group up to the cistern. They could not enter the house, owing to the wax seals the justice of the peace had affixed to the frame of every window and door. These would only be removed, Martin-Caille explained, once Olive's will had been approved by the authorities.

None of them had ever paid the cistern much attention before. They knew it was there, but the only part that had ever entered anyone's consciousness was the retaining stone wall that sloped above the path to Olive's studio. The structure had always been dwarfed by the rocks above. Now, it took on a looming aspect of its own.

A ladder rested against the side, left over from the operation to retrieve Olive's body. Grateful, they clambered up: none of the men were of an age to scale the wall with any dignity, and Kay's stockings would have been ruined. Yet, according to the events the solicitor now described, less than forty-eight hours earlier Olive had done just that – scaled the wall, revolver in hand, and then lowered herself into the water through a hatch at the rear and shot herself.

As they stood looking at the expanse of wet flagstones at their feet, Martin-Caille pointed to where her body had been submerged, stretched out along the back wall. Her revolver had been lying near her left side, where it had dropped from her hand as she sank.

This last fact was disturbing. They all knew that Olive had not been left-handed. Arthur had known her since she was a child, Kay had witnessed her domestic pottering, Baltus had observed her drawing and Leroy was her physician. She had always favoured her right hand. Martin-Caille said there were witnesses to the contrary, and that Dr Cot and Sergeant Fabre had been thorough in their analysis of the scene, but they held their tongues until he took his leave to return to his office in Tarascon. Olive's right-handedness, after all, was just one of several factors that cast doubt in their minds over the thoroughness of the investigation.

For his part, Baltus had been convinced of foul play from the moment he'd seen Olive's contorted body dripping on the flagstones. He'd never been enamoured with the local population – in fact, he did his best to avoid them – and found it easy to believe that one of their lumpen number had dispatched his friend out of spite or jealousy.

While Arthur disagreed with this assessment of the Baussencs, he did struggle to see why Olive would have taken her own life. She wasn't the type. The dark times she had navigated in her adult life were proof enough of that. Furthermore, even if she had been tempted, her conscience would have compelled her to leave a letter – for his wife, if no one else – explaining her reasons. Kay believed the very thought of her sweet mother would have stopped Olive in her tracks: the cousins had supported each other through thick and thin, and Olive would never have burdened May with the guilt of having 'failed' someone whom she regarded as a sister.[7]

Dr Leroy, however, was keeping an open mind. He had been the resident doctor at the Saint-Paul-de-Mausole asylum in Saint-Rémy since 1919, and knew a thing or two about mental illness.

He was also a fastidious physician. During the war, he had been honoured both for his work on the treatment of gas victims and for halting an epidemic of diphtheria in the Somme. He even had a syndrome named after him: Fiessinger–Leroy disease, a form of reactive arthritis he and a colleague had noted after an outbreak of dysentery in the army in 1915.

He had known Olive since she arrived in Provence, both as a friend and as a patient. In fact, he had been the one to recommend she move to the area permanently. They shared a crusading spirit, although Leroy was more overtly political than Olive had ever been. (In 1926, for example, he and his wife Claire had taken their eight children, the eldest of whom was seventeen, to Normandy for a month-long, anti-fascist peace congress for French and German youth.)

Olive had been very fond of his family and had often joined them for lunch at their large house on the Avenue Pasteur. The last time was in March. Baltus had been there, too, which made for an awkward scene when the children started playing up: while the Leroys and Olive cheerfully continued bawling their conversation over the din, Baltus had just sat there with his hands over his ears until Claire restored order.[8]

Baltus felt everything deeply. Olive had, too, although in a less immediately reactive way. Leroy had witnessed first-hand the depression that had sometimes taken hold of their friend, leaving her stranded in an emotional wilderness. It had been at its worst the previous summer, when, to her mortification, she also started bursting into tears with no warning. 'I can't help it – it's ridiculous!'[9]

The three-month rest cure he prescribed had been a success for a while – she returned to Les Baux cheerful and clear-headed – but in the new year she confided in him that her sense of detachment had begun to return. In Leroy's view, suicide was not outside the bounds of possibility.

The practicalities of her having done so, however, were another matter. Leaving aside the effort required to clamber onto the platform, the only way to get inside the cistern was through an opening in the grille at the rear. As Leroy understood it, this had been closed when Joseph Girard first looked inside, meaning Olive must have lowered it herself after climbing into the water.

He volunteered to test the mechanics of this. With the others' agreement, he stripped down to his singlet and underpants. Although largely bald, the doctor's round face still sported a thick black walrus moustache and, in his long underwear, the overall impression was that of a hearty sea bather of yesteryear. The mood, however, was sombre as he eased himself through the opening.

The first problem Leroy encountered was that the wire mesh surrounding the hatch had raw edges, forming dozens of sharp needles which scratched his skin and snagged his underwear. Even with the most careful of movements, these were impossible to avoid. Yet, from what he had heard, Olive's body was free of abrasions.

The practicalities became even more doubtful once his feet had sunk into the sludge at the bottom of the tank. Standing up, his head and shoulders still poked out through the opening. He could look around at the house and garden, rest his arms on the platform and carry on talking to the others. Olive had been nearly five feet nine inches tall, just one and a half inches shorter than him. To close the hatch, she would have had to crouch down in the water, taking care to keep the revolver dry, while simultaneously reaching up and lowering the mesh above her head. Not only did Leroy struggle to mimic this, it seemed an unlikely and pointless undertaking for a woman focused on oblivion – especially one not known for her tidiness.

*

When the group arrived at the Hotel Monte-Carlo a short while later, they were met by Joseph, Marie-Thérèse and François. Kay, of course, knew the trio well and submitted to the Girards' effusive greetings. Arthur had only met them on a couple of occasions, but their characters were lodged in his mind with disproportionate vibrancy thanks to Olive's letters.

> *– François . . . sitting next my bed with the perfect manner of a West End Physician while we discussed the latest upheaval . . .*[10]
> *– Madame G is searching for a powerful motorbike for herself! She is a sporting soul . . .*[11]
> *– I have just had another white hot scene with my Joseph*
> *– & I trust all will go more peacefully now . . .*[12]

François led them up through the damp streets to the cemetery. It was dark and musty inside the mortuary. Olive's coffin lay on a wooden bier in the centre of the room and everyone hung back as Arthur knelt down beside it, lowering his head in prayer. Kay, briefly hesitant, wiped her eyes and followed her father's example.

On the way back down to the village, they were largely silent as their footsteps crunched on the uneven, rocky path. As Arthur and Kay walked ahead, however, François stopped and turned to Jean Baltus. 'Do you think they'll do an autopsy?'

'Of course,' Baltus replied, although he didn't know.

Dr Leroy confirmed it was indeed likely, and they walked on in silence.

Back at the hotel, Arthur sat down with François and Marie-Thérèse to discuss a few practical matters. Olive had kept her family informed as to the contents of her wills. Arthur knew that there were two, both written the previous year. The first, her English will, had been drafted by her cousin George. Other than a number of specific bequests, it left all her English property to

Kay's sisters, Phyll and Bet. The second, prepared according to French law, bequeathed her assets in Les Baux to Kay herself. This meant that Kay would be the new owner of the hotel.

Marie-Thérèse and François asked him what they should do. Could they keep it open while the estate was sorted out and Kay decided how to proceed?

'I'm not one of the executors,' Arthur replied, 'so I can't tell you.'

'All the same, you're still her family,' said François.

Seeing their predicament, Arthur relented. He suggested they carry on as usual for the time being.

It was a relief when Louis Vigne arrived to take them back to Saint-Rémy. It had been a draining afternoon and the village scandalmongers were beginning to gather around the hotel, hungry for gossip. One of the older villagers had already informed Kay that Olive had 'tempted the devil.'[13]

Just as they were driving off, however, Marie-Thérèse called for them to stop. Speaking to Arthur through the passenger window, she said, 'We've got to bury Miss Branson as quickly as possible. The mayor doesn't want us to leave her at the mortuary.' She suggested they use her family's vault, before adding, 'Although, once you bury her, you can't touch her body for a year.'

Arthur was confused. But, before he could reply, Louis drove on, telling him to ignore her: the mayor would never have said such a thing, and not moving the body for a year was just superstition.

Either way, Arthur had no intention of speeding up Olive's burial. There were too many unanswered questions.

The following evening, sixty-seven kilometres away in Marseille, the public prosecutor Auguste Rol was reading the late edition of the *Petit Marseillais*. With the municipal elections due to take place that weekend, much of the right-leaning paper's front page was given over to a list of candidates, along with an editorial excoriating the taxation policies of the city's long-standing socialist leaders. Also prominent were that day's updates on the talks taking place in Paris regarding Germany's war reparations, and those in Geneva to prepare for the League of Nations' upcoming disarmament conference. What caught Rol's eye, however, was a short piece at the bottom of the page.

Au fond d'une citerne on trouve le cadavre d'une Anglaise établie aux Baux

Elle avait la tête trouée d'une balle

It concerned a wealthy Englishwoman – a 'Miss Brampton' – whose body had been found in a water tank in a wild valley somewhere near Les Baux. The gendarmes had determined it to be a case of suicide: the woman had a bullet wound in her head, and her revolver had been found with her body. Apparently, however, this conclusion had not been universally accepted. As the *Petit Marseillais* reported, those who'd known Miss Brampton said she had no reason to take her own life. In fact, she had been notably cheerful at a luncheon the previous day.

'So?' the article continued. Here, the journalist had paused for dramatic effect, employing that coyest of punctuation marks: the ellipsis. 'So, in the village, people recall that recently Miss Brampton was the object of blatant threats . . .'[14]

The piece ended with the mundane fact that two of the woman's nephews were now in Les Baux and had been to view their aunt's remains. But those three dots had hit their mark. Rol picked up the telephone and placed a call to Félix Martin, the head of the Marseille Flying Squad.

II

Alexandre Guibbal was the best of Félix Martin's four *commissaires*. He'd only been with Marseille Flying Squad for two years, but was a detective of undoubtable talent. Good humoured, dependable, shrewd and dogged, he was destined for greatness – as, indeed, time would attest in the form of entry into the Légion d'honneur and a series of promotions through which he would become head of the Flying Squad and then of the regional Sûreté as a whole.

Physically, Guibbal was built to be a *commissaire*. When the Marseille Flying Squad – the ninth *Brigade Mobile* – had been set up in 1907, it had only admitted men shorter than five feet five inches, so they would blend in with the city and dockside crowds. To Guibbal's advantage, that rule had since fallen by the wayside and the twenty-strong brigade now comprised men of all shapes and sizes, from the ferrety Laforgue to the giraffe-like Mercuri, their fedoras and berets bobbing around in the throng without undue incident.

Guibbal was more of a bear. His solid body carried an air of trust and authority, which was enhanced by the cut of his suit, his neat tie and crisp pocket square. On colder days, he would add a thick, double-breasted coat. Whatever the weather, he wore a grey homburg that would be discarded the moment action beckoned to reveal greying hair, slicked back in an ever-inching widow's peak.

His mouth, poker straight and a fraction too wide, was set in an expression of amiable neutrality, with only the faintest twitch up or down needed to denote humour or displeasure. Most expression came from his eyes, which danced with intelligence.

He had arrived in the Flying Squad by a circuitous route. The eldest son of a postman, he grew up in Sainte-Marthe on the outskirts of Marseille, where, after leaving school, he trained as a mechanic. When the time came for his military service in 1908, the young Alexandre joined the navy, where he stayed for four years. At the outbreak of war in 1914, he reported back to the fleet, but instead of being assigned to a ship or naval depot, he caught the eye of his superiors and was whisked away on secondment to the special commissioner for counter-espionage in Marseille.

Other than the happy fact of his marriage in 1916 to Denise and the subsequent birth of their daughter Clairette, Guibbal would never speak of what he did during those years. Anyone consulting official records would find his war a curious one: eighteen months of invisibility, followed by a sudden appointment as the police superintendent in a sleepy north-eastern town, then back south to Port-de-Bouc as a deputy special police commissioner for the Paris–Lyon–Méditerranée railway, alongside a series of mysterious promotions within both the Ministry of the Interior and the Ministry of War, the details of which were redacted for reasons of national defence. At one point, he was knighted by Alexander, the semi-exiled king of Greece, for services rendered but unknown. Post-war, he spent some time in army intelligence during the Allied occupation of the Rhineland.

It was unsurprising that a man of his experience had been snapped up by Félix Martin. The Marseille Flying Squad needed men like Guibbal, dealing as it did both with the criminality of an international port favoured by the Mafia and the general baseness of human behaviour throughout the region. Guibbal himself had hunted down all manner of offenders, from rapists and murderers to a large gang of *carambouilleurs* dealing in stolen silks and cars.[1]

But it was Old Provence that had been calling him recently. The previous Friday, while Olive Branson was spending her last hours reading in her deckchair, Guibbal had been at the courthouse in Aix, testifying against a widow and her farmhand lover for the murder of the woman's husband. The case had not unduly stretched Guibbal's powers of deduction: Madame Négrel had been trying to kill her husband with poison for months and had finally delegated the task to young Lucien Jaume, who finished the job with an easily traceable gun.

A more complex investigation, and arguably Guibbal's greatest coup on behalf of the Flying Squad to date, was scheduled for trial in September. The Valensole murders had shocked the whole of France with their brutality and had raised Guibbal to prominence for his relentless pursuit of the culprits. It had, admittedly, been a fine bit of police work.

He had been called to the isolated farm near Valensole one wet evening in December. It was dark by the time he and his team found the cluster of dilapidated buildings a few miles outside the town. Electricity had yet to reach the farmhouse, so they only had the beam of their headlights to light the interior as they opened the door, but that did little to diminish the scene of unimaginable horror that awaited them.

They encountered the first blood-soaked body as soon as they stepped across the threshold. This was later identified as that of the farmhand, Amaudric. Further on, they discovered four more: the woman of the house – Madame Richaud – and her three young children. Amaudric and Madame Richaud had both been shot, but the children had been beaten to death.

Drawers had been emptied and mattresses slashed, and evidence of the family's attempts to defend themselves could be seen in the kitchen utensils scattered on the ground and the chairs splintered in desperation. The baby's highchair had suffered the most.

Behind the house, they found the body of Monsieur Richaud lying on a stone threshing platform. He was still clutching the hurricane lamp he'd been holding when shot from behind. His dog lay inconsolable by his side.

It was a Thursday night, but Guibbal, noticing the family was dressed for church, deduced that the attacks had occurred five days earlier, on the Sunday. He was equally sure that there had been at least two assailants and that they were known to the Richauds – the only reason he could see for such savagery against innocent children was to prevent them from naming their parents' attackers.

At first light, he was about to return to Marseille to check the criminal history of all the Richauds' former employees, when word came from nearby Voix that two young men wheeling Amaudric's distinctive bicycle had visited a local moneychanger the day after the murders. A waitress at Voix station confirmed the men had eaten at the station buffet before taking the train to Apt in the Vaucluse. At Apt, a railway employee said they had gone on to Cavaillon. But from there the trail went cold.

Meanwhile, in Valensole, a witness reported seeing one of the Richauds' old farmhands the day before the murders. She had been surprised, as he had long since left the area. Eighteen-year-old Jules Ughetto matched the description of the taller man with Amaudric's bicycle. 'Everything now fitted perfectly,' as Guibbal would later recall. 'An identified criminal is half caught . . .'[2]

It was now the second night. Guibbal and his team hadn't slept and were caked in mud from traipsing around in the heavy rain, but they set off again for Ughetto's home town of Lauris, some twenty-five kilometres away. When they arrived at the local gendarmerie early the next morning, however, it was to the news that the Ughetto family had long since left the region. But Guibbal wasn't entirely out of luck. On entering a nearby bakery to buy breakfast for his men, he was greeted by a familiar voice.

'Hey, Monsieur Guibbal, there you are! So, you're looking for the bandits of Valensole?'

It was his old baker from Marseille, who had swapped his metropolitan *boulangerie* for a quieter enterprise in the country. Furthermore, the baker was familiar with Ughetto.

'Jules? Hell, I know him! He doesn't live here anymore, but I bumped into him only two weeks ago on the train. He was going to . . . he was going to . . . I don't remember the name, but it's in the Gard. He told me he was working in the mines.'[3]

There were coal mines all over the Gard. The region kept the railways running and the navy afloat, and thousands of men went there to work, bunking down in barracks, hotels and private lodgings. It was the perfect place to go to ground. But Guibbal's luck continued when he returned to the gendarmerie: a standard request form had arrived in the post from the mining town of La Grand-Combe. The authorities wanted to check the identity of a new resident, one Jules-Baptiste Ughetto.

By the time Guibbal arrived in La Grand-Combe, the local gendarmes had detained Ughetto and his companion on the pretext of an irregularity with their paperwork. Ughetto's partner in crime had been his boyfriend, a baby-faced Pole going by the name of Joseph Witkowski. It was then simply a matter of playing one off against the other to secure the necessary confessions.

The whole exercise had taken less than three days. Guibbal had been rightly lauded for his work, although he would always be keen to stress that it was a team effort – and an unusual one at that: 'Seldom have I worked on an investigation with such team spirit among the various law enforcement agencies . . .'[4]

*

As he headed to Les Baux that day, however, Guibbal assumed he was just enjoying a spring trip to the countryside. After digging out the gendarmes' report into Olive Branson's death, which had been forwarded to Marseille as a matter of routine, he'd quickly realized that the facts reported in the evening edition of the *Petit Marseillais* bore little relation to the truth. In its haste to break the story, the paper had got the victim's name wrong, along with the location of the supposed crime and a number of other details.

As far as Guibbal was concerned, his mission was a political one, a matter of appeasement for the purposes of international diplomacy: the dead woman's cousin, one Sir George Branson, was a judge in the English High Court and had already spoken to the British press. With the hounds of Fleet Street now haranguing their French colleagues for details, the situation threatened to get out of control.

He therefore intended to poke around Les Baux for a while, chat to a few witnesses, take a few photographs and then return to Marseille. There, he would write his own summary, which would no doubt find its way to the British consul and then on to Sir George, and the matter would be closed.

His first stop was Saint-Rémy, where he spoke to Sergeant Fabre and the justice of the peace, Dominique Muselli. Nothing either man told him suggested that the case was anything but a tragic case of suicide. He then went to find Arthur fforde, who he understood disagreed with Fabre's verdict. Such denial was not unusual. The overwhelming combination of sorrow, disbelief and guilt wreaked by a suicide often sent relatives on a frantic search for an alternative explanation where none existed. Reasoned discussion was rarely any use in such cases.

On arrival at the Englishman's hotel, however, Guibbal found him to be remarkably calm and composed. As he would later learn, Arthur fforde was a kindred spirit, having also worked in intelligence, albeit in India rather than Europe. He therefore knew that facts – and their clear and rational transmission – were his best chance of rectifying what he and his family saw as a gross error of judgement by the gendarmerie.

Speaking in a near-perfect Tours accent, fforde began with his cousin's state of mind in the weeks leading up to her death. The view in Les Baux was that something had upset her during a recent trip to London, but fforde had collated a list of her activities from that visit, none of which had the potential to drive an otherwise contented woman to suicide.

As he explained, Olive had arrived in London on Saturday, 13 April and booked into her usual hotel, the Astoria in Soho. The purpose of her trip had been twofold. Firstly, she needed to see her dentist. She had booked two appointments, at least one of which required anaesthesia. Secondly, she wanted to visit Shoolbred's storage warehouse on the Fulham Road, where the furniture from her London flat had been kept since she moved to Les Baux. There, she had selected some pieces for use in the Hotel Monte-Carlo and arranged for them to be shipped to France. The shipment was expected to arrive any day.

She had spent the rest of the week recovering from her dental treatment and catching up with friends and family. Arthur fforde had not seen her himself – he'd been laid up with flu – but knew from those who had that she was in good spirits. On the Sunday, for example, she had treated his daughter Phyll to lunch at the Astoria before accompanying her back home to see his wife. Both said that Olive had been her usual delightful self.

She'd also had lunch with Karel Ruckl, an impoverished Czech actor who she'd been supporting in his attempts to build a theatrical career for over half a decade. Although Olive – and indeed fforde himself – had sometimes found Karel's lack of organization exasperating, he was a gentle soul and she had been very fond of him. As far as anyone knew, the lunch had been nothing out of the ordinary.

She had left London early on Saturday, 20 April, arriving in Les Baux late in the evening. On the Sunday, she had written to his wife, who had sent a card to welcome her home. Perhaps she had been feeling a little out of sorts, as one line had read, 'I often wish I hadn't been born a Misfit! But you never make me feel one!' – but the rest of her letter had been full of optimism. 'All well here,' she'd reported. The Channel crossing had been cold and rough, and the train to Paris overcrowded, but she had described the journey with her usual humour. The Girards, she'd said, had been excited to hear news of Kay and Phyll.[5]

As far as Arthur fforde had ascertained, nothing untoward had happened in the five days after that. If Olive seemed quieter than normal, as some had reported, then she had reason to be. She'd been rushing around for months, entertaining his daughters, chasing up the work at the hotel, and juggling money between England and France to pay for it all – all on top of finishing drawings to submit to the Royal Academy Summer Exhibition and a group show with the New English Art Club. That week had been the first opportunity she'd had to relax since Christmas.

Continuing his list of concerns, fforde then described an experiment he had conducted two days earlier with his cousin's doctor in Les Baux, which had shown it was impossible to get inside the cistern without scratching oneself, a fact at odds with the reported lack of abrasions on the body. Lastly, he pointed out that Olive had been right-handed and therefore unlikely to have fired a gun with her left, as the gendarmes seemed to believe.

Guibbal remained unconvinced. Granted, it was an unusual suicide, and one the family might think had no motive, but where was the motive for murder? According to Sergeant Fabre, Olive Branson had no known enemies. Money could also be ruled out: no valuables had been taken from the house and the beneficiaries of her wills were ffordeʼs own daughters. Nor had the attending doctor noticed any signs of a struggle or assault.

'For my part,' he said at last, 'suicide still seems most likely. Nevertheless, I'll take a good look, although, as we say in France, I'll be looking for a hair in an egg.'*

The location, at least, was captivating. Like many visitors to Les Baux, Guibbal travelled by the road that snaked through the limestone hills of the Alpilles before descending into the Val d'Enfer, Les Baux's infamous Valley of Hell. This soulless landscape was filled with colossal white rocks, up to eighty feet in height, which had been sculpted by the wind into a maze of grotesque and unearthly shapes. It was said by some to have inspired Dante's descriptions of the Inferno itself. More recent quarrying works had only added to the sense of unease it provoked: giant geometric portals had been hewn into the rock at the sides of the valley, which receded into the darkness via a series of staggered chambers, as though one had stepped into a painting by Mondrian. In the words of the artist Archibald Stevenson Forrest from 1911, 'One could imagine it inhabited by strange monsters of human shape bereft of man's feelings and emotions.'[6]

And that was just the *amuse-bouche*. At the far end of the Val d'Enfer, towering against the horizon, was the precipitous rock upon which stood Les Baux itself. Even from a distance, the ancient citadel was an extraordinary sight. On a plateau at

---

* Something that doesn't exist.

the rear, the jagged walls of the medieval castle rose into the sky. Below that, a jumble of dilapidated buildings sprawled towards the deserted scrubland of the promontory. At the very front, where the cliff face dropped down to a small, verdant valley, the buildings and town walls seemed to meld with the rock. To quote Forrest again, it was 'half-built, half-excavated, more than half-ruined, a strange confusion of man's and nature's architecture.'[7]

Following the road as it made another steep descent through the rugged terrain, Guibbal turned off before it climbed again up to the village, driving straight into the valley. The Vallon de la Fontaine was less than a kilometre long and no more than 200 metres wide, with the telltale white rocks of the Val d'Enfer beginning to rise to the right and the village towering above to the left. He passed a cluster of buildings sitting around the fountain which gave the valley its name, among them an old olive mill, a decaying domed pavilion and a low-roofed communal wash house daubed in red paint with the words *Liberté! Egalité! Fraternité!*.

A moment later, the view opened up into fields bursting with the fresh green of spring. Despite the chilly and cloudy weather, it was an idyllic spot. A smattering of farmhouses, their red-tiled roofs bleached by the sun, kept watch over small olive groves, neat squares of vegetables and rows of vines. Here and there, lines of cypresses provided protection from the wind that swept up from the plain.

Just past the promontory of the village, a dirt road cut across the fields to the far side of the valley before disappearing into the hills. Guibbal followed it for a short distance until he saw the large Carita farmhouse mentioned in Fabre's report. Turning right, he joined a small track hugging the edge of the valley, where he'd been told he would find the entrance to Mas de Chiscale.

Two things changed Guibbal's mind about the case during the few hours he spent in Les Baux that day. The first was the cistern. As soon as he set eyes on it, he knew there was more to Olive Branson's death than he'd first assumed. He couldn't comprehend how anyone, sane or otherwise, would choose to strip off, climb such a high wall, wrestle open the grille and slip into the cold water to shoot herself, when she could have achieved the same result with much less effort and in far more comfort indoors.

The second was Joseph Girard, whom he found at home a little way down the valley. Joseph, as ever, had a lot to say – about finding the body, his late employer's character, his work at Mas de Chiscale and his doubts that Olive could fold herself into the cistern 'like an acrobat'. What really caught the detective's attention, however, was a story Joseph told about Olive's dogs.

The four that had been with her on the night she died were still in Joseph's care, so Guibbal asked to take a photograph for his records. Joseph therefore wrangled them into the courtyard, warning somewhat needlessly that they were lean, loud and *méchante*. This, in turn, got him talking about their ancestry. Frida, he explained, was part wolf; the three youngsters were her pups, and their father had been Miss Branson's late greyhound. And it was what Joseph told him about the greyhound that had Guibbal scribbling in his notebook.

By all accounts, Spring had been a sweet old boy and something of a favourite in Les Baux, especially among the children. He'd reached an extraordinary age – seventeen or eighteen – but had still tottered about quite happily. His ageing mind had even occasionally turned to romance, causing him to slink off without a sound and prompt a search of the local farmyards. Yet, despite his advanced years, Spring had not died of natural causes.

He had passed away the previous August while Olive was visiting her family in London. Spring would usually have accompanied

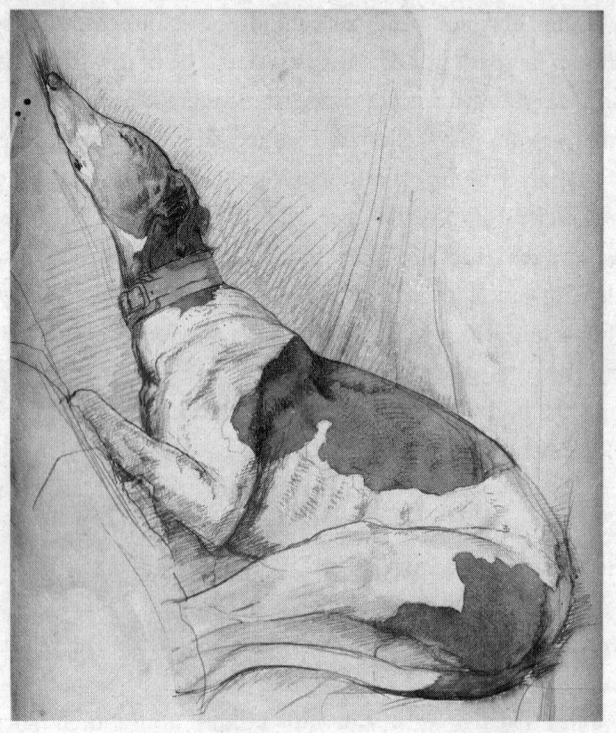

Sleeping greyhound by Olive Branson (pen and wash).

her – he had fans in England, too – but it was high summer and his old bones were no longer up to the journey. All he'd wanted was a cool corner in which to doze and a bit of fuss, so he stayed behind under the care of Joseph and Marie-Thérèse.

One day, Spring had become violently ill. They sent for Abert, the vet from Saint-Rémy, who suspected that the dog had ingested some poison. It had taken three agonizing nights for Spring to die. Abert had later performed an autopsy, which confirmed his suspicions, although he had not investigated the exact nature of the toxin.

On her return, Olive had been distraught – and furious. She

believed Spring had been deliberately poisoned. The thought festered in her mind until she became convinced that the culprit would return for her other dogs. Just before Christmas, in fact, she had sent a letter to Sergeant Fabre, pre-emptively offering a reward of 4,000 francs should her fear be realized.

> *Nothing has happened. I accuse no one – but if a malheur happens to my young dogs I'll let you know – & I beg you then to come at once . . .*[8]

The next day, the gendarmes had turned up at Mas de Chiscale and Joseph had shown them into Olive's bedroom, where she was recovering from flu. There had been a long discussion, and she had seemed satisfied with the outcome.

Olive may have refused to name any names, but Joseph was less discreet when recounting the saga to Guibbal. The man with a bounty on his head was Etienne Patin, Olive's former gardener. And she had been right to suspect him; the pair had a long and turbulent history.

Guibbal took note. He would follow it up, if necessary. For the purposes of his current commission, however, it was enough to know that, contrary to Fabre's assertion, at least one person in Les Baux had wished Olive Branson ill.

In the handwritten report he delivered to Félix Martin the following morning, Guibbal recommended three things: firstly, a deeper probe into 'some particularly delicate points' he had unearthed during his visit to Les Baux; secondly, a search of Mas de Chiscale; and, thirdly, an autopsy.

After reading Guibbal's report, Félix Martin telephoned the public prosecutor Auguste Rol at the Palais de Justice. In turn,

Rol informed the British consul and summoned the examining magistrate Joseph Rochu up from his office in the basement. Rochu's clerk, Emile Jeanpierre, finding himself at the end of this chain, fetched his notepad and braced himself for an outpouring of instructions.

A thousand trees quivered as the French justice system, with all its attendant paperwork, heaved into action: forms were fetched, reports requested and summaries distributed. A flurry of telegrams flew out of the basement of the Palais de Justice, ordering Bouches-du-Rhône's finest forensics experts to assemble at Mas de Chiscale the following morning. Joseph Rochu would direct the judicial investigation as the examining magistrate, with Alexandre Guibbal as lead detective. They would be joined at the farmhouse by Auguste Rol's deputy, as well as Félix Martin, Sergeant Fabre, Fabre's superiors from Marseille, various local officials and all their associated hangers-on.

The people of Les Baux had no idea what was about to hit them.

III

The first cars began to arrive from Marseille at nine o'clock on Friday morning, rumbling through the valley and spilling their occupants into the yard of Mas de Chiscale. They were soon joined by more from Saint-Rémy, carrying the local officials.

There was a sense of expectation in the area around the farmhouse. A smattering of villagers had gathered in the lane, but most of the activity came from members of the press, who, with cameras and notepads in hand, were stumbling about in the undergrowth at the front and side of the property, trying to find the best spot from which to watch events unfold.

By ten o'clock, there were easily two dozen men milling about the yard, awaiting instructions from Joseph Rochu, the examining magistrate. Clusters of kepis and blue serge denoted the gendarmes, the glint of silver on black the Sûreté. While the reporters noted down familiar faces among the sea of civilian suits, their camera-wielding colleagues focused on two in particular: Alexandre Guibbal – still the man of the moment after his victory in Valensole – and the dashing young head of the Marseille police forensics laboratory, Dr Georges Béroud. Guibbal, with his piercing eyes, always made for a striking picture, but Georges Béroud was in a class of his own. Towering above his colleagues in a fine wool suit, with his thick, black hair oiled to perfection beneath a jaunty fedora, Béroud had the looks of a matinee idol and the ambition to match.

The photographers at the side of the property soon got their opportunity when Rochu called the assembly to order and asked the justice of the peace to lift the seals on the house in the presence of its official guardian, Joseph Girard. While this was happening, Guibbal took Béroud up to look at the cistern, offering a perfect shot of the celebrated pair on top of the most infamous water tank in Provence.

Guibbal pointed out to his colleague the height of the wall and the sharp edges of the wire inside the grille. He called for Sergeant Fabre to indicate the original level of the water before it had been drained, and for Joseph Girard to describe the position of Olive's body as he'd found it.

Then, like Dr Leroy four days earlier, the investigators tried to recreate her alleged suicide. This time, Béroud was the one to lower himself into the tank, albeit fully dressed, preferring to sacrifice his immaculate suit to the sharp edges of the mesh than disrobe in full sight of the press. Just shy of six feet tall, Béroud was nearly four inches taller than Olive, but it was the headroom above the waterline that interested him. Discarding his fedora, he asked to borrow Guibbal's pistol. He crouched down inside the tank, taking care to keep the weapon out of the imaginary water, and pulled the hatch down above him. The water, he reported through the grille, would have been up to his chin at this point.

After some experimentation, Béroud's top half emerged, triumphant. Lighting a cigarette, he reported that there had been just enough room to hold the pistol to his forehead if he leaned his head back. But a revolver? To accommodate the extra length of the barrel, Olive would have had to slide down and brace herself against the back wall – 'almost to the point of sitting double,' as he put it. This would have meant her mouth and nose would have been under water at the moment of death.

Dr Georges Béroud and Alexandre Guibbal at the cistern.

This was a crucial observation, he explained. It meant that the autopsy would give a definitive answer as to whether she had taken her own life or not. If she had, there would be water in her lungs and stomach; if not, there would be none. Of course, it was also possible that someone had forced her into the cistern and shot her from above, causing her to breathe in water as she sank, but that could be determined by a bit of trigonometry. It all depended on the angle at which the bullet had entered her skull.

When the house was ready, they entered through the studio door. Guibbal took in the mess before walking over to the table, where the dishes from Olive Branson's last meal still sat on the chequered cloth. The banana skin was now black and the asparagus ends shrivelled to sharp, green shards. The dregs in her wine glass had dried to dark purple flakes.

He noted the inkwell next to the pepper grinder, and the reading glasses next to her abandoned book. She'd been reading *The Silver Spoon* by John Galsworthy, the latest instalment in the ongoing Forsyte Chronicles, set in the kind of London circles she'd presumably once known. There were hundreds more books on the high shelves in the bedroom and crammed into a low bookcase at the top of the stairs. Some were in English, others French. Rudyard Kipling nestled against Honoré de Balzac, George Borrow's *The Romany Rye* shared houseroom with a French translation of Turgenev's *Virgin Soil*. A half-used pad of request forms for *The Times'* postal book club, along with a reader's ticket for the public library at Arles, suggested that more came and went all the time.

Police photograph of Olive's bedroom.

To a detective's eye, the house was full of clues about its late occupant, from the framed picture in the kitchen of Saint Roch, the patron saint of dogs, to the unusual ring on the bedside cabinet, with a coral cartouche engraved in Hindi. As a potential crime scene, though, it was less than ideal. Fabre's report said her handbag had been found on the floor by the table, but it now hung from the back of the chair. In the bedroom, the covers on the bed had been pulled back and the top mattress removed. Who knew what else had been disturbed by the gendarmes and villagers after the body had been found? All Guibbal could do was to call in the police photographer to record everything as it was.

The primary task for Guibbal and Béroud, however, was to search for evidence of a crime. Although yet to be confirmed, it seemed fair to assume that Olive Branson had been killed by a single bullet to the head, so they weren't expecting pools of blood. But if the revolver had been fired by a second party inside this house, it was still likely that there would have been a struggle beforehand, or at least a moment of violent surprise that could have left some mark. The challenge was separating such evidence from the general chaos of Olive Branson's daily life.

Olive's studio, as viewed from the external door.

Once the photography was complete, they decided to start with the floor. It would not be easy. Although there was linoleum in the bedroom, the studio had a traditional *béton* floor, formed by lacing cement with gravel and chalk and beating it as it dried. The resulting dusty surface soaked up every spill, and there were stains and splashes everywhere, which formed notably dense clusters under the table and in front of the hearth.

Still, they got down on their knees, magnifying glasses in hand, and began to inspect every inch. It was hard to shuffle around without kicking something: the legs of the inordinate amount of furniture crammed against the walls, for example, or piles of ink-stained rags, or the dogs' giant, heavy water bowl. Guibbal had barely got started at the entrance to the studio, however, when he noticed a line of small brown spots. He called Béroud over, and the scientist confirmed his suspicions. It was blood.

The kitchen, with arrow indicating the bottom curve of the stairs.

The path outside had been washed clean by the rain over the last week. Inside, though, the spots formed two trails: one that led to the dining table, and another that ran towards the bedroom door and then down the stairs into the kitchen. The kitchen wall at the bottom of the stairs was spattered near the base, but from there all was clean.

Back in the bedroom, they found more small stains on the side of the mattress at the foot of the bed. The surrounding linoleum, in contrast, was surprisingly clean. There had been a large sponge in the kitchen, which still felt damp to the touch despite the house having been shut up for a week. Had someone been in to tidy up? All the doors and windows may have been sealed, and there hadn't been any evidence of tampering, but it wasn't beyond the wit of man or woman – especially one armed with a spirit lamp and a hot knife – to remove one of the wax discs and replace it afterwards. The farmhouse was isolated and shielded from view. They could have taken their time.

With nothing else obviously untoward inside the house, Rochu agreed it was time to gather up the evidence and reseal the doors and windows. While Dr Béroud took scrapings of the dried blood from the studio floor and kitchen wall, Guibbal called for Sergeant Fabre. They would be taking the pile of clothes on the bedroom chair, but were they in the same order as when the sergeant had first seen them? Fabre couldn't remember, but suggested Marie-Thérèse Girard might know. A gendarme was dispatched to find her.

Meanwhile, Béroud cut away the stained portion of the mattress and boxed it up with the bedclothes, the sponge, and the box of ammunition from the bedside drawer. Guibbal, having been alerted to the arrival of Arthur fforde, went outside to ask for his help in sifting through a pile of papers he had gathered from the house. The detective had already set aside the official documents – Olive's passport, bank statements and cheque stubs – but there were a number of personal letters that would be better appraised by a native English speaker.

Arthur did this crouching on the terrace. None of the letters proved of any interest – just other people's news – but he told Guibbal that he would ask his wife to forward a selection of letters Olive herself had written in recent years. These would provide the most comprehensive view of her daily life in Les Baux.

More immediately, Arthur was able to give Guibbal an overview of Olive's pocket diary. The detective would have been able to decipher most of it himself, the entries being predominantly written in French, but Arthur explained the English weather notes and unfamiliar names, as well as the appointments she had recorded during her trip to London two weeks earlier. The pages since her return were blank, other than some financial jottings on the Friday, and the only future appointment was for a court date in June relating to the hotel.

When Marie-Thérèse arrived, it was only to say she could not recall the order of the clothes on the bedroom chair, either; she had only taken a few items from the armoire to wrap the body and prepare it for burial. Joseph, hovering by the studio door, meanwhile directed Guibbal's attention to a white napkin with a red border discarded on a sideboard, saying he'd found it in a plant pot outside when he'd first arrived on the Saturday morning.

Guibbal took the opportunity to ask the pair about the dishes on the table. What food had Marie-Thérèse prepared on the Friday evening? This she remembered perfectly. It had been a tin of fish soup with vermicelli, followed by three lamb cutlets and asparagus. She'd also left some Roquefort, a banana and an apple on the table for dessert.

Finally, under the eye of Rochu and the justice of the peace, Sergeant Fabre handed over the items he'd seized during his own investigation: Olive's identity card, the cash from her purse and

– most importantly – her revolver, the cylinder of which still contained the spent cartridge and an unfired round.

It was time for the autopsy.

The pathologist Dr Louis Rey was waiting for them in the small cemetery at the far end of the village, where the dilapidated buildings gave way to the scrubland of the promontory. It had once been the garden of an old mansion and still retained the high garden walls on three sides, with a double iron gate giving access from the street via the old courtyard. A low wall at the far side offered a view over the valley, with Mas de Chiscale in the distance.

The site was filled with pale tombs and grave markers embedded in the stony ground. Each family had staked a claim to their own section according to their means: the deceased Vayssières, for example, occupied a temple-like vault in one corner, while the Pinets huddled more humbly to the side. A smattering of leafy trees offered little respite from the constant scrutiny of the heavens.

Dr Rey, a quiet mountain of a man, had set up his portable autopsy table among the graves, out of sight of the entrance. On such a fine day, it made no sense to fire up a generator to work in the dim and cramped mortuary, when perfect illumination was available outside. Once he was satisfied that the gendarmes at the gate would keep any onlookers at bay, Olive's coffin was brought out and her body transferred to the bench.

He invited Béroud to assist, an honour that Béroud gladly accepted. Louis Rey, at fifty-one, was the region's foremost forensic pathologist. Though self-effacing and discreet, he also had a whiff of celebrity about him: his older brother Félix, also a doctor, had treated Vincent van Gogh during his time in Arles, and was said to have kept the artist's ear pickled in alcohol for a number of years. The ear had since been mislaid, but this collecting instinct spoke to Béroud, who had been gathering items for his own 'Black Museum' modelled upon that of Scotland Yard.

Above all, the Reys were dedicated and talented physicians. Louis himself was now the head surgeon at Arles Hospital, having previously excelled in radiology, pulmonology and paediatrics. As an expert witness, he had played his part in many of the most sensational and baffling murder cases to plague Provence in recent years.

Unbeknownst to Béroud, Rey's invitation to assist in the autopsy may have had an ulterior motive. Having read the gendarmes' report, Rey knew that the doctor who had made the initial diagnosis of suicide was his old intern, Pierre Cot. The pair had once been close. Rey, in fact, had acted as a witness at Cot's wedding in Maussane just before the war. Now, he had been called upon to challenge his judgement in a very public way. This was not something Rey relished, especially if Cot had been in error. To have the backing of another forensic expert was therefore most welcome.

Their first observation was that the body was clothed in a strange assortment of garments. Some of them they recognized from Fabre's report – a pink cotton shirt, a white vest and a pair of beige stockings – but whoever had prepared the body for burial had simply added a second pair of stockings and a long, black evening cloak. No underwear, no skirt. The poor woman had been left to knock at the pearly gates looking as though she had stopped at a rummage sale on the way.

Of more forensic significance was the state of her stockings. Neither pair was in the slightest bit dirty or torn, as one might expect had she clambered up the retaining wall of the cistern. Her body was also free of abrasions.

The bullet wound gave the doctors further pause. Although its burned and blackened edges were consistent with the gun having been fired at close range, the bullet had entered the head at a downward angle of forty degrees. Experience told them that a self-inflicted shot would either travel slightly upwards or at a straight ninety degrees, in line with the natural movement of the wrist.

After removing the top of the skull, they could see the bullet's exact path. It had not gone far. Rather, it had pierced the frontal bone and lodged in the outer grey matter of Olive's brain. In itself, this would not necessarily have been fatal, but the force had also driven a fragment of bone deep into her cerebellum, which would have resulted in the end of all motor function and instant death.

As Rey and Béroud moved on to examine Olive's internal organs, they were able to say with certainty that she had been dead before dropping into the water: there was no trace of fluid in her lungs, no signs of asphyxiation. Nor did they require Béroud's trigonometric gymnastics to rule out the idea that she had been forced into the cistern and shot there. That could be done by the mouthful of chewed yellow fruit – probably banana – that they discovered in her oesophagus. It had been stopped in its tracks on the way to her stomach, meaning she had been eating at the moment motor function ceased.

Moving on to the stomach itself, they found its contents corresponded to the menu relayed to them by Guibbal. The pelvic organs displayed no signs of sexual assault or pregnancy: it was possible, in fact, that she had been a virgin.

Leaving Béroud to close up the body, Dr Rey reported their findings to Rochu. To his regret, his old friend Dr Cot had been entirely wrong. This was no suicide: Olive Branson had been murdered. There was no indication that she had struggled. In fact, considering her height, the trajectory of the bullet suggested she had been seated at the time, most likely at the table, finishing her dessert. Someone had stood above her, held the revolver against her forehead and pulled the trigger. It had been a cold assassination.

In the afternoon, Joseph Rochu set up a temporary office in the *mairie* with Jeanpierre and sent the gendarmes to fetch the witnesses from Fabre's original report. This exercise was largely for the record: more in-depth interviews would be left to Guibbal and his team.

The examining magistrate had a principle of displaying unwavering courtesy and patience to everyone he met in the course of his work. The first Baussencs to test this were Joseph and Marie-Thérèse. Joseph took the opportunity to repeat his concerns about Olive's lack of acrobatic ability and his doubts that she had been left-handed. These were noted, despite having been made redundant by the results of the autopsy, before Rochu guided him to talk about his employer's demeanour in the days leading up to her death.

Joseph said she'd been tired after her return from London, and perhaps a bit downhearted, but she had soon eased back into her normal routine. She hadn't left Mas de Chiscale for four days, though, other than for her daily walk. Nor had anyone come to visit her. On the Thursday, however, she had walked up to the hotel for lunch. The same day, she'd asked him to run some errands in Saint-Rémy. He handed Rochu the list she had given him. It was worn and dirty, having been in his pocket all week, but read:

La Banque (he had cashed a cheque on her behalf at the Société Générale)

L'ordonnance de Dr Leroy (this he had collected from the pharmacist Monsieur Bonnet)

6 paquets Jaunes (her usual cigarettes; she had favoured the smoothest Gauloises)

6 bananes

Rochu gave it to Jeanpierre for safekeeping as Joseph continued. On the Friday, he said, Miss Branson had again stayed at home. It had been sunny, and she had spent most of the day sitting outside reading while he'd done some gardening and walked the dogs. At her request, he'd also gone to Maussane on his motorbike to buy a small barrel of oil for her stove and a case of condensed milk for the dogs, both of which he'd arranged for his brother-in-law to collect later.

In the evening, he said, he and his wife had served Miss Branson's supper at the usual time – seven o'clock. Miss Branson had come inside by then and was sitting by the fire. She was wearing a beige jumper and a brown cotton velvet skirt. As they were leaving, he had reminded her to expect François with the oil and milk. She had smiled and handed him her crumpled copy of *Le Matin*, saying, 'Have a good evening, Monsieur Girard. Good night.' And that was the last time either of them had seen her alive.

Marie-Thérèse, with her lank, bobbed hair, and dressed in a sensible jumper atop a sensible skirt and sensible shoes, had stood sullen and silent while her husband spoke. After six hours in Les Baux, Rochu was beginning to get a sense of the Baussencs' aversion to outsiders. Joseph Girard was clearly an exception. His wife, however, was not. When faced with questions only she could answer, she did so with as much brevity as possible. It was also evident that she had little time for the notion that Olive had been murdered.

One topic, however, prompted a brief burst of defensive animation: that of her cleaning, or implied lack of it. What did she know about the blood Guibbal and Béroud had found? At first, she refused to believe they'd found any blood at all, but then remembered that there had been a fight between the dogs earlier in the year. She hadn't been there herself, she said, but Miss Branson had told her two of the pups had gone for each other. If there was blood, it must have been from that.

Rochu also extracted from her the circumstances and details of Olive's purchase of the Hotel Monte-Carlo, and the management arrangement through which her family got to keep the day-to-day profits. The initial beneficiary of this had been her brother François, she said, but he had stepped down a few weeks before Easter and she had taken his place. When asked if this had suited her, Marie-Thérèse said it had: she'd been looking for a business opportunity for herself since the birth of her youngest daughter.

François was brought in next. Neatly dressed and polite, he seemed more amenable than his sister, but it was still hard to get him to talk. From what Rochu could gather, this was his natural disposition: he was not given much to speaking at all. His account of dropping off the oil and tinned milk at Mas de Chiscale, therefore, yielded little information. He and Miss Branson hadn't exchanged more than a few words, he said. She had come down to the gate to let his car into the yard and had offered to carry the case of milk, and he'd declined. As soon as everything was put away, he'd got straight back in his car and returned to the hotel for supper with his family. As far as he knew, she had been alone. This had been around eight o'clock.

Despite the gendarmes' best efforts, only one of the other witnesses Rochu wanted to question could be found: Félix Tougay. The Baussencs, it seemed, were good at hiding. At just five foot three, Tougay might have been expected to be especially talented in this regard, but he'd made the mistake of returning home for lunch, which meant walking past Mas de Chiscale, where gendarmes were stationed at the entrance.

The dark-haired, dark-eyed Tougays had once been numerous in Les Baux, but their numbers had dwindled over the years due to a combination of marital poisoning, suicide, misadventure and war. Félix's own father had died when Félix was just six years old. His brothers had also been dispatched early, one at fourteen in a ploughing accident and the other at thirty-five during the Battle of Verdun. And so, Félix, the youngest, had been running the family farm on his own for the past ten years, ever since returning only slightly maimed from his own three years on the front. He now had a wife and two young children of his own.

With this family tendency to attract misfortune, one would have thought the Tougays were used to talking to the authorities. But, as Félix stood before Rochu in the *mairie*, he too had little to say. When asked about the moment he'd heard the gunshot, he merely repeated what he'd told Sergeant Fabre the previous weekend: that he'd been at the water trough behind Carita at the time, talking to the Spanish farmhand, Vincent Aracil.

The report, he said, on further questioning, had been clean and sharp, and sounded like it was coming from Mas de Chiscale. As no other noise had followed – no screaming, no barking – they had thought little of it. In fact, when Aracil had remarked, 'Someone's shooting a badger,' Tougay hadn't even felt the need to reply.

Rochu noticed one small anomaly between Tougay's original statement and his current recollection: he'd told Fabre that the shot had rung out at nine o'clock; now, he said it had been eight forty-five. That, however, would be for Guibbal to clear up once Aracil and the other witnesses had been located. They couldn't hide in the fields forever.

*

At five o'clock, Rochu summoned Guibbal, Martin and the representative from the public prosecutor's office to formally instigate a murder investigation. With the delay and isolated setting, not to mention the attitude of the local population, it would not be a simple case to solve. As things stood, they were looking for an unknown killer with an unknown motive who had arrived at Mas de Chiscale between eight and nine o'clock and could have left at any time during the night. Fortunately, Alexandre Guibbal enjoyed a challenge.

IV

Guibbal was back at his desk early on Saturday morning. The offices of the Marseille Flying Squad were a discreet affair, occupying as they did a slice of bourgeois real estate on the Chemin des Chartreux, where the tall apartment buildings were dressed in golden stone and adorned with elaborate wrought-iron balconies. Any passer-by glimpsing the tiled lobby behind the oak doors of number 26 would have seen nothing to suggest that the small doorway leading into the ground-floor apartment concealed anything other than urban domesticity. The only clues as to the Flying Squad's presence were the fleet of black cars parked outside and the large radio antenna erected in the rear garden.

The four *commissaires* and fourteen inspectors of the Marseille Flying Squad were expected to cover a vast area: not just Marseille and the wider Bouches-du-Rhône, but also the neighbouring departments of Var and Vaucluse, and the island of Corsica (some 320 kilometres to the south-east and a haven of the Mafia). The rough and tumble of Marseille alone would have been enough to keep them occupied: the previous year, the Sûreté as a whole had made over 4,000 arrests in the city and had investigated a further 28,000 individuals for all manner of offences, from vagrancy to armed robbery and murder. The vice squad had been equally busy, with close to 6,000 cases under their belt, as had their counterparts in the ports, who fought a constant battle with opium smugglers and other undesirables.¹ The overstretched Flying Squad had to liaise with them all and take on the most complex cases, including those emanating from the shadowy world of organized crime.

As a result, their offices on the Chemin des Chartreux were abuzz with activity both day and night. Although the more exuberant aspects of their work took place elsewhere – in interrogation rooms commandeered at local police stations, for example – there was always someone dashing in or out on some urgent assignment or with a favour to ask, and the clattering typewriters and shrill telephones rarely let up. It was not the ideal place to concentrate.

Regardless, Guibbal turned his attention to the Branson case. His instinct and experience told him that the murder had been premeditated, that Olive Branson had been killed for a specific reason and by someone she knew. On the one hand, this increased the odds of finding the person – or people – responsible. On the other, he was frustratingly late to the game. It had now been over a week since the crime had occurred, giving his prey plenty of opportunity to cover their tracks or disappear altogether.

There were also some puzzling questions to ponder. If the bullet had caused so little blood – there had been no exit wound – what were the blood spatters in the house? Were they from a dog fight, as Marie-Thérèse Girard had suggested, or had the killer been injured? And, if so, how? By those same dogs or by Miss Branson herself? And why, if she had been killed in cold blood while eating, was she naked from the waist down?

At least the house had been sealed for most of that time, although that hardly made up for the disturbance to the crime scene caused by Fabre's botched investigation: half of Les Baux seemed to have gone into the house at the gendarme's invitation. To make matters worse, those same people were now displaying a distinct aversion both to the Sûreté's authority and to scientific fact. If the morning papers were anything to go by, they were still clinging to the idea of suicide despite clear evidence to the contrary.

Luckily, Guibbal had before him a bundle of documents seized from Mas de Chiscale the previous day. It was a small bundle – just a pocket diary, cheque stubs and bank statements – but one he hoped would provide some indication of the best way forward.

The pocket diary was a small, black Hachette number, already showing signs of wear after only a few months of use. Each day had its own page, which Olive Branson had used not only for her appointments, in themselves scarce, but also to record books she wanted to read and observations about the weather. Here and there, the diary turned into a commonplace book, with short passages in French that had caught her eye. One day in March, for example, she had noted various aphorisms from *Le Livre d'Or de la Comtesse Diane*, first published in 1889:

– 'Is it amusing to say whatever comes to mind? Not nearly as much as doing it.'
– 'With what can one replace Faith? With Charity.'

She had chiefly used it, however, to note down her daily spending. Every meal or drink taken at the Hotel Monte-Carlo was recorded – '*1 Porto, 1 dejeuner, 2 cafés*' – as were payments to the Girards and the contractors working on the hotel renovation.

As for her travel expenses, Louis Vigne's name cropped up regularly, as expected. On another page, she had also written 'Car – François', followed by a list of dates, towns and distances, all within three quarters of an hour of Les Baux: Maussane, Saint-Rémy, Avignon, Arles. It wouldn't be hard to find out what she had done in those places. If Vigne or Pinet didn't know, someone was sure to remember having encountered a tall, eccentrically dressed Englishwoman.

Guibbal had chosen as his assistant for the case Inspector Antonin Laforgue, a small, wiry man of forty-one who had been with the Flying Squad for nearly a decade. All that would be a job for him, along with a careful analysis of Miss Branson's bank statements and cheque stubs. Nothing about them stood out as unusual – no suggestion of blackmail or, indeed, any other financial difficulty – but there might be something. Laforgue was good with numbers. He'd been a bookkeeper before the war.

Of more immediate interest to Guibbal was his own trusty black notebook that had accompanied him to Les Baux. Despite the general reluctance of the locals to talk, he'd jotted down enough information during his two visits to get some sense of Olive Branson's life in the village. Arthur fforde had been particularly helpful, thanks to the innumerable letters Olive had sent to his wife May over the past five years. She had, it seemed, been an unrestrained correspondent, especially when it came to the latest goings-on in Les Baux.

In due course, Arthur would hand over a small selection of these letters to the investigation, causing no small headache for the translator engaged to decipher them. Not only were they written in a mix of idiomatic English, French and phonetically transcribed Provençal, they mostly took the form of impulsive streams of consciousness scrawled at great speed.

To be fair, Olive had usually started normally enough – 'Darling May, A moment now to gossip with you . . .' or 'Darling May, Just a scrap before lunch . . .' – but then she would be off, darting here and there, bouncing from one tale to the next without so much as a breath. Long dashes leapt across the paper where one might expect a comma or full stop, were commas not so backward looking or full stops so final. Her dashes meant *onwards!* because there was more – there was more – there was *always* more.

Ampersand tumbled after ampersand – *& more & more & more* – and *Oh!* the exclamation marks – three, five, ten in a row? Why not?!!!!!!!!!! It was as though, by the very force of her pen, Olive thought she could propel the whole of Les Baux towards England – which, in a way, she had.

For the time being, however, these exuberant outpourings were shut away in a bureau in Golders Green. Still, Arthur fforde had been able to furnish Guibbal with the essence of their contents: Olive's worries, her joys, her health, her friendships and – perhaps most importantly – her many, many quarrels.

You know how a scrap amuses me when I'm well . . . ![2]

Where to start? With the minor rucks? There were certainly enough to choose from, although most had blown over quickly enough. Take, for example, an incident with Madame Sous and her beloved donkey.

The donkey, a portly beast called Friquet, was something of a fixture in the village. He was forever being called out on small missions, to haul wood up from the valley, move building materials from A to B, or simply pull Albert Montfort and his bottle of beer around in a dog cart while Albert sat back with his legs spread out along the shafts. Friquet was rewarded for his efforts by palatial accommodation at the Roi René and the pampering of Madame Sous, who liked her pets plump and docile.* It was this pampering that had prompted words between the two women when Olive had first moved into Mas de Chiscale.

---

* Madame Sous also owned an extremely round cat named Thaïs and a waddling fox terrier called Franchette. In contrast, Monsieur Sous, kitted out in a drooping jacket, white cord knickerbockers and slightly too short black stockings, was as thin as a rake.

> *The other day Louis Montfort borrowed Friquet – to bring me down a stone he'd found. He was working here – cutting out some rock – for the cistern – & it began to rain – & there was Friquet – tied to an olive tree – & there was Madame Sous – suddenly appeared from nowhere! – & in a state of mind! – & gesticulating – 'Mon Pauvre Friquet – et tu est tout mouillé!' ['My poor Friquet – and you are all wet!'] Louis hid in the cistern – & I told her that it was the custom in England to leave asses in the rain – but I would dry him on a towel to please her – (& it wasn't real rain – more Scotch mist!!!).*[3]

Andrée Sous had claimed to be Olive's closest friend in Les Baux, but other letters suggested that their friendship was less cosy than the antiques dealer wanted people to believe.

> *Madame Sous is wearing scarlet & white Catalan slippers & always bare legs – & she's the last woman who should wear bare legs – unless she stains them coffee colour – or wears the whole of herself bare – they're too big.*[4]

It seemed more likely that, to Olive at least, their friendship had been little more than a convenient social contract based on the provision and dissemination of gossip, that essential rural currency of which Madame Sous was widely acknowledged to be Les Baux's banker-in-chief.

Gossip was traded, however, at virtually every fireside in the village. Knowing that no one could survive in a place like Les Baux without it, Olive had joined the other women in their kitchen chats and proved herself an adept anthropologist in the process. Over time, she perfected the gentler Baussenc arts of polite sniping ('I believe the very best is to treat her with a cold deference . . .'), subtle displays of allegiance ('Madame Sous was pleasant – but a bit spiteful – & got her knife properly into the Girards & the Pinets . . . Later on, I shall appear in the 150-year-old shawl Madame Pinet has given me . . .') and, most deadly of all, stone-cold silence ('My revenge was to say not a word.').⁵

The majority of her quarrels, however, had been with the men.

*I've learned some time ago that patience is no use here – one's got to come down instantly like a cartload of bricks.*⁶

She had a particular word for her side of these arguments, one which she had picked up during the war: *strafing*. And, in the five years she had lived in Les Baux, she had seemingly strafed her way through the entire village.

Her earliest targets had been the unsuspecting stonemasons brought in to restore Mas de Chiscale. Later, with her place in the village more secure, she had moved on to strafe on behalf of other people. She hadn't been afraid to make a 'white hot scene', whether it was with Joseph for ignoring her advice when Marie-Thérèse was ill ('Dear dear – what a scene – me walking up & down the studio in the beat style! If I could have blasted him on to the floor I'd have done it – I was so angry!')⁷ or the parish priest who had failed to attend an event she had hosted ('. . . [it] made me want to ride straight over to Paradou – & have it out in the Presbytère . . .')⁸

Above all, Olive had been unable to abide anyone – herself included – being taken advantage of. It was this abhorrence of injustice that had led to her feud with the alleged dog poisoner, Etienne Patin.

At one time, she had been on very good terms with the Patins, a young couple who owned a smallholding just past the Carita farmyard. Etienne's wife, Marthe Montfort, had been one of the first friends she had made in Les Baux and it was through her that Olive found Mas de Chiscale. When she decided to hire a couple to look after the house and garden, Marthe and Etienne were a natural choice.

For the first two years, the arrangement had gone well. Marthe was an excellent housekeeper and cook, and Spring took an immediate liking to Etienne. Olive, too, enjoyed his company. He taught her the Baussenc names for the local wildflowers as they ran errands together in his mule cart.

A testament to their friendship still sat in Olive's studio: two of the monumental carved stones balanced on the high mantel had been a gift from the Patins. They had been salvaged from a dilapidated farmhouse once belonging to Etienne's grandfather and were thought to have come from the twelfth-century chapel on nearby Mont Paon, which had been sacked during the Revolution.

That friendship, however, had been tested in April 1927, when Marthe was diagnosed with renal tuberculosis. In line with the doctor's recommendation of complete bed rest, Olive hired a live-in nurse to look after her.

The arrangements were simple: Marthe and Nurse Druz would stay at the Patins' home, while Etienne and their young daughter Yvonne moved in with Etienne's parents over the lane. Instead, taking advantage of the free household help, Etienne had stayed put and also invited his elderly parents to join him for their meals. The additional money Olive had given Nurse Druz to cover food and daily expenses was soon eaten up by the enlarged household.

When Nurse Druz plucked up the courage to raise the issue, Olive was furious with Etienne for taking advantage of her generosity – and promptly sacked him. In return, Etienne vowed revenge and hounded the nurse out of Les Baux, revealing a hitherto unseen violent temper.

Nevertheless, Olive refused to compromise on Marthe's treatment and paid for her to stay instead at a sanatorium four hours away on the Riviera. Etienne had constantly harangued her with evidence that Marthe wanted to return home and have another live-in nurse, but Olive stood her ground.

> *I know it may sound harsh – but those folks are the utter limit – they only want to get money out of one – & she's absolutely under Etienne's thumb – it relieves me to know that for quite a while he has known what I think of him – !*

Angry letters flew back and forth between Etienne, Olive and the directrice of the sanatorium. Village opinion was also divided, with the usual consequences.

> *I said 'Good evening' & Madame Suares turned sideways & cut me dead – quite quite dead . . .*

In the end, Marthe had stayed at the sanatorium for four months, returning in time for the autumn fêtes looking younger and healthier than ever. But Etienne had neither forgotten nor forgiven. His new job in the Bauxite mines was gruelling compared to the work he'd enjoyed at Mas de Chiscale, and he also blamed Olive for the burden he'd had to bear in looking after his daughter and parents while, in his view, his wife had holidayed on the Riviera.

Olive, sensing that Etienne still intended to exact some sort of revenge, worried that he would do so through what was most dear to her: her beloved Spring. Oblivious to the falling-out between his mistress and his former caretaker, the old greyhound would still sometimes turn up at the Patins' house in search of treats or fuss, often taking his new companion Frida and their young puppies with him. Reluctantly, Olive had fenced her yard to keep the dogs from wandering.

She was especially anxious when she had to return to London that summer, just as the hunting season got underway.

> *This year the 'Chasse' opens late – 28th August – & now that Etienne is back it will be his opportunity – when I've gone – for a mishap with the dogs . . . I hope Etienne realises that I should make every effort to have him – if he does some mean trick – but that wouldn't replace Spring . . .*

As it happened, the expected mishap didn't occur for another year: Spring was poisoned in August 1928. With no evidence that Etienne had been responsible, however, Olive's desire to 'have him' through the courts came to nothing. Her appeal to Sergeant Fabre a few months before her death, however, suggested she felt that Etienne Patin was not quite done with her dogs – or, indeed, with her.

Olive had also collected a fair number of enemies through her participation in the old Baussenc sport of property disputes. Her first taste of this local pastime had come soon after she moved into Mas de Chiscale, when her elderly neighbour, the tall and patrician François Moucadel, appeared on her doorstep while a flood raged through her kitchen. He wanted to arrange a boundary survey, he explained, and it was a matter of great urgency.

> *He . . . said, 'I'm in a bit of a hurry! Death never announces the day it will come – and I have heirs – and I don't want them to say "Boun Dieu – that old man – what did he do!!!!!"'*[9]

Olive, having enough on her plate with the flood, naively agreed, despite knowing that Moucadel's family had owned the surrounding land for centuries and the boundaries with her own five acres were clearly marked on the ancient maps held in the *mairie*.

The subsequent row lasted eighteen months and centred around a steep stretch of hillside covered in thickets of gorse, dwarf holly and neglected olive trees. The land was of no use to either of them, but teams of experts were drafted in as Moucadel tried in vain to prove it was his.

Amid all this, the old man's sheepdog – an Alsatian cross – had decided it would prefer to live with Olive and Spring, causing Moucadel's pettiness to intensify. He started to hack away at the ancient olive trees on the hill simply to annoy her.

> *. . . he told a neighbour – who told Etienne – that he is going to cut down a bit each day – to make me mad – that even if the President of the Republic comes to fix the boundary, he will not accept it . . .*[10]

Moucadel had underestimated his opponent. Olive summoned the *garde champêtre* over the trees, and then the gendarmes. But it was her threat to take the matter to tribunal and donate any damages to the hospital at Maussane that had ultimately persuaded him to back down. The sheepdog was encouraged to return home and peace reigned for a short while.

Early in 1928, however, fresh trouble had begun when Moucadel's 'bandit shepherds', as Olive called his seasonal workers, started to hunt on her land. Their bullets were bouncing off the rocks above the cistern and endangering her dogs. Moucadel refused to intervene, the right to hunt freely having long been established in Les Baux.

Once again, she took matters into her own hands, at first pleading with the men, and then ordering them to hunt elsewhere. Finally, one Sunday morning, she cornered a lone Spaniard on the rocks and berated him in her best 'dog telling off voice' until he agreed to her demands. This perhaps worked a little too well because, within twenty-four hours, the Spaniard and his friends had all left Les Baux in order to find work – and peace – elsewhere. None of this had endeared Olive to those with Moucadel blood.

Her greatest feud over property, however, was undoubtedly that with Raoul Dumas following her purchase of the Hotel Monte-Carlo. The sale had been completed that January and the money distributed between Madame Pinet and her offspring. It had not, however, been an easy decision for the family.

Following their father's death, the five Pinet siblings had met a number of times to decide what to do and how to take care of their mother, whose mental health had always been delicate and was now compounded by severe deafness. The hotel and its associated land represented almost their entire inheritance, which could only be shared out if sold. But there was also their family pride to consider, not to mention the ongoing dispute with the Hotel Reine Jeanne. The latter, in particular, complicated matters: Dumas's lawyers were still trying to force through the aborted sale that had led to the Great Turning Out of 1926, and the case had yet to be heard by the Court of Appeal.

Most of the siblings were keen to sell – to Dumas, Échenard, or whomever – and divide the profits. It was Marie-Thérèse who held out.

> *I went into the kitchen unexpectedly & found her crying – most unusual for her – she is not Madame Patin's type at all. She said straight out, 'They talk of nothing but selling the Hotel.'*
>
> *It's all very difficult . . .*

Even François, who was finally his own master and could run the hotel in any way he desired, wanted rid of it. Such freedom was of little comfort compared to the family arguments and the escalating pressure coming from Raoul Dumas.

> *He is fed up to the eyes – told me that if it depended only on him he'd shut the Monte-Carlo at once – clear off, look for a job & hope for a purchaser.*

Both Marie-Thérèse and François had approached Olive for advice, but she maintained a stance of absolute neutrality. Privately, she thought the property ought to be divided, despite having her own reasons to maintain the status quo.

> *If the place is sold, it will be a bore – particularly if it goes to Dumas! I can't see myself a client there – or paying Dumas' prices!!! But we shall see.*[11]

Once Dumas's appeal had been dismissed by the Court of Appeal, however, Olive proposed a solution that would keep the whole family happy: using her own inherited money, she would buy the hotel as an investment and François could remain as manager. Other than some much-needed repairs and renovations, nothing need change.

> *. . . I want the place to run as it does now – the rooms for painters – & hard up tourists – who can't think of the Reine Jeanne prices – & the Grande Salle for the country people. They've been used to coming since Madame Pinet's father's time . . .*

Nevertheless, she proposed one change to improve the hotel's reputation. This was to evict the rowdier locals who sometimes made the bar unwelcoming to visitors. The only other licensed cafe in the village was run by Madame Pinet's brother, Charles Cornille, and Olive decided to use that to her advantage.

> *I've told Uncle Charles I shall send Journet & a few other drunkards along to him!!! He is very good at dealing with them. It is so simple. One has only not to stock the abominable stuff they ask for . . . Luckily, I get on well with these folks. It's very like a Y.M.[C.A.] hut* – without those ghastly Christians!!!!*

And if François decided to leave and Marie-Thérèse changed her mind? Olive had thought of that, too.

> *. . . I have only to shut the Hotel – & what a house! in the very best position – Place on one side – & Valley on the other – & what a studio the Grande Salle would make – & what a bedroom with the terrace on the valley the new dining room would make – & what a dining room the old vaulted dining room with the monumental fire place would make!!!*

She paid 75,000 francs, cash, for the hotel. The sale included three separate parcels of land: the hotel itself; the sizeable Maison du Four opposite, which housed five further guest rooms, the family quarters, a bakery, a big lock-up garage and stabling for seven horses; and an acre of land outside the old city walls which was used for grazing and extra parking for sightseers.

Also included, at no additional cost, was the opportunity for revenge.

---

* She had been a volunteer for the YMCA during the war.

> *... what really tickles me is that I'm beginning to wipe out some of the score against Dumas & Co. <u>You don't know</u> how black & long that bill is!!!!*[12]

Olive waded into battle even before the sale had been finalized, with a challenge over the rights to a small terrace at the rear of the two hotels.

> *I attack – <u>I have actually attacked</u> – a few days before Xmas...*

The first round of this was awarded in her favour, and that was just the start. In the months leading up to her death, she had instigated three more legal processes.

Naturally, Raoul Dumas was fuming ('Of course he's mad!'). But so, by extension, was someone else.

Fifty-three-year-old Vernon Blake, Les Baux's only other British resident, had never warmed to Olive. Nor she to him. In fact, they had been on exceedingly black terms for years.

Blake lived by the Porte d'Eyguières – the old water gate – in a ramshackle house that he'd been restoring with extreme thrift since 1911, when he'd arrived in the village with his Parisian wife and young daughter. Like Olive, he was an artist and wore his bohemian credentials on his sleeve. The sleeve in question was invariably made of pink linen and attached to a shirt unbuttoned to the chest above a pair of white Oxford bags. His intellect was similarly advertised through a pair of wire-rimmed glasses, a sharp goatee and a waxed moustache.

Blake was an acknowledged genius, and not merely by himself. A good number of respected figures of the day agreed with him. Besides sculpture and painting, the various strings to his substantial bow included art theory and criticism, amateur archaeology, philosophy, chemistry and small-scale mechanical engineering. He was said to be fluent in at least nine languages.

Blake's greatest passion, however, was cycling, which he had pursued both as an engineer and an athlete since he was at Westminster School. Despite poor health,* he still relished a ride around the Alpilles and was perpetually tinkering with his latest experimental gear system to attack the slopes in the most efficient manner. His passion for innovation, and his advocacy of the latest French ideas, had gained him wide respect in cycling circles. British touring clubs would often stop off at Les Baux for an audience with the great man of gears.

His dream was to make enough money to continue the travels he had started in his youth: back then, he'd explored the Balkans and India, and had travelled through war-torn Sudan to Egypt before returning to Paris and Rome to complete his art training. Now, his dream was to travel to China, which he had come to view as his philosophical and spiritual home.[13]

In the meantime, Vernon Blake was stuck in Les Baux with his haughty wife Marie, a former model he'd plucked in her prime from the gaiety of Paris (and whom Olive referred to as 'Madame Blot' or 'La Blake' depending on her level of ire). The Blakes' personal difficulties notwithstanding, the couple were enthusiastic hosts, often welcoming parties of visitors from the intellectual centres of Europe, with whom Vernon would pontificate late into the night on the terrace of the Hotel Reine Jeanne. Over the years, he had become close friends with Raoul Dumas, the air of refined intellectualism he brought to the establishment more than making up for his lack of personal funds.

---

* Among other medical misfortunes, his lung had once been pierced by an ice axe during a climbing expedition.

To most in Les Baux, however, he was an angry and difficult man, a dogmatic teetotaller who existed in a cloud of caustic intransigence. He had little time for those he considered his inferiors and, as was clear from Olive's letters, he placed her firmly in that category. She, in turn, loathed all that he was and did.

In years to come, some would speculate that the contempt between the two artists stemmed from a disagreement over aesthetics. Yet, while this had been Vernon Blake's great theme when it came to art criticism, none of Olive's papers suggested she had any strong opinions on the subject. Nor were her enmities ever based on abstract principles: her crusades, like her art, were grounded in reality. She may, however, have had an opinion on a piece Vernon Blake wrote for *Artwork* magazine in 1926, which read, in part:

> Too often a woman Strives to rival the certainty of virile outlook. The crowd applauds for the moment, expresses surprise that a woman's work should be so Strong, generally fails to realise that the seeming Strength is more allied to recklessness than to the controlled and measured decision of great things . . . Another, and more usual form of woman's artistic activity is the transcription of feeble and pretty sentiment, rendered by little clevernesses of hand designed to hide the lack of vision which penetrates to ultimate relations, to irrefutable formulae . . .[14]

Blake was currently putting the finishing touches on a longer work of grand and irascible thoughts. It would be his eighth substantial publication and was believed to be about the local area. Olive's letters suggested there had been some trepidation among local artists as to what would be in the book.

> *It will be Jou – and I – who are most 'for it' if he is personal
> – possibly also De Hérain (who is in Morocco).* Anyhow, if
> there is any ground for fighting – Jou will fight – so will I – but
> probably we will both be damned with faint praise. I want that
> book as soon as it comes out . . .*[15]

Their trepidation was due to the fallout from a court case in which Blake had been involved. A few years previously, in need of extra funds, Blake had begun producing wooden tourist souvenirs of Provençal figures. After drawing the designs, he'd enlisted a sixteen-year-old girl from Maussane to cut out and paint the silhouettes. As soon as they hit the shops, however, he was faced with a lawsuit from an artist from Arles who had patented similar designs. Blake was fined one hundred francs, but swiftly appealed, arguing that the responsibility rested with the girl who had physically produced the figures.

The village, of course, had revelled in the drama, with Olive, Jou and de Hérain publicly condemning his treatment of the girl. Olive had also reported to her family that Blake had threatened a court official, saying, 'I am not an *électeur* but I am a *littérateur* and I am writing a book upon [sic] Provence. I shall not forget you, and I shall not forget any of the inhabitants of Les Baux & their spite.'[16]

It had come as a shock, therefore, when the appeal court ruled in his favour. No one was more outraged than Olive, who had been following his troubles with some satisfaction.

---

* Olive's fellow artists Louis Jou (1882–1968) and François de Hérain (1877–1961) both split their time between Paris and Les Baux. Jou was an engraver, printer, typographer and book artist; de Hérain a painter, sculptor and engraver.

> ... *Blake has won his appeal – shuffling all the responsibility for the toys on to a girl at Maussane!!!!!!* <u>What a sweep</u> *– & La Blake has been parading Les Baux – I've told Joseph to be most careful with the dogs – & most polite – or I shall be 'for it'. If she makes one scene, I shall go straight to Maître Martin-Caille.*[17]

A number of vitriolic showdowns had indeed followed between her and 'Madame Blot', who blamed Olive for turning the village against her husband. For her part, Olive made enquiries in London about who would be publishing Blake's book, but took no further action – as far as anyone knew.

The Blakes, Raoul Dumas, François Moucadel, Etienne Patin, plus other sundry foes? It was fair to say that Guibbal did not have a shortage of suspects. But did any of them have enough reason to commit murder? He was developing a theory, but first he needed to return to Les Baux.

V

The village was full of tourists that afternoon, the springtime visitors seemingly undeterred – and a few perhaps even encouraged – by the thought of a murderer on the loose. The valley, however, was quiet, and it was there that Guibbal found Etienne Patin at home with his wife.

Olive's former gardener lived not far from the Girards, in a small house 200 metres from Mas de Chiscale. He had a surprisingly jovial appearance for an alleged dog poisoner. When questioned, he admitted that Olive Branson had not liked him. This was due, he claimed, to lies told by the nurse she had hired to look after his wife. For his part, he'd never harboured any ill will and certainly never harmed her dogs or threatened her in any way. He was merely grateful, he said, for the 'delicate attentions' that she'd paid to Marthe during her illness.

Patin did not deny, however, that he'd been in the valley at the time of Olive's death, although he made it clear that he thought she had taken her own life. He knew for a fact she had been suicidal in the past: two years earlier, he'd told her that he was struggling with life and she'd replied, 'Me, too,' before confiding that, shortly after moving to Les Baux (or was it just before? He couldn't remember), she had almost killed herself. She'd advised him to take courage, yet it seemed to him – and to many others who had known her – that her own courage had since failed.

Patin was firm in this conviction. Nevertheless, finding himself under Guibbal's steely eyed scrutiny, he was equally keen to remove himself from suspicion for any 'murder' the authorities were looking to solve. This he did by way of an alibi that placed him both near the scene and out of the frame. After finishing work that evening, he explained, he'd had a few drinks in the village before making his way home via his father's house, which adjoined the back of Carita. Seeing Félix Tougay in the Carita courtyard, he had stopped for a chat. Then, as he was leaving, he'd spotted Vincent Aracil heading to the water trough with his horses. Everyone knew that Tougay and Aracil had been talking to each other when they heard the gunshot at around nine o'clock, but by that time he'd been inside with his father.

Guibbal's sense was that Patin was telling the truth – about his movements, at least. Neither Tougay nor Aracil had mentioned seeing him, but then they hadn't been asked and few people in Les Baux, it seemed, gave up information willingly. Making a note to speak to them later, Guibbal took his leave and drove up to the village.

At the Hotel Reine Jeanne, Raoul Dumas gave a simpler alibi for both himself and his wife: they had been serving in the hotel dining room from six o'clock until nine thirty. The chef and sous-chefs were able to corroborate this, as were three of the guests who had been in residence that night: an English vicar and his wife, along with a distinguished-looking explorer named Luxmoore, who had spent a good portion of the previous year – his fifty-sixth – hacking through 5,000 kilometres of Amazonian jungle in an attempt to find the missing archaeologist, Percy Fawcett.*

---

* Colonel Percy Fawcett had famously disappeared in 1925 while searching for the fabled 'Lost City of Z'. Charles Luxmoore and his partner – both amateur explorers – had abandoned their rescue mission after losing Fawcett's trail less than a hundred miles from his last known location. After six

Guibbal was not surprised that the hotelier was in the clear. His interviews with Dumas and Patin were just formalities to eliminate the most obvious suspects. His thoughts were still drawing him in another direction, and it was towards this that he now intended to put his energies.

It was hard to do this discreetly, however, with reporters following his and Laforgue's every move. The first trench-coated figure had approached him four days earlier when he'd first gone to Saint-Rémy, and their numbers had been growing ever since. Having exhausted the findings of the autopsy, and with the people of Les Baux being a closed book, the press were having to work hard to keep the story alive.

A number of rumours had been circulating, which Guibbal had batted away to little effect: it was still widely reported, for example, that a pair of gold cufflinks had been found by Olive Branson's bed, and that she had foreseen her own death in the form of a black butterfly. (This last rumour, admittedly, was perhaps Guibbal's own fault. He had given a Reuters correspondent a brief glimpse of Olive's pocket diary, and the man had leapt upon a scrawled entry from early March which read, 'Warm – the first butterfly of the year – a dark one.' It had been a simple nature note, but, by the time it had undergone various translations from English to shorthand to French and back again, it had been transformed. The word 'one' had become 'omen', and readers throughout the world had been led to believe that Olive had written, 'I saw a butterfly to-day for the first time – it was a black butterfly. I see in it a bad omen.')[1]

But these were harmless, if irritating, inaccuracies. They might lead armchair sleuths a merry dance, but they made no difference

---

months, they arrived home to Devon empty handed, apart from two jaguars, a few parrots and a homesick interpreter named José.

to Guibbal. Besides, he was not on the whole opposed to red herrings, especially when they got the press off his back. He'd even been known to fling a few about himself. And, to give him his due, the details of the 'suspect' Guibbal leaked that day in 1929 had some basis in fact. Over a year earlier, a Spanish vagabond had been causing trouble in the valley, which had led Olive to call in the gendarmes:

> ... an alien undesirable, knowing Madame G was alone, went & made himself a nuisance – luckily the door was locked. On Xmas Eve at 5.30, he came round here!!! My word!!! That sort of sauce can't be allowed – I went after him with the dogs!!! but had no luck.
> ... On Xmas day ... there was the most awful storm – a deluge – lasting till midday Monday – & the telephone lines smashed. On Tuesday morning I got a message through to Louis – he fetched me – I interviewed all the police who were charming – & I settled the alien's little affair – he's gone – good luck to him![2]

The alien had not returned, but what better diversion for scoop-hungry journalists than a mysterious Spaniard who had threatened the victim with a revolver? And it worked. With much of the pack sent on a wild goose chase, Guibbal and Laforgue were left to pursue more pertinent lines of inquiry in peace.

MAN HUNT IN THE BRANSON MYSTERY

Police Search Countryside for a Spaniard

DIARY PREMONITION

Meanwhile, across the Channel, the British press had been working to one objective: to find out as much about Olive Branson as possible. Despite the earliest French reports offering wildly different versions of her name – Brampton, Bramson, Bronson – they had soon found their mark. Before Guibbal had even received his orders to visit Les Baux, they'd sniffed out details of her orphanhood, her art career, her wanderings in her caravan and her Romany and circus friends. The icing on their cake was that this bohemian free spirit was the cousin of a High Court judge.

Reporters had swarmed on Frimley Green in Surrey in the hope of speaking to Sir George Branson himself. At first, only Lady Branson was at home, but her statement did little to diminish their sense that a delicious Gallic scandal was brewing. 'I think that the idea of suicide can be "washed out" altogether . . .' she'd said. 'In Les Baux she took full part in the village life, and was very popular. I fancy, however, that her recent business speculation in a small hotel there may have made her some enemies.'[3]

Nor had Sir George disappointed. On arriving home that evening, he spoke at length about his 'bright and cheerful' cousin and confirmed that 'suicide would be the last thing she would contemplate.'[4]

Back in London, the *Evening Standard* had tracked down the Soho hotel that Olive had always favoured when visiting England. The Astoria's manager remembered her well, saying, 'We all liked her, even to the humblest member of the hotel staff. She was charming to everybody. She was reserved, and never spoke of herself; but she had a nice word for everybody.'[5]

A reporter from the *Daily News* had also located Olive's former flat in nearby Greek Street and had spoken to her landlady. 'I can only say that she was a very charming woman with eccentric ways, and a heart of gold . . .' Madame Poli said. 'We used to talk together nearly every day, and she was obviously a woman of culture and breeding . . . everyone liked her in Soho, although, strangely enough, she had few close friends.' Madame Poli added that Olive's clothing had attracted a certain amount of attention, as had her equally incongruous greyhounds: 'She once told me that she loved the life of a Romany.'[6]

The press also dug up some details of Olive's war career, thereby adding a dash of heroic daring to the portrait they were painting of her as an intriguing and complex murder victim. In anyone's eyes, Olive had done her bit for king and country. For a time at the beginning of the war, she had volunteered in London, carting milk from Paddington Station to Bow, along with other essential tasks that had suffered from the exodus of young men. Her limited first-aid skills had been rejected by the Red Cross, but, in late December 1914, she had joined a recruitment committee for the City of London Royal Fusiliers.

Olive's real experience of war, however, began in April 1915 on the outskirts of Rouen, in a large, wooden refreshment hut operated by the Young Men's Christian Association (YMCA). Topping up tea urns and wiping down tables had not been Olive's first choice of war work; nor was the 'C' in YMCA much to her liking ('those ghastly Christians!!!!'), but she knew the vital role their huts played in boosting troop morale, and threw herself into the work with gusto.

For three years, she topped up, wiped down, smiled and chatted. The daily grind took a toll on her health, being far removed from the gentle caravanning-and-art lifestyle she had developed to suit the twin demands of her delicate constitution and adventurous spirit. But she persevered, aided by regular recuperative trips back to Gordon Square. Then, one night in spring 1918, everything had quite literally come crashing down around her.

Rouen was over a hundred kilometres from the front, but, as a major base for British and Commonwealth forces, it was still subject to air raids. Olive had been working an evening shift, when the sound of German planes came from overhead, followed by a deafening explosion. The next thing she knew, the hut was ablaze and she was being carried to safety by an army officer who, just moments before, had been enjoying a cup of tea. Others in the hut were not so fortunate.

Olive never wrote about the horrors of that night, other than a few vague acknowledgements about the damage the war had done to her nerves and spirit. The *London Gazette*, however, was less circumspect and recorded that she had been mentioned in despatches on 7 April 1918 for her 'gallant and distinguished service in the Field.'[7] She also received the British War Medal in 1919.

But these were not the only things Olive kept quiet about her wartime experiences, as the Sunday papers now revealed. For six days, an explosive word had gone unnoticed in the death certificate drawn up by the mayor of Les Baux from her identity papers. The word? *Divorcée*.

THE ENEMIES OF MISS BRANSON.

Relatives Tell of Threats to Murder Victim.

WEDDING SECRET.

This had led a reporter from the *Evening Standard* to Somerset House and then back to Frimley Green, where a member of Sir George Branson's household reluctantly confirmed his findings: 'It is quite true that she was married, but it was an unhappy marriage . . . Her husband was a Mr. Wilson, of whom we have heard nothing for a long time.'[8]

The *Daily News* tracked down Mr Wilson to an address near Bognor Regis, where he was living with his new wife. Wilson himself had gone to ground since the secret of his earlier marriage had surfaced, but his brother-in-law Mr Marshall spoke on his behalf.

When asked what Wilson thought of the murder, Marshall said, 'What could Colonel Wilson possibly say about the crime? He had forgotten about the marriage, or, at least, he had tried to do so. It was just a war-time romance which did not last. It was a period of his life that he wanted to forget.'

Marshall also warned the press to stay away, saying, 'He is distressed that his previous marriage should have been dragged into the limelight. Not even his brothers and sisters know about it.'[9]

The statement about his siblings was a lie – one of his sisters had attended the wedding – but the rest was true. The short-lived marriage had been a source of regret for both parties. The ceremony had taken place in July 1918, after a whirlwind romance. At the time, Wilson had been an officer in the Railway Transport Establishment, responsible for liaising with the French and Belgian railways to ensure the smooth movement of British troops and supplies. He had met Olive in Rouen in the spring of 1918. In fact, Major Wilson (as he was then) had been the one to scoop her from the blazing YMCA hut and carry her to safety.

After such a gallant rescue, the pull of romance had been hard to resist. The pair married four months later, on Wilson's first available leave. Olive was thirty-three, Wilson thirty-six, and the only guests at the Marylebone registry office were Wilson's sister, Olive's cousin William and her Aunt Mary. Following a quiet lunch at a hotel near Olive's flat in York Street, the newlyweds had travelled to Cornwall for their honeymoon.

The relationship was doomed from the start. In civilian life, Arthur Wilson had been a clerk at Euston Station. Despite his burst of heroic daring during the bombardment, he was a practical person who gained quiet satisfaction from the punctual departure of the 4.52. Olive, on the other hand, was the kind to fling herself into a carriage at 4.51 and fifty-nine seconds: 'very artistic and temperamental', in Mr Marshall's words.

Within weeks, it had become clear that the marriage could never live up to either party's expectations, even in the bedroom.

> *I told May of the honeymoon episode, when the Monthly arrangement came on a week early – just a few days before his leave finished, and I thought I was naturally Out of Action – & he said 'Well – do it with your hands, friction is all that's required –' She was much more shocked than I expected.*[10]

The decree nisi had not, however, been issued until October 1927. The nine intervening years had been an awkward – and, for Olive, depressing – burden. She and Arthur had only seen each other on three occasions after the honeymoon – twice in Paris and once on the Riviera – before retreating back to their individual lives.

For a time, Olive had been torn over whether they should give the marriage a go despite their obvious differences. Neither wanted to attract the stigma of divorce. In the end, Arthur was spurred into action by a desire to remarry, and applied to have the whole mess annulled on the basis of Olive's incapacity to consummate. Olive didn't even respond to the petition.

When they found their way back to French newsrooms, these findings were leapt upon by editors eager to add further colour to the unfolding story. Those reporters tasked with trailing Guibbal on the ground, however, found themselves at something of a loss. Although the savvier among them had dismissed his tale of the mysterious Spaniard for the fiction that it was, they still struggled to work out what he and Laforgue were really up to.

The detectives had been on the move all weekend. As well as questioning various people in Les Baux, they were spotted in Marseilles, Tarascon, Arles and Saint-Rémy. Word also got round that agents had been visiting all the local notaries, and that Arthur fforde had been summoned to appear before Joseph Rochu. Was there a discrepancy with a will or other legal document?

It was the special correspondent for the *Daily Express* who claimed the scoop – or as much of a scoop as was on offer. In an exclusive interview with Guibbal on Sunday morning, the detective told him: 'You can take it from me that to-morrow at the latest I shall be able to lay my hands on the murderer, or murderers, of Miss Branson – for although I am certain that she was murdered, I cannot be absolutely positive that it was the work of one person only.'

Guibbal added that his main suspect was a man – a man who had known the victim, her habits, her dogs and her house very well. He refused to elaborate any further, other than to say that certain things about Olive Branson's life in Les Baux had only just come to light, which, when revealed, 'will surprise most people. Even those who knew her intimately, and saw her nearly every day.'[11]

VI

The excitement in the village had calmed over the weekend, but was reignited on Monday morning when, just before seven o'clock, two black cars swept into the valley and up the track to Mas de Chiscale. There, Alexandre Guibbal, Antonin Laforgue, Félix Martin and two gendarmes stepped from the cars and into the yard.

The sky was low and grey. While the gendarmes headed back down the track on foot, the three detectives hauled Olive's large, green outdoor table into place on the lower terrace under an almond tree. They arranged two bow-armed garden chairs on one side, lined up pen and paper, and waited. Olive's absence permeated the silence. The doors and windows of the house were shuttered and sealed, the dogs gone.

The gendarmes returned shortly afterwards with their quarry, who was invited to stand in front of the table, facing the cistern. The gendarmes were directed to hover at the edges of the property to stop any onlookers from getting too close. People had already started to drift down from the village: rumour had it that the gendarmerie in Saint-Rémy had been told to ready itself for prisoners, and here was Joseph Girard, called in for questioning by the Sûreté.

The reporters would also arrive in due course, taking up their previous positions at the end of the track and in the undergrowth by the lane, straining to hear what was going on. Those who brought cameras had more luck: the police had set up the interview table in full view of the low wooden gate and had placed the chairs with their backs to the cistern, offering a perfectly framed tableau below the fruiting almond tree. The line between theatre and policing could be whisker thin, and the Flying Squad was a master of both.

Joseph was dressed for the cool of the morning in a blue serge jacket over a thick shawl-collared cardigan and linen shirt, his hands clutching his large, soft cap. Félix Martin and Inspector Laforgue were installed at the table, while Guibbal paced back and forth on the path behind.

They started gently, with Félix Martin asking questions while Laforgue, all angles and bones beneath his black fedora and ill-fitting suit, took notes. The table was slightly too high for the petite inspector, and his elbows were splayed as he hunched over his notebook. Guibbal occasionally stopped his pacing to lean forward against the back of a chair, listening intently to Joseph's replies.

The first questions were about Joseph's movements on the Friday that Olive had died, which he seemed happy to provide.

'I showed up here at seven o'clock, my usual time, to take the dogs for their walk. My work kept me here until around ten o'clock, and then I went to Maussane to run some errands for Miss Branson. I returned at midday and found her eating lunch outdoors beneath the cherry tree over there.'

'Who prepared her lunch?'

'My wife, although I didn't see her. She must have come down while I was at Maussane.'

'What then?'

'After about ten minutes, I went up to the Hotel Monte-Carlo. I came back down around quarter past two to feed the dogs and water the trees.'

'And Miss Branson?'

'She was still under the cherry tree. She had cleared away her plate herself, as she always did, and was resting on a deckchair with her hands behind her head. She didn't move from there until about four o'clock, and then only to make herself some tea, which she took back to her chair to drink.'

'What did you do after watering the trees?'

'I prepared some asparagus for her supper, weeded the terrace and, at around five thirty, took the dogs for another walk.'

'What time did you get back?'

'About six thirty. I found my wife in the kitchen. Miss Branson was in the studio, sitting by the fire. My wife brought in her supper tray, put it on the table and covered it with a cloth.'

'And when did you leave?'

'About seven o'clock. Miss Branson was getting ready to sit down to eat. I wished her a good evening and good night, and she handed me her copy of *Le Matin*. My wife was standing beside me, and we left together.'

'Where did you go?'

'Two of my girls were playing at a nearby farm, so we went our separate ways there. My wife fetched the children and took them back to the hotel, and I went on to our house to collect my motorcycle.'

'Where were you going?'

'To Fontvieille.'

'And what did you do when you got there?'

'I left my bike at the garage to be filled up and—'

'Which garage?'

'The first petrol distributor on the left, coming from Les Baux.'

'And then?'

'I went to see the tinsmith Montfort's family to ask if their daughter wanted a job at the hotel. I then called on Monsieur Desmaries, the butcher, and chatted with him for over an hour. After that, I went to collect my motorcycle and pay for the petrol.'

'What time was that?'

'It was almost dark by then, so between eight thirty and nine?'

'And how long is the journey back to Les Baux?'

'About twenty to thirty minutes; it must be nine or ten kilometres.'

'Did you pass anyone on the road?'

'No.'

'And what did you do when you returned to Les Baux?'

'I went straight to the hotel. There were no customers in the cafe, only my family – that is, my wife, her mother, our three daughters, my brother-in-law François and my niece Madeleine. We ate our evening meal together. After a while, my mother-in-law, my two eldest daughters and François left us, as they sleep in an annexe that adjoins the hotel.'

'And you and your wife?'

'After settling our seven-month-old, my wife went to bed. I joined her almost immediately afterwards.'

These questions, in various iterations, were repeated over and over, along with even more about the following morning, when he had found Olive and her revolver missing. The persistence was designed to wear him down, to catch him out, but Joseph appeared untroubled and his responses never changed.

One question which he struggled to answer, however, and which seemed important to the detectives, was why Marie-Thérèse had failed to prepare Olive's usual lunch the following day. When François had stopped to drop Marie-Thérèse off at Mas de Chiscale, she hadn't even unloaded any of the provisions she'd bought for her employer in Arles. As the body hadn't been found until early afternoon, why had they assumed that Miss Branson wouldn't return in time for lunch? Each time, Joseph's answer was the same – that his wife had probably simply forgotten on account of the anxiety – but this didn't appear to satisfy the investigators.

They brought out Olive's pocket diary, in which she had jotted down her expenses. Had Joseph himself forgotten to mention that he had settled accounts with Miss Branson on the Friday morning? He had. She had given him a cheque for 2,407 francs earlier in the week, he said, which he had cashed for her at the Société Générale in Saint-Rémy. On Friday morning, she had handed him 800 francs of this, nearly half of which was the weekly wage for the housekeeping work he and Marie-Thérèse undertook; the balance was to be used for household purchases, a large proportion of which were dog related. This had since been spent – exceeded, even.

The questioning continued for hours. Joseph, shifting from foot to foot in his heavy work boots, proved to be increasingly overdressed as the sun rose higher in the sky and began to break through the clouds. Occasionally, he rested against the edge of the table, dangling one foot and then the other for relief.

At one point, Guibbal took him up to the top terrace to look at the cistern. Martin and Laforgue followed, and the interrogation continued. What was the position of the body? Was the wire mesh like this, or this, or this? What exactly did he mean by his statement that Miss Branson would have needed to be an acrobat to enter the tank? Joseph had already discussed all this with Guibbal the previous week, but he repeated everything with his customary attention to detail.

Around midday, some bread and sausage was produced, which the men ate as they continued the interview, going over the same ground again and again. Other questions were scattered between the endless repetitions. No, he hadn't been wearing these clothes that day ... Well, the dogs either slept in the studio or at the foot of Miss Branson's bed ... No, they didn't have any recent wounds, as far as he knew ... Yes, they would bark at everyone, except him, his wife, their nephew Pierre, and François ... No, he didn't know what time François had arrived at the hotel because he'd been in Fontvieille, but his wife could probably be more specific... Yes, it was he who'd asked François to go to Maussane to buy oil and milk for Miss Branson, along with a few things for the hotel... Yes, he had informed Miss Branson that François would be delivering her provisions that evening...

François... François... François... It was clear where things were heading.

Félix Martin fetched François from the village at one o'clock. The young man was wearing pale grey striped tennis trousers, a blue jacket and a soft-collared shirt. When one took into account the rakishly thin tie tucked into his waistcoat and his thick, carefully styled hair, the whole effect was that of a playboy somewhat down on his luck: his skin may have given the impression of having been tanned by the sun of Cap Ferrat rather than the crude rays that beat down on his fellow Baussencs, but he could not escape the dust from their fields.

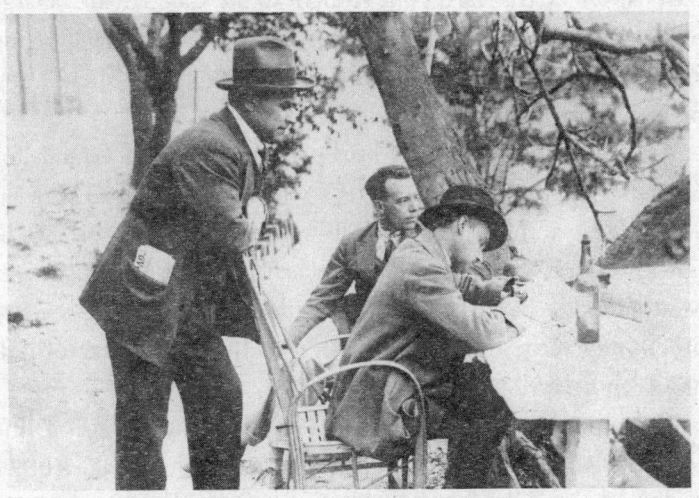

Alexandre Guibbal, François Pinet, Inspector Antonin Laforgue.

He took a seat in Félix Martin's vacant chair and leaned back, resting his elbow on the table. Reports that he was a strange boy were not unfounded: from his demeanour, one wouldn't think that he was sitting just yards away from the scene of a crime that had taken the life of his former employer. His composure barely shifted, even after he was met by the same barrage of questions as Joseph.

Guibbal started with his movements on the day of Olive's death. François responded that he had got up around nine o'clock and spent the morning painting the hotel annexe. There was little he could say about that – it was just routine maintenance – although he had taken a break for lunch in the hotel. He couldn't remember the precise details, but he'd probably eaten in the kitchen and alone.

At about three o'clock, he said, Joseph had asked him to fetch some provisions from Maussane, which he'd done a few hours later: he estimated that he'd arrived in the town at about six o'clock. On arrival, he'd gone straight to the Café Dinard, a large bar on the main square. Sorro the postman had been there enjoying an after-work drink with a cheese merchant called Michel, and he had joined them.

Afterwards, François said, he'd run a few personal errands for his family before going to Rieter's wholesale market to pick up a fifty-litre can of oil for Olive Branson's stove and forty-eight tins of 'Gloria' condensed milk for her dogs. He'd then gone to Moucadel's the butcher to collect the hotel's meat and charcuterie order, only to be told that it wasn't ready as a delivery of veal had been delayed.

To pass some time, he'd stopped by the Café de la Fontaine to find his friend Adrien Sautel, with whom he'd had another drink. After leaving Sautel, he'd tried again with the meat order – still no luck – and then returned to the Café Dinard. There, he'd found the butcher talking to a painter and decorator from Saint-Rémy. The two men had just returned from Arles, where they'd been chasing up the missing veal in the decorator's van. François had joined them for a glass or two and then returned to the butcher's with Moucadel and waited while he cut up the veal. He'd finally left Maussane at around eight o'clock.

Laforgue noted down all the timings and names; they would be checking them later. But first, Guibbal wanted to know about François's subsequent – and presumably slightly inebriated – arrival at Mas de Chiscale.

According to François, it had been brief and uneventful. Pointing to the wide gate at the top of the track, he said, 'Miss Branson came to meet me and I drove my car into the yard. I put the can of oil in the storeroom and the case of milk in the kitchen. She offered to help, but it wasn't necessary.'

'Do you know if she'd eaten by then?' Guibbal asked.

'I think I remember her telling me she'd had dinner.'

'Did she seem strange in any way?'

'Well, there was nothing to suggest that she was going to kill herself.'

When asked to describe his route home, François explained that he had driven back to the village via the family's old olive mill, which sat on the crossroads near the fountain and public washhouse. It was a useful place to sort and dry laundry, and Marie-Thérèse had asked him to collect a basket of linen that she had prepared.

'What time was this?'

'I'm not sure. I had to turn on my headlights when leaving, but it was well before nine o'clock.'

'Did you pass anyone on the way?'

'There was a car, a Donnet, which belongs to a travelling salesman from Tarascon. I'm not sure of his name, but I do know that he bought the car from Monsieur Gras, who runs the Charité in Tarascon.'

Laforgue made further notes, while Guibbal continued the interview.

'Who was at the hotel when you arrived?'

'The stonemason Noël Journet was in the cafe with his wife, along with the Brussets and Albert Montfort, who works in the quarry.'

'And your brother-in-law?'

'Joseph arrived afterwards. I remember because my sister scolded him for being late.'

François's account of eating supper with his family and then walking back to the annexe with his niece Madeleine adequately matched that given by Joseph. He added that he had gone to bed at about eleven and had not left his room until morning.

The following day, he said, he'd gone to the market in Arles with his sisters and had only found out about Olive Branson's disappearance when they'd stopped at Mas de Chiscale on their way home to drop off Marie-Thérèse. Joseph had met them at the gate in a panic. François had helped him search for a quarter of an hour or so, before driving his sisters back up to the hotel while Joseph went out again with the dogs.

When Joseph had joined them at the hotel, the brothers-in-law had forgone lunch and headed straight to Saint-Rémy to see Louis Vigne and the gendarmes. He had been cleaning out the hotel garage when he heard that the body had been found. At about four o'clock, he'd packed everything away and gone back down to Mas de Chiscale. The body was already out of the water by then and Sergeant Fabre had been taking statements. After providing his own, he'd driven to Tarascon to see Bruno Martin-Caille, their family solicitor, who also managed Olive's affairs.

Why? Because Marie-Thérèse had told him to go. She'd actually asked him earlier in the day, before he'd gone to Saint-Rémy with Joseph to alert the gendarmes, but he hadn't got round to it until later. His sister, he explained, had anticipated that, if the gendarmes found their employer had killed herself, Mas de Chiscale would be sealed while they completed the necessary investigation. She had wanted to know whether the hotel, being Olive Branson's property, would also have to close. If so, they would have had to tell the organizers of a private banquet that was due to take place the following day.

In any case, François continued, he had not seen the solicitor. It being a Saturday afternoon, the only people in Martin-Caille's office had been a clerk and a typist. The clerk, however, had assured him that no seals would be necessary, as the hotel was under separate management. When he'd arrived back in Les Baux and passed the group wheeling Olive Branson's body up to the village in a handcart, he'd therefore been able to tell them to lay her out in one of the rooms at the hotel.

By the time they had gone over François's account several times, with ever-increasing focus on the tiniest of details, it was late afternoon. The three detectives had been working non-stop for nearly twelve hours and they'd barely touched on the fruits of Guibbal's inquiries over the weekend. François was looking less than fresh and Joseph had been sitting under the eye of the gendarmes for hours. It seemed a good time to take a break.

But first, Guibbal asked François one final question. 'Did the dogs ever bark when you came here?'

'No. Not as much as they would with a stranger.'

Guibbal decided to go straight to Maussane. It was the end of the working day and he'd be able to catch some of François's friends before they went home or began to descend into unreliable drunkenness.

Baptistin Moucadel was still at his shop. He remembered the Friday in question well. He'd been waiting all day for the delivery of veal. When it hadn't arrived by four o'clock, he'd paid the decorator Aristide Perret to drive him to Arles to track it down; they'd returned with the meat at around six thirty or seven and gone straight to the Café Dinard. François had arrived half an hour later and joined them for two aperitifs.

When asked about François's mood, the butcher struggled to describe it: he'd been calm and composed as usual, yet also preoccupied; not quite himself. Moucadel had asked what was on his mind, and François had said, 'There's something I've been putting off.'

At around half past seven or quarter to eight, the butcher recalled, François had accompanied him back to his shop. Moucadel had cut up about six kilos of veal for the hotel and then watched as François got into his car and drove off. It had been around eight o'clock, certainly no later, and Moucadel hadn't seen him since.

Guibbal's next stop was the Café Dinard, where the paint-spattered Aristide Perret was already installed. The forty-two-year-old decorator had been working on a job in Maussane for about three weeks and had got into the habit of visiting the cafe each day before heading home to Saint-Rémy. He said that he'd actually stopped by twice on Friday, 26 April: once in the morning, for a quick tot before work, and then again in the evening for a more leisurely drink after returning from Arles with Baptistin Moucadel. He'd seen François one of those times, but was it the morning or evening? He couldn't be sure. Either way, he said, it couldn't have been after seven o'clock because he usually went home for dinner around then and would remember if he'd been late.

*

Back in Les Baux, Guibbal went straight to the hotel, which he found in a state of commotion. Félix Martin had brought François and Joseph up from Mas de Chiscale and locked them in separate rooms while he and Laforgue searched their living quarters. This had not gone down well with the family.

Marie-Thérèse Girard was particularly distraught: her face was red and puffy, and someone said she had been crying all day. Guibbal had hoped to interview her, too, but was aware that he'd need to pick his moment. Her current distress aside, she'd encountered Félix Martin before, in circumstances that were unlikely to have left her with a favourable view of the Flying Squad. There was certainly no point in questioning her that evening.

Nor had the searches turned up anything useful. Nevertheless, Guibbal sketched a floor plan of the freshly painted annexe where François's bedroom was located. It was an old bakehouse tucked away in a side street opposite the hotel. Once, it would have been full of the aromas of warm bread and simmering cassoulet, but now it smelled only of paint, stale clothes and sleep. The door from the street opened directly into a short corridor giving access to three rooms. The one at the rear belonged to Madeleine Vayssière, with beds for the Girard girls as needed. François slept at the front, opposite his elderly, deaf mother.

'Pinet can leave without being seen,' Guibbal noted above his sketch, before closing his notebook and walking back to the main building.

The gendarmes had rounded up the men François had said were in the hotel bar on the evening of Olive's death. The two stonemasons – Noël Journet and his younger colleague, Félix Brusset – confirmed that they had been there with their wives that evening, but their memories were hazy. The Journets had stayed until about nine o'clock and Noël Journet had seen François at some point, but couldn't even guess at the time. Brusset had left with his wife at eight thirty, but couldn't recall seeing François at all. Albert Montfort was equally vague: he'd seen François arrive, but had no idea when. He'd gone home soon after, but he didn't own a watch and, although he had an alarm clock at home, it didn't work.

Guibbal returned to the hotel reception to use the telephone. It was time to apply a bit more pressure.

VII

Tarascon sat thirteen kilometres north-west of Les Baux, on the banks of the Rhône. It was getting dark by the time the detectives' cars rumbled over the cobbled streets and drew up outside the police station. The local police commissioner, François Maury, was waiting for them. He had placed two interrogation rooms at their disposal and arranged for food to be delivered to the prisoners once they had been searched and transferred to the cells.

Maury also had something for Guibbal and Martin: some unexpected news from their colleagues in Marseille. Earlier that day, the owner of a charcuterie on the Boulevard des Dames had contacted the Sûreté about a strange assistant he had recently employed, and a member of the Flying Squad had gone out to interview him.

Monsieur Pélissier had been reading the evening newspaper on the day the first reports emerged of Olive Branson's death, when his new employee snatched it from his hands and said, 'This is about my family!' The man had jabbered on about knowing the victim and her farmhouse, that he spoke English, that the cistern was very close to the house, and how it was easy to get to Les Baux and back in an evening.

The man had started work on the day Olive's body was found. He'd been vetted and sent by the local *charcutiers*' guild, but a few things about him seemed odd. Although he appeared destitute and was living out of a suitcase in a cheap hotel on the Boulevard d'Athènes, he'd shown the butcher's boy a cheque for over a thousand francs. And had he come from Les Baux or Avignon? He had claimed both at different times. He also seemed burdened by something. One day, when the butcher's boy had remarked that the mistral was blowing hard, he replied, 'I'd like it to carry me ten thousand leagues from here to an unknown land.'

And perhaps it had, because the man had since disappeared. On Friday evening, just as the news was breaking that a murder investigation was underway, he'd unexpectedly announced that he was leaving for a hydrotherapy cure. The next morning, Monsieur Pélissier had seen him talking to a man with a suitcase on the nearby Rue Colbert. He had then returned to the charcuterie to leave the suitcase, along with his own travelling bag, while he attended to some business. At six o'clock that evening, he had collected both bags and had not been seen since.

On receiving this report, an inspector from the Flying Squad had gone to check the guest register at the dingy hotel on the Boulevard d'Athènes where the man had been living. The register identified him as Etienne Girard of Saint-Rémy: Joseph's older brother. Further inquiries with the port police established that Etienne Girard had recently returned from America after being expelled by the immigration authorities for having insufficient means. His current whereabouts were unknown.

It was an intriguing development, but whether it had any bearing on the investigation remained to be seen. Guibbal was certain he'd identified the right suspects – or one of them, at least – but he was still piecing together his findings from the weekend. The hours ahead would tell. He and Félix Martin would take one man each and continue the questioning all night, if needed. Eventually, one or the other was bound to let something slip or break down altogether.

After Guibbal had knocked back a fortifying glass of raw egg and milk, he was ready to begin. Alone with Joseph, he chose not to ask about his brother but returned to his previous line of questioning. He still wasn't sure exactly what had led to the fatal gunshot, but he had a good idea of motive. How Joseph Girard fitted into that was unclear, but Guibbal was sure he knew something. Fortunately, the gardener was just the type to crumble under pressure.

Some of that pressure would be provided by the excellent work Inspector Laforgue had done looking into Joseph's past. It had been an average life – and an honest one, if truth be told – but still easy to present in a way that would make him feel wretched.

Over the weekend, Laforgue had unearthed how Joseph had grown up as one of seven children of a Saint-Rémy butcher and left school at thirteen to work in the shop; how his military service had coincided with the start of the war and he'd spent five years as a foot soldier with the Eighth Colonial Infantry Division; how he'd fought in the Marne and the Somme, and then the Balkans, where he'd been captured and sent to a German prison camp in Ingolstadt for nearly two years; how minor infractions meant that he'd been refused a certificate of good conduct when he left the army in 1919, thus restricting his already limited employment options even further.

But then, a happy event: the work he eventually found with a butcher in Maussane had led him to meet Marie-Thérèse Pinet. The couple dreamed of a better life than Les Baux could offer, so he'd taken a well-paid job on board the SS *Providence* as second butcher, but had only endured one miserable crossing from Marseille to New York before returning to the village to work as a day labourer.

The births of his daughters had stretched his meagre earnings even further. Most of Marie-Thérèse's siblings had done well for themselves and could support their families without undue hardship: Marguerite had even married Louis Vayssière, heir to the wealthy Baumanière estate that dominated the end of the valley. And there was Joseph, barely scraping by.

The arrival of a rich Englishwoman in the village would have been an opportunity to improve all that. Hadn't he been at the front of the queue when she was seeking men to renovate the crumbling Mas de Chiscale? It can't have been hard for him to stand out from the others, most of whom had arrived late, packed up early and left empty bottles all over the place. And when the Anglaise's relationship with her housekeepers had broken down in the spring of 1927, hadn't he and his wife stepped forward to offer their services? Hadn't he advised her never to take the Patins back and thus ensured their continued employment?

Of course, it hadn't always been easy. Olive Branson had given him a dressing down or two in her time, and his in-laws were difficult. He and Marie-Thérèse continued to talk of getting out and starting afresh elsewhere. But that changed when Olive bought the hotel. Everyone knew that François – her preferred manager – never intended to stay long term. When François stepped down in March and Joseph and Marie-Thérèse took his place, their future must have felt secure.

But then Olive had begun to worry about money. In recent weeks, she had told Joseph to sell the mare and talked about making other savings. On the day of her death, she'd received the final bill for the renovations at the hotel, along with an update on the ongoing boundary disputes with the Hotel Reine Jeanne. Had she become tired of it all? Was she thinking of selling up and surrendering to Raoul Dumas? Had she perhaps even confided as much to Joseph? And where would that have left him and his family?

Had there been an argument about broken promises? Had he seen red after all those years of struggle? As he'd told Sergeant

Fabre, he knew where she kept her revolver. It wasn't meant to have gone so far, of course – what use would she be to him dead? An accident, though . . . ?

Joseph, wide-eyed with alarm, denied it all.

In another room, money was also the focus of Félix Martin's grilling of François. Inquiries at the Société Marseillaise in Arles had revealed that the young man was surprisingly short of funds for someone who had recently come into an inheritance. François, unfazed, admitted as much. 'About a month ago, my brother Pierre gave me eleven thousand francs, which was my share of the sale of the hotel. But I had debts to pay, so there's only four or five hundred left now.'

One of his debts had been for his Renault, which he bought the previous March from a garage in Arles. It was second-hand and cost him 8,000 francs, which he'd arranged to pay in instalments. He could barely afford those, however, and had taken out a loan of 5,000 francs. While he'd been running the hotel following his father's death, and during the two months he had acted as Olive's *gerant*, the loan repayments had been manageable. Since handing over the reins to Marie-Thérèse two months earlier, however, he'd had no income at all. Recent advertisements in the *Petit Marseillais* showed that he'd been trying to sell the car for 7,000 francs, without success.[1]

'How did you intend to make a living?'

'I was going into business with Louis Vigne. I'd already given him five thousand francs about a month ago and I was to pay another five thousand a fortnight after the machine was switched on.'

The machine in question was a commercial ice machine, which was to be installed in a building in Saint-Rémy. The plan was to start a small ice factory, serving local butchers and bars. It had been Louis's idea – such services were few and far between in rural areas and good profits were almost guaranteed – but he couldn't do it alone. The machine, a clanking behemoth, would need round-the-clock supervision. François had therefore come on board as a partner. He would sleep at the factory and take his meals at a nearby *pension*.

'And when was the business supposed to start operating?'

'Around the fifteenth of May.'

'So, at the end of this month, you were to pay Vigne another five thousand francs, yet you say that you only have four to five hundred francs to hand. How were you going to pay?'

François shrugged. 'I'd have borrowed it somehow.'

His use of the past tense was telling, as though he already knew he wouldn't be borrowing money anytime soon. He had good reason for this belief. He and Joseph had been searched on arrival at Tarascon police station. While Joseph's pockets offered up nothing of interest, folded inside an interior pocket of François's wallet was a letter, which Félix Martin now produced. It was written in French, in the formal *vous*.

Sunday, 2 Dec. 1928
Dear François,

This letter is for you. The other one – the long one – is for your family. I am writing in bed with a pencil because my right arm hurts.

The damages case will be heard in Marseille on Wednesday 5th December. Be a darling – as always – and accompany me to Marseilles on the 4th – Tuesday – We can leave in the afternoon from Les Baux. You will go to the theatre with your sister-in-law and we'll come back late on Wednesday . . .

If all goes well, as soon as I've bought the hotel and taken possession, I shall add a few lines to my French will and leave the property to you. You never know what might happen. Chances are I'll live to be a good old girl of 90 – but if next door should give me a blast from a revolver for Christmas, the hotel will be yours.

Keep this letter as it may be very useful to you.

O. Branson

Olive had added the last line and her signature in ink. It was undoubtedly her handwriting and François had no choice but to admit it was intended for him.

'Did she give it to you in person?'

'No. I think she asked my brother-in-law to deliver it to me, or maybe she sent it by post.' Its contents, however, hadn't come as a surprise. 'When Miss Branson bought our hotel, she told me that one day it would be mine. She repeated this on several occasions.'

Félix Martin returned to the question of François's visit to the solicitor on the Saturday afternoon after Olive's body had been found. Had it really been to check whether the hotel could stay open? François insisted it had. But, he admitted, he had since spoken to Bruno Martin-Caille about Olive's bequest.

The letter found in his wallet also opened up another line of questioning. 'You will go to the theatre with your sister-in-law . . .' Not *you could*, but *you will*. Either it was an order, which seemed strange, or Olive had been giving him a cover story for their overnight stay in Marseille. But why would he need one?

Félix Martin already knew the answer to that, thanks to Guibbal's efforts over the weekend. On Saturday, Guibbal had visited the hotel at which they had stayed, after noticing its name in Olive's pocket diary. The large Hotel Beauvau dominated one end of the Vieux Port, overlooking the pavement cafes and street stalls of the Quai des Belges, and was popular with well-heeled tourists.

The hotel director had confirmed that Olive had made a number of bookings in the six months leading up to her death. For the first two, in mid-November and early December, she had taken two rooms, one with a private bathroom for herself and another on a higher floor for her driver. On two later visits, however, she had requested an additional room next to her own. Each booking had been for just one night. Guibbal had subsequently returned to question the chambermaids, taking along various photographs he'd snapped in Les Baux the previous week. One of the girls had identified François as the occupant of the third room.

Confronted with this evidence by Félix Martin, François saw that it was pointless to deny the truth and agreed to make a further statement.

'I previously omitted to mention that I had been Miss Branson's lover for about a year,' he began. 'The first time we slept together was at the beginning of 1928 at the Hotel Beauvau. We'd gone in the evening to see *Un Coup de Mistral* at the Alcazar Theatre on the Cours Belsunce. After that trip, I was obliged to sleep with her four or five times more – never in Les Baux, always in Marseille . . . and once this last winter at the Hotel du Tourisme in Embrun, when we spent a couple of days in the Alps.'

'When was the last time?'

'Before her last departure for England – on the eleventh of April, I think it was. The Hotel Beauvau was closed, so we stayed at the Continental next door. On Miss Branson's advice, Louis Vigne and I had gone to the Varieties. I went to bed with her when we got back to the hotel.'

'Did she give you money on these occasions?'

'Well, she used to slip money into my pocket at restaurants so I could pay for our meals.'

François would later claim that he'd been reluctant to disclose the affair out of respect for Olive. Yet, going by what he said next, chivalry had not been the only reason. He also had his own vanity to wrestle with. Olive had been nearly twenty years older than him, a fact that clearly caused him some embarrassment.

'There's one final detail I must give you, a rather delicate one,' he said. 'It's that I never took any pleasure in the sex we had. I was never able to achieve *coït complet* with her. That is to say, I could never ejaculate inside her. Not even extensive petting on her part could change how I felt.'

'And how did Miss Branson feel?'

'I never noticed any great dismay . . . Only once – the first time – did she seem disappointed.'

Leaving Joseph to stew in his cell, the detectives drove François back along the dark roads to Les Baux, where they drew up outside the annexe of the Hotel Monte-Carlo.

As François stood silently in his bedroom, Guibbal and Laforgue gathered the clothing he had been wearing on the night of Olive's death: a sweater, a pair of light grey trousers and a cream trench coat, along with the navy blue jacket currently on his back. That done, they started to search the rest of the room again. Eventually, François pointed wearily towards a small, brown leather travelling case tucked beneath a chest of drawers. Inside, Guibbal found a document, handwritten in ink. It was the promised codicil to Olive's French will, dated Christmas Eve. In it, she had bequeathed the hotel to François in its entirety.

Guibbal looked at the piece of paper and then at François. 'What would you do in my situation?'

'I'd arrest me,' François replied.

And he was right.

PART III:

A MATTER OF TIME

1

The Palais de Justice stood behind a large fountain in the leafy Place Montyon, in Marseille's sixth arrondissement. It had been the city's main courthouse for nearly seventy years and, for many, left much to be desired. At the building's inauguration ceremony in 1862, the imperial prosecutor had given a rousing speech about French law and Napoleon III's devotion to the welfare of the people, unaware that the design of the new courthouse had condemned a portion of those people – that is, all future Marseillais magistrates and their staff – to an eternity of gloom. The architect had put all his energies into the public-facing areas – the elevated, neoclassical facade with its monumental Ionic columns and the grand entrance hall decorated with red Languedoc marble – and had hidden the offices in the building's extremities, almost as an afterthought.

Take, for instance, the magistrates' accommodation in the basement. Cramped and inadequate, it was poorly lit, freezing in winter, and the waiting room was far too small for the number of miscreants the police brought in each day. Admittedly, the basement could be pleasantly cool in summer, but then the misery was transferred to the archivists in the attic, who would be doubly attacked by the sun's rays on the roof and all the rising heat. Plans were afoot to build a large annexe to solve these problems, but these were on a strictly need-to-know basis to avoid alerting nearby property owners that their old mansions would soon be bought and demolished. As it had been decided that most of the courthouse's basement dwellers did not need to know, they continued to work without hope in their dreary offices, aided by spectacles and lamps, tunnelling through paperwork like short-sighted moles.

It was into these depths that François was brought on Tuesday afternoon. Joseph had been released that morning after Guibbal checked his alibi in Fontvieille: Gabrielle Desmaries, the butcher's wife, had confirmed that he was with her husband on the evening of Olive's death. The men were old friends, she said, and her husband had been showing Joseph some paintings. Joseph had left sometime after eight thirty, saying he would need to get some petrol on his way home.

François, therefore, was on his own. A large crowd had gathered in Tarascon to watch him being led from the police station in handcuffs, and now he was surrounded by Guibbal, Martin and Laforgue after a long and tense journey in their car. It was nearly three o'clock by the time Jeanpierre ushered the group into Rochu's office.

The examining magistrate sat behind a desk obscured by stacks of reports and memoranda. After reading the statements handed to him by the detectives, Rochu looked at François.

'This bequest. Why didn't you tell me about it when I interviewed you on Friday?'

'You didn't ask me.'

'Or that Miss Branson was your lover?'

'It would have been indelicate of me to mention it.'

Rochu pondered this before continuing. 'And when did Miss Branson return from England?'

'She arrived at Avignon on the Sunday – the twenty-first of April.'

'Did you go to the station to meet her?'

'No. I didn't see her until the Thursday, when she took lunch at the hotel.'

'And after that?'

'Not until eight o'clock the following evening, when I dropped off the oil and milk.'

'What did she say when you arrived?'

'"Good evening, François."'

'And you said . . . ?'

'"Good evening. Where should I put these?" Miss Branson replied, "Put the oil in the storeroom and the milk in the kitchen." She accompanied me as I did so, and then I left.'

'You said nothing else?'

'I asked her if she would be taking lunch at the hotel the next day, and she said, "I don't think so." I said, "No doubt you're saving your energy for the banquet on Sunday." She didn't answer, so I returned to my car while she went to open the gate.'

'What was she wearing?'

'I don't know. I didn't notice.'

'You didn't notice how your mistress was dressed?'

François shrugged. 'She often criticized me for not noticing people or things.'

Rochu was clearly perplexed by this behaviour. It wasn't how Frenchmen usually treated their lovers, especially when they had been apart for over two weeks. It reeked of a falling out of some sort. Still, other than a compelling theory and a clear financial motive, there was no evidence that the young man was guilty of any crime. The law, however, allowed for a suspected murderer to be held for up to eighteen months without charge while evidence was gathered. Rochu therefore ordered that François be transferred to the city's Chave Prison, and instructed Guibbal to continue his investigation.

*

Back in Les Baux, the atmosphere was one of outrage. With Joseph's return, the village soon learned the reasons for François's arrest. Further details were gleaned from those who'd had the misfortune to receive a visit from Guibbal that morning to provide further statements.

Olive's bequest of the hotel was a surprise to all, but no one in Les Baux believed it could have enticed François to murder. He didn't have a violent bone in his body, they said. He had always been a gentle boy – a bit closed off, perhaps, but harmless all the same. If the authorities had any evidence against him, it must have been fabricated. Besides, it was quite obvious the Anglaise had killed herself – and her reasons for doing so were now clear.

Far from being the shocking revelation that Guibbal had anticipated, François's admission that he had been Olive's lover merely confirmed what many in the village already suspected. Affairs were impossible to keep quiet in a place like Les Baux. However discreet a couple might be, it only took one person to notice a change in demeanour or an ill-timed glance and the rumours caught fire. Indeed, there were at least two other secret entanglements known to be underway in the village, with the paramours having been spotted, respectively, in a wood near Maussane and alighting from a train at Avignon. With François and the Anglaise, there had been no conclusive evidence, but they had sparked a great deal of speculation with all the overnight trips they had taken with Louis Vigne, along with other outings à deux to God-knows-where.

François is in great form . . . he whirled me off to the St Eloi*
at Chateau Renard [sic] on the motorbike – another scandal for

---

* A parade held in honour of Saint Eligius in the market town of Châteaurenard on the first Sunday in July.

Les Baux – I made him promise, before we started home again, that if he shed me by the way – & arrived without me, he'd give the dogs their supper – ![1]

The age difference was unusual but, as was agreed, that was more than made up for by the Anglaise's wealth and François's reputation as a ladies' man. As was his way, François kept the details of his romantic escapades to himself, but there were said to be broken hearts all over Bouches-du-Rhône.

That said, one of his girlfriends had been quite serious for a while, or so everyone had thought. Little Wiesje Falkenhayn had only been fifteen, François twenty-two. She was from the Netherlands, but had spent a few months visiting Les Baux with her mother and stepfather, the Zondags. Madame Zondag had done everything she could to keep the pair apart, but François had finally won her over.

I took Madame Zondag to St Remy with me – I had to go to the bank & the moment she got in the car she began about François. He's vanquished her!!! She didn't like him – & couldn't see that he had any charm. Now she finds him 'très sympathique' & she can't understand how a family like the old folks & Marie Girard can possess a cultivated being like François . . .

François was bidden to call – & did so, said he was very fond of Wiesje & ready, later, to marry her. Madame Z said she was an idle child, not at all the sort of wife he ought to have & he said 'If one loves one's wife & she is idle – one is ready to work harder oneself – if one doesn't love one's wife – what is the use of working?'

She said he might come to the house as much as he liked – but she trusted he would respect the youth of her daughter – &

*he said 'Madame, I understand the difference between a child
of 15 and a girl of 22.'*[2]

It had been assumed that François was ready to settle down, but
when Wiesje and the Zondags left for Paris, François seemed
unconcerned.

*Not a word of Wiesje – but I hear indirectly that she may soon
be sent back to Holland – to an Aunt. François is very cheerful
& has told Madame Patin – who said 'Et ses amours?' that he
had NO intention of marrying yet, that he was extremely well
(bien) as he now is – & he intended to have several more
mistresses before he got married – !*[3]

At one point, the local gossips deduced that one of those other
mistresses was Phyll or Kay fforde. Not only had François joined
them on their day trips with Olive, he'd also accompanied them
both to dances in Saint-Rémy. Their chaperones at these dances
– Louis Vigne and the Saint-Rémy tobacconist, Madame Passa
– had never reported anything untoward, but that did not stop
tongues wagging.

And tongues continued to wag now, as all the morsels of gossip
were gathered, sifted, arranged and rearranged, until everything
finally made sense: François, of course, had never been serious
about the Anglaise – what young man would be? – and had broken
it off either before she left for England or on her return. Ageing
and prone to neurasthenia, the Anglaise had brooded over the
rejection until she could bear it no longer. Seeing François on the
Friday evening had presumably been the final straw. It was a
tragedy worthy of Mistral.

*

The affair was more of a shock to Olive's family and friends. Over in Saint-Rémy, Jean Baltus, the incurable romantic who marked his diary with a big, red 'K' after every chaste encounter with his beloved Katie Schloop, was finding the whole thing particularly difficult to digest.

Johnny B . . . he always looks too fragile for anything . . .[4]

Although he had no problem accepting that the uncouth Baussencs had a murderer in their midst, the idea that Olive had been conducting an affair with one of them floored him. Surely, François had to be lying? The only time Baltus had spent any time with the two of them was at a small lunch party Olive had held the previous January. It was to celebrate François's victory over Raoul Dumas in the long, drawn-out court battle over the hotel. François aside, the guests had been a selection of the Monte-Carlo's higher-class patrons: Madame Sous, the antiques dealer; old Madame Pinet's brother, Charles Cornille, who was something of a poet in addition to running his cafe and acting as Les Baux's *gardien des ruines*; and Madame Melville, Louis Jou's erudite and beautiful mistress. Jou himself had been in Paris.

It was a delightful afternoon. The food and champagne were excellent, and Charles Cornille treated them to a few songs of his own composition and read one of his Provençal tales. Much to Olive's amusement, Baltus himself had relaxed into an innocent and happy flirtation with Madame Melville. Yet, he had noticed nothing in Olive's behaviour towards François. In fact, despite being the guest of honour, the young man barely joined them at the table, busying himself instead with topping up glasses and helping to serve the food. There had been no signs of attraction. Indeed, as Baltus would later tell a reporter, he found it 'quite incomprehensible' that his charming friend had indulged in 'a vulgar liaison with a peasant lad.'⁵

To make matters worse, Baltus owned François's old car, 'La Bonne Vieille',* the sale having been partially facilitated by Olive. He had always been a reluctant and timid driver, and he would now have to deal with gears, pedestrians and narrow streets in a vehicle infused with vulgarity, all while clutching a steering wheel tainted by a murderer's hands.

Earlier that day, another car had whisked Arthur and Kay fforde away from Saint-Rémy and Les Baux altogether. Having received advance notice of the developments from Rochu, they had left the Hotel de Provence and sought refuge from the press with Arthur's father in Grasse, nearly 200 kilometres away. With a more worldly view of Olive than Baltus, however, both had taken the revelation in their stride. In fact, as Arthur was about to find out, his wife had known about the fling for a while.

*I think Madame Sous knows!*⁶

Indeed, it would become evident that Olive had written to May about the very trip to Marseille during which François claimed the affair began. Her letter had not said as much, but it was easy to see how events might have taken such a turn. This was due, in large part, to a haircut.

The trip had taken place in February 1928. Its main purpose was for Olive to see Dr Vigne, the specialist who had been treating her ailing scalp, but she suggested that François join her. He was in need of a break, having been left holding the fort at the Monte-

---

* 'The Good Old Girl'

Carlo while Marie-Thérèse, ill and pregnant, languished in a rest home in Saint-Didier. Marie-Thérèse's absence hadn't been a problem in itself, but Marguerite had gone with her for support, leaving Joseph and the Vayssière men to mope around the hotel, apparently unable to fend for themselves.

After a few weeks of this, François had confided in Olive that he wanted to 'chuck the whole lot of them out', a sentiment that drew her sympathy.

> *I consider François has shown the patience of an angel – he has for weeks & weeks fed Joseph, lodged & fed Pierrette – lodged & fed Louis Vayssière & Pierrot – who don't do one hand's turn of work – & don't pay for their food – & has had his waiters – or his cook – snatched from him, to go to St Didier to be with Madame G . . .*[7]

Olive herself had been dealing with Joseph's drinking and further drama in Saint-Didier, where Marie-Thérèse was proving to be a reluctant and headstrong patient. The plan, therefore, had been to let off some steam, stay at a hotel overnight and return the next day.

Louis Vigne had picked them up on the Thursday morning in his Citroën. It had been blowing a gale as they set off.

> *Louis suggested going across the Crau!! – So we went – I don't think I've ever been on such awful roads – Since the rain there are deep holes everywhere. When one side of the car is up, the other side is down – & then the car jumps! Men were shooting in wading boots in the marshes the other side of Maussane – & there was water shining between the stones on the Crau – we saw one little herd of bulls – all the others are away still because of the wet.*

> *When we got to Martigues, the road was up!!!!!! That meant turning into the little alleyways & they were all placarded 'Sens Unique' ['One Way'] and 'sens unique' was always the wrong way for us – we somehow dodged into a little 'place' where we found more lost cars. Louis said 'Hé! Bê! Par example!' several times – & at last we got away. The road from Martigues to Marseille is good – up to the Cote de L'Assassin – a zigzag like Les Baux – but much larger – then down 8 kilometres of garden city & manufacturing suburbs into Marseille.*

They went straight to the Vieux Port on arrival, where they ate outside a restaurant on the sunny side of the harbour. After lunch, they wandered over to the Hotel Beauvau to check that the rooms Olive had requested had been reserved.

> *They had – mine with two windows looking right down the Vieux Port – & a bathroom (Mo* expected any moment – & I thought this time I'd be comfortable). Then we went to the Doctor – where I shed François, telling him to amuse himself & to find out what theatre we could go to laugh . . .*

Dr Vigne had been overseeing the treatment of Olive's scalp for some time. This involved the regular application of tar poultices, administered by Marie-Thérèse ('. . . she has very gentle hands . . . & shows great ingenuity in bandaging on the poultices – it's awkward – 3 on a head!!!!').[8] The bandages, Olive said, forced her to sleep 'very gingerly & straight – like a Templar – with my hound at my feet.'[9]

Most of her hair was so damaged that it had to be shorn off. Although Marie-Thérèse had saved what she could, Olive kept

---

* Her monthly period.

A Matter Of Time

her head covered by a silk scarf. On that visit, however, the specialist delivered good news.

> *The Doctor said 'C'est parfait – vous êtes complètement guéri et je suis très, très content.' ['It's perfect – you are completely healed and I am very, very happy.'] . . . I said, 'May I go to a hairdresser?' & he said 'Yes' & gave me the name of the best one – he said 'He is expensive, but in every way admirable – you cannot come to any harm with him.'*

She went straight to the salon, a discreet establishment occupying a first-floor apartment on the corner of the Place de la Préfecture. Louis and his Citroën had looked out of place among the uniformed chauffeurs waiting outside. Victor Pellet was not used to customers arriving unannounced, but he took pity on Olive, with her headscarf and two lonely ringlets dangling from her temples. He told her to return after five o'clock.

> *At 5.15, I went again – such a funny visit . . . I told him Dr Vigne had sent me – & what had happened. I was sat down in a little recess, lit as if I was to make up for the stage. Monsieur Victor & two young men attendants arranged themselves, & I took off my silk handkerchief. Monsieur Victor said, '<u>Quel dommage</u> – évidemment il fallait le faire – <u>mais quel dommage</u> – C'est affreux – <u>c'est affreux!!!</u>' ['<u>What a shame</u> – of course, it had to be done – <u>but what a shame</u> – It's awful – <u>it's awful!!!</u>'] He then had a good look all round me – said 'Je ferai tout mon possible' ['I will do everything I can'], selected one young man, Paul – explained minutely to him what to do – & went away.*
>
> *Paul began – with great care – & in a few moments he stopped & called 'Monsieur Victor – qu'est ce que je ferai maintenant?' ['What should I do now?'] & Monsieur Victor would come –*

fatherly & elderly – & very business-like – he was called every few moments – & the young man did the cutting & at last Monsieur Victor said 'C'est bien – je suis content.' ['That's good – I'm satisfied.']

It was fascinating to watch! Like Orpen pulling together a bad student drawing. They have faked my head! No waving, no shaving – but they've somehow thinned out the hair so that it is cut almost to my skull – & yet looks solid. Then where it is a little longer, they have cut so that the longer bits lie in place – & the very, very short back hair gives you the impression somehow that it is the end of the proper ordinary shingle, starting on the top of the head!!

It defeats me! They haven't touched the top – that is to grow – but they've trimmed the two flower girl curls – & three sweeps of a brush finished it! Now, in a strong light – full face – I have a close-fitting silver helmet – which turns dark gunmetal, sideways – & full back – & it shines again!!!

The tar is worked out . . . I think the man is a genius.

When she and Louis returned to the hotel, François complimented her new look. He also reported that he had arranged the evening's entertainment: a variety performance entitled *Un Coup de Mistral* at the glittering Alcazar music hall. Louis decided to occupy himself elsewhere.

. . . François said one would see the best of the Midi artistes there – & we have suffered too much to go to the opera.

The Alcazar is large – comfortable and packed full – a 'Revue Régionale' beginning with the Aerodrome of Marignane . . . Then a gem of a scene of the Vieux Port . . . two women & two men ran the scene – a hefty Vieux Port Fishwoman – shingled head – blue wooly [sic], blue apron – purple socks – & clogs – a little Marchande de Légumes, a lovesick Policeman – & an electrician in overalls – admirable. I'd have loved K & Phyll to be there – & how we laughed.

There was also a lot of good dancing . . . One of the English girls, Iris Rowe, is very pretty & dances divinely – they did a marvellous Argentine apache dance – part of 'Les Sylphides' which Karsavina used to do – & the funniest & prettiest Harlequin with a helpless Columbine – if he held her by so much as one finger – she danced perfectly. Then he'd let her go – & her arms & legs went wobbly & she'd collapse where she was left – in a little heap – & the Harlequin's surprise & concern made it a joy. I'd have loved the girls to have seen that –

But the comedy! Midi of the Midi – indescribably funny – we sat quite helpless – & my handkerchief was a wet rag at 12 o'clock – & being there – one of a French audience – all tickled to death. It was quite all right – a completely primitive show, & comic to the last degree – but I wouldn't have borne it if I'd been with a party of English or Americans – & I would NOT have liked the girls to have been there.[10]

It was the first time Olive had truly enjoyed herself for months. She and François got back to the Hotel Beauvau well after midnight, their faces flushed with laughter and the thrill of the bawdy comedy still tingling in their bones. In her letter, Olive had not mentioned what happened next. Considering her cousin's shocked reaction to the 'honeymoon episode' involving Major Wilson, however, that was perhaps for the best.

II

Two days after François's arrest, the front page of *Le Matin*, France's premier newspaper, carried a short piece echoing the mutterings that had been growing since the affair had become public knowledge. Written by the paper's chief leader writer, Louis Forest, the piece lambasted wealthy foreign women for treating France and its colonies as their sexual playground.

The problem, Forest wrote, was not new. He gave as an example the town of Biskra in French Algeria, known as the gateway to the Sahara and a popular destination for pleasure seekers in the late nineteenth century. One year, he said, there had been a 'veritable epidemic' of foreign women trotting into the desert with Arab guides to 'see the sights.' Such women were now flocking to France itself, a fact which Forest attributed to favourable exchange rates. (The latter, at least, was true: dollars and pounds could buy a woman a lot of time and fun in France. Olive herself had commented on it in a letter to her cousin George that January, in terms of purchasing property: 'It's amazing . . . The Monte Carlo, the Maison du Four – & the Vayède, with the Quarry included – has cost me about £800!!!!! The exchange, at Paris, is 124 to the pound.'[1])

The good people of France, Forest continued, would have gladly averted their eyes from such behaviour had these women not then returned home and prudishly griped about French debauchery. He related this moral hypocrisy directly to Olive, or at least to one version of her that was emerging in the press. Falsely quoting François as saying that she had valued her reputation above everything, Forest played on an old French proverb, writing, 'She had a golden girdle, but she wanted a good name.'*

Olive and her kind, as he saw it, did great damage to France's reputation abroad, and this latest scandal had moved him to speak out on behalf of those who suffered as a result: 'This cannot harm Miss Branson's reputation, which is dead, as is she; but it will partially avenge a few old families who are ignored because they have no voice.'[2]

Meanwhile, parts of the British press had also been attempting to paint Olive as a sad, washed-up adventuress. Their most prominent source was a writer called April Day, who claimed to have received many letters from Olive over the years. 'She wrote so frequently that I felt at last that I had to reply,' Miss Day told a *Daily News* reporter. 'I think she fancied we would be twin souls.'

One of these letters, allegedly written just days before Olive's death, read:

> I was delighted, on going through the spring lists of various publishers, to see in Herbert Jenkins's list that you have written a book ... A Spanish friend of mine suggests I should write my romances, but really I am so disillusioned. I find romances fade in dust and bitterness.
> Many good wishes for 'Cameos From My Life.'
> – Yours sincerely, Olive Branson[3]

---

* The proverb 'A good name is better than a girdle of gold' refers to the old practice of carrying money in a belt around one's waist.

In another, she had supposedly stated that 'Frenchmen make the best lovers in the world.'[4]

It wouldn't be until the following March that *John Bull* magazine would expose April Day as the latest incarnation of a notorious fraudster, blackmailer and bigamist who had been plaguing British society for over a decade.* In 1929, she had published a volume of memoirs filled with Baron Munchausen-like claims about her exploits as an aviatrix, lady detective, literary agent and socialite. To publicize this book, Miss Day piggybacked on the press coverage of Olive's death, fortuitously 'discovering' new bogus correspondence as the case progressed.[5]

Those who had actually known Olive, however, were keeping their lips tightly sealed. From his father's villa near Grasse, for example, Arthur fforde was doing his best to maintain Olive's reputation through judicious silence. When he did speak, it was only to express mild doubts about François's guilt. In his experience, François had always been gentle, respectful and honest, and he struggled to believe that he, or indeed anyone in Les Baux, was capable of her murder. As he told a correspondent for the *Daily News* who had caught him as he left Saint-Rémy: 'The mystery of her death may be deeper and darker than we imagine. The brutality of the crime seems to me to be inconsistent with the theory that its perpetrators may have been the people who knew Miss Branson, and to whom she showed every kindness.'[6]

Arthur refused to discuss, however, the fact that Olive had bequeathed the hotel to François, nor did he comment on their relationship. Privately, he knew that neither was particularly out of character. It was strange that she had not informed him about

---

* The magazine was unable to establish April Day's true identity, but it did reveal four of her other known aliases and warned that she should 'be avoided at all costs.'

the codicil to her French will, affecting as it did Kay's inheritance, but also understandable given the explanations that would have been required were she to do so. Olive had never been one to lie.

She had, however, always had a soft spot for young men. Ever since her art-school days, when she had sought out wrestlers and acrobats to model for her action drawings, a few had invariably found their way under her wing. As Alfred Munnings had noticed at the Calderon summer school, mothering had come naturally to her; she couldn't help it.

Olive had never hidden these friendships from her family. Fortunately, her young men had been easy to like. Their manners may not have been as polished as Aunt Mary would have preferred, but they were always kind, gentle and striving towards some great dream.

She had met Jack Gorman, for example, in 1910. At a lean nine stone, Jack was a young Mancunian boxer enjoying some success on the circuit but struggling to make ends meet between matches. In addition to engaging him as a model, Olive had supplemented his winter earnings from the boxing ring with regular five-shilling postal orders. She had also introduced him to her circus friends, enabling him to secure work in the spring and summer months. During the circus 'tenting' season, he either played in the band for John Swallow's or 'Sir' Robert Fossett's circus, or acted as Olive's groom when she took to the road herself.

Jack had always kept her informed of his successes and failures, signing his letters 'Your faithful Watch Dog, Jack'. He also strived to repay the winter postal orders from his summer wages. It had been a principle of Olive's that the help she offered her poorer friends was given on business lines to preserve their autonomy and dignity. Besides, she wasn't wealthy enough to indulge in limitless charitable acts; she still had to sell her work to make ends meet. Privately, however, she didn't always expect to see her money returned.

Jack Gorman, Olive and Spring with her caravan.

By the time of her death, for example, she had been sending cheques to her friend Karel Ruckl for six years and had not seen a penny back. But then, Karel's dream had always been more of a gamble. The pair had met in 1923, when he was twenty-two and fresh off the train from his native Czechoslovakia. His ambition was to take to the stage. Although his English was stilted, he was chronically disorganized and he couldn't afford drama school, Olive – then almost forty – had seen something in his passion and intellect. He was also, of course, very handsome, with a brooding brow and chiselled features.

She had taken Karel for tea at Gordon Square to meet their fellow theatre lover, Aunt Mary, in the months before Mary's death in December 1923. From there, Karel had charmed the whole family, and they all became invested, to a greater or lesser degree, in his acting career. Through persistence and determination, and an anglicized stage name, Karel found work with a company that toured provincial theatres. Writing from dismal lodgings in Kidderminster or Weston-super-Mare, he would enthuse about his work as second assistant stage manager or stepping in for one of the Three Musketeers to swashbuckle to a half-empty house. He advised Olive on Russian literature; she provided money and encouragement.

By the time Olive settled in France, Karel had been transformed into a bona fide thespian of the endearingly pretentious type. His now-impeccable English sprang off his tongue with many a 'my dear' and a 'splendid'. He'd also picked up Olive's idiosyncratic way of writing, and his letters became increasingly littered with dashes, declarations of 'What a life!!' and more exclamation marks than were becoming. At the same time, his work had become more regular, prompting him to decline some of the Coutts' cheques. In 1927, he even got a foot in the door of the film industry, with a background part in Anthony 'Puffin' Asquith's acclaimed silent film *Shooting Stars*, leading the family to refer to him affectionately as 'the cinema villain.'*

From what Arthur had seen, François had been another of Olive's Karels or Jacks. He even had the same gentle demeanour. The sexual element appeared to be a new departure, but the pattern was the same: instead of fame in the boxing ring or on the stage, François wanted to break free of Les Baux and its stifling atmosphere. Whether it was arranging to view the hotel in Embrun or merely giving him the opportunity to escape to Marseille for a

---

* Although fame as an actor would continue to elude Karel Ruckl, meeting Asquith brought about a gratifying alternative. As Peter Russell, he later became the director's longstanding private secretary and occasional film production partner.

night or two, she had been encouraging him to seek freedom and independence, just as she had done in her own youth. Leaving him his family's hotel in her will was an extension of that. She was restoring it to its proper place, where it could do the most good – although, of course, she had not expected it to be restored so soon.

But how could Arthur – or anyone else – explain any of this to a press that dealt in caricatures and absolutes? No one could truly understand Olive, unless they had witnessed her personal evolution or seen the interplay between her belief in individual authenticity and the empathy and generosity that came so naturally to her. It was therefore better to keep quiet, despite aggravations such as the *Le Matin* article.

It was perhaps with all this in mind that Arthur arrived in Marseille later that day to see Joseph Rochu. The public prosecutor had summoned him to clarify a few matters.

The first was that of Olive's wills. Arthur confirmed that her English and French wills had divided all her property between his three daughters and that it was Kay who was due to inherit the assets in Les Baux. He also admitted that, when he had spoken to Marie-Thérèse and François about this the previous week, François had given no indication that Olive had left him the hotel.

The conversation then turned to more personal matters. This was Arthur's chance to demonstrate that, whatever Louis Forest wanted to insinuate, Olive had been no carefree adventuress dripping with gold. For a start, as he pointed out, her income had been a modest five or six hundred pounds a year, which she'd had to supplement through sales of her drawings. As for her past relationships, there had only been two of note. Each had been tragic in its own way, but both were beyond reproach. Rochu already knew of Olive's marriage to Major Wilson, but, Arthur confided, she had also once been engaged to a French airman by the name of La Place who had died during the war.

Emile Jeanpierre was diligently writing all this down, ready for the stamps and signatures that would make it part of the official record, unaware that Arthur had just played a blinder. If the press subsequently caught wind of his deposition and assumed, as indeed they would, that Monsieur La Place had been a dashing French flying officer shot down in battle, that would be their own doing. And if their subsequent reports went some way to rehabilitating Olive in the eyes of Louis Forest's patriotic readers, who could complain? Certainly not Arthur, who had seemingly chosen his words very carefully.

The truth was that Harry La Place had not, in fact, been French. He'd had a French father, but Harry himself was a Londoner through and through, having been born and raised in Lambeth. Nor had he been obvious officer material, at least by the standards of class-obsessed Britain: both his parents had worked in the circus. His father Auguste had been a clown and an acrobat, and his mother Violet performed as 'La Belle Atalante', whose disrobing act on the high wire had earned her the title of the 'Venus de Medici of the Arena'.[7]

Perhaps inevitably, Harry had become an entertainer himself. Under the name Steele Cohen, he had worked the music halls as a 'Hebrew comedian', seeking cheap, anti-Semitic laughs with the aid of a fake nose and a cod-European accent. In some respects, therefore, it had been fortuitous when war broke out in August 1914, wresting the twenty-two-year-old off the stage and into the Army Cyclist Corps.

After a year of pedalling back and forth along the Western Front, Harry had caught malaria and found himself at an army hospital in Rouen, a hop and a skip from Olive's YMCA hut. The precise details of how the pair met have been lost, although presumably a tea urn and gossip about their respective circus friends were involved. In wartime fashion, they soon became engaged.

The engagement lasted less than eighteen months. On 18 March 1917, Sergeant Harry La Place had been killed while on secondment with the Royal Flying Corps, the only casualty in a plane accident at an aerodrome. His death had left Olive bereft and, arguably, vulnerable. Twelve months later, she was scooped out of her burning hut and into the arms of Major Wilson.

The truth was that men of her own class had never attracted Olive. That's not to say none had tried to catch her eye, as a letter she had kept from July 1908 demonstrated. It had been written by candlelight under canvas on a lonely hill in the Lake District. The signature was formed by an 'A' and an 'R' intertwined to look like a tent tethered to the page by a row of tiny, inky pegs. A kettle propped over a campfire steamed nearby. 'Ain't this a tweaky monogram?' the author had asked.

In the body of the letter, 'A.R.' begged Olive to join him in the Lakes:

I am still hermitting, a solitary camper. Can't you manage to come up here for a little. Noble subjects for etching. You can put up here for 23/- a week. The railway fare return is two golden sovereigns. Three guineas in all for a week, and only four for a fortnight. Be a delightful independent person and come, tent or no tent. You need not see more of me than you want to, and I'll be working like 'ell. But it would be awfully jolly for me to have you up here, and I think you would find it worth your while from the sketching point of view . . . Just you come along any day after Monday, bring your etching apparatus, and Indian ink, as well as your painting things; and we'll have a great time. I don't at all see why you should not come by your wild lone. I'll take great care of you.[8]

The hermit was Arthur Ransome, who was spending the summer at Low Yewdale near Coniston Water. At twenty-four, he had yet to bring the Swallows and Amazons to life, but had just had great success with a book called *Bohemia in London*, an autobiographical guide to the literary and artistic world that he and Olive inhabited. His letter had been prompted by a parcel Olive had sent him containing a couple of etchings – including one of a charcoal burner's camp – and the news that five of her other pieces were on display at the Royal Albert Hall as part of the Allied Artists Association's first annual salon.

Arthur Ransome's intentions would have been clear to Olive. It was widely known in bohemian circles that he had recently decided to get married and, to everyone's amusement, had been declaring his love to almost all the women he knew. Olive, being outdoorsy, independent and cultured, had been an obvious, though unenthusiastic, target. That November, when some of their set had decamped to Paris and Olive was wondering whether to join them, her best friend Edith Wolfe had summed up the general exasperation at the situation:

> I <u>refuse</u> to go there if the Author is going to come & propose to you every other evening. I really cannot gather up sufficient strength for that! And besides, I hate being gooseberry, & a disapproving gooseberry would be a most wearing part to play: I see a vision of myself sending agitated telegrams to your cousin William!![9]

As it happened, Arthur Ransome had moved on by Paris. That autumn, he had met Ivy Walker, to whom he would be indifferently married until 1917, when he discovered the real love of his life: Leon Trotsky's secretary, Evgenia Shelepina.

Nevertheless, his brief interest had raised the Bransons' hopes that Olive would settle down with *someone*. She played along with this. That same December, she wrote to her cousins to announce her engagement to a mysterious suitor named Rodney, whom she had met through Edith Wolfe's father and intended to bring to London. After describing his various flaws, she declared that she was going 'to go through with it, whatever happens.' They had all been horrified – it was clear from her letter that Rodney was completely unsuitable, even by bohemian standards – until they discovered that Olive's betrothed was, in fact, a horse. ('You're a PIG,' May wrote, while George went along with the joke, acknowledging that 'the artistic temperament cannot expect to be happy in normal situations . . .')[10] Olive had announced no further suitors until she met Harry La Place.

The year after her run-ins with Arthur Ransome, Olive had stumbled across the hop-pickers' camp in Hampshire that would have such a profound impact on her lifestyle and sense of liberation. With the harvest in full swing, she made preliminary sketches of the Romany women and children among the towering rows of hops, with a view to creating some etchings. She also did a number of more refined pencil drawings of her new acquaintances at rest.

Two of the latter appeared in print the following year. One portrayed a young man called Sonno Barney in thoughtful repose, the other his fair-haired friend in proud profile. Both were in their shirtsleeves and waistcoats, Sonno wearing a newsboy cap and his friend a neckerchief and bare head. The portraits were arresting for their serenity and simplicity, and for Olive's facility for capturing the bloom of youth with achingly tender care.

Portrait of a young man by Olive Branson, published in *The Tramp*.

They had been published in the May 1910 edition of *The Tramp*, a short-lived periodical set up by Douglas Goldring, a former subeditor at Ford Madox Ford's *English Review*. Subtitled 'An Open Air Magazine', its name paid tribute to the popular bohemian pastime of 'tramping', a form of voluntary and part-time rural vagrancy funded by a healthy bank balance. Each monthly edition comprised a blend of fiction, poetry, art and reportage, the latter having titles such as 'Afoot by Night' and 'The Character of Roads'.

In many ways, *The Tramp* occupied an awkward space. In terms of literary content, it swayed between modernism and nostalgia. Many of its contributors highlighted the poverty and reality of the lives of the working and travelling classes, and yet did so through a romantic lens, treading the fine line between a search for authenticity and fetishizing the 'noble' poor. Nor did 'going off the beaten track' necessarily mean heading into the wild: some pieces covered middle-class expeditions into, say, the East End of London.

The magazine folded after only a year, but had nevertheless pulled in some big names in that time. Using his contacts from the *English Review*, Douglas Goldring had gathered together an impressive array of writers and illustrators. His old editor Ford Madox Ford and Ford's lover Violet Hunt were a given, but other contributors included Rose Macaulay, Jack London, Arnold Bennett, Arthur Ransome, Constance Garnett, Edward Thomas, Wyndham Lewis and E. H. Shepard.

There were some unknowns, too. Olive's portraits of the two young men had accompanied a short story entitled 'The Castle in Spain' by a woman named Sarah Girdlestone, which addressed head on part of the intelligentsia's longstanding fascination with Romany culture: that of sexual attraction.

The story explored the frustrations and impossibility of inter-class romance and was Sarah Girdlestone's one and only foray into print. In telling the story of a female artist's yearning for a young Romany hop-picker called Jim, she turned the usual gender roles of such tales on their head. From her first encounter with Jim and his greyhound at the edge of a wood, the narrator focused her gaze hungrily upon the young man.

> He was a big young man, with the same appearance of easy strength and abundant energy as the dog, trained also to the same perfection of condition.
>
> The spare, tanned face was very attractive in its insolence and good temper. It was a face built of definite planes and an

uncompromising framework of bone, the eyes set wide and rather far back, grey-blue eyes, slightly aslant, the lines running up to the outside edge, light eyebrows and long curving eyelashes, just dark enough to escape the charge of being too light.

His hair was cut to the limit of shortness, I should imagine amateurly with horse clippers – all but the curl in front, which was natural, and bleached golden brown by the sun.

He leaned upon the stile, making the dog snap at his cap. The rough hands were well shaped and the carriage of the head upon the neck very graceful.

The artist fantasized about employing Jim as a groom for the caravan she intended to purchase, and mentally clothed him as her ideal squire:

The coat with dark brown velvet collar and cuffs and many buttons, made to fit him truly and show his beautiful figure – can't you imagine him – the swagger, the immense self-esteem it would occasion. He should have shapely breeches and cord gaiters and I think a purple silk handkerchief round his neck . . .

Sarah Girdlestone was, of course, a phantom. Tucked away in Mas de Chiscale was the original manuscript for 'The Castle in Spain', written in Olive's own hand. Girdlestone was her mother's maiden name. As for the title, a phrase denoting an impossible dream, it had perhaps been influenced by a trip to the Royalty Theatre that Olive had taken with her Aunt Mary in 1906 to see Cosmo Hamilton and Eustace Ponsonby's *Castles in Spain*, a comic opera involving maidens, matadors and forbidden love.

The artist in Olive's story certainly appeared to be a version of herself. Written in the first person, the tale described her routine when in Hampshire for the hop-picking and even mentioned the first names of some of her Romany friends. What else was autobiographical, however, remained a matter of conjecture – except, that is, for her eternally optimistic view of human nature.

In the story, once the 'hopping' was over, and with Jim having promised her two hares and some mistletoe for Christmas, the narrator met one of the camp's missionaries in London, who informed her that Jim was a savage prize-fighter who would no doubt end up on the gallows for murder – a 'terrible! . . . terrible!' young man. Still, as Christmas came and went, with no sign of her gifts, she found it hard to let go of her impossible dream.

> After all, wouldn't a prize-fighter be the most efficient bodyguard one could find? . . . I tell myself he is a blackguard – but secretly I fear that he may have fallen off a tree, gathering the mistletoe, and killed himself . . . or he may be in jail for poaching my hares.[11]

III

The Marseille Police Technical Laboratory was situated at the top of the Évêché, the old bishop's palace where the Marseille Sûreté had been in residence since 1908. Although the lab itself had only been operating for two years, the head of this new service, Dr Georges Béroud, hoped it would soon lead the global field in forensics.

The competition was strong but limited. Forensic science was still in its infancy and there were only fifteen other dedicated laboratories in the whole world: four in Germany, two in Switzerland, two in France (in Paris and Lyon) and one each in Britain, Belgium, Italy, Spain, Portugal, Argentina and Brazil. The services they offered varied wildly. Some conducted full crime-scene investigations, others only processed evidence. The majority focused on identifying individuals, dead or alive, through fingerprint analysis and other methods of physical identification. A smaller number offered services to identify stains and analyse handwriting and forgeries, but few had a dedicated forensic pathologist on their staff.

France was already leading the pack with its laboratory in Lyon, created in 1910 and the first of its kind in the world. Its founder and director was Edmond Locard, who had established the underlying principle of modern forensic science: that every contact leaves a trace. The laboratory in Paris, created in 1923, served the

Parisian Sûreté and, while acclaimed, was more restricted in the scope of its operations. One of its main specialisms was anthropometry, the identification of individuals through biometric measurements, which, although still in use throughout the French prison system, was falling out of favour as a primary identification technique.

Georges Béroud had dabbled in this dying science himself during the war, when his interest in criminal psychology had been piqued by the company of ex-convicts and disgraced soldiers whom he'd found under his command. Although just a young officer, he'd had the chance, as he put it, to study the 'character and mentality' of such men.[1]

On discharge, he had enrolled at the medical school in his home town of Lyon with a view to pursuing a career in this field. When he graduated in 1923, however, he landed a coveted position as assistant to Dr Locard himself, and henceforth switched his allegiance from man to microbe.

While working for Locard, Béroud collected further diplomas in forensics, pathology, physics, chemistry and natural history, as well as undertaking stints at the city's prisons, psychiatric hospital and dedicated pathology and fraud laboratories. Two years later, in 1925, he sailed for South America on Locard's behalf, summoned by the US government to join a team of American lawyers and officers who, under the direction of General Pershing, were providing neutral oversight of a critical referendum on disputed territory in Chile and Peru. Béroud's role was to examine the electoral registers for signs of fraud. While he was there, he also helped set up a new forensics laboratory in Santiago and trained the Chilean police in the latest forensic techniques.

On his return, he settled in Marseille, working in the prison system and biding his time until the city's long-promised new laboratory was in place. He was the obvious candidate to become its inaugural director and took up his post a week after his thirtieth birthday in July 1927.

Béroud was determined that, under his direction, the Marseille laboratory would one day provide unrivalled expertise in everything from poisons to explosives. Indeed, he had already secured a major upgrade: a new suite of seven rooms was due to open that November, with additional staff and dedicated spaces for firearms experiments, chemical analysis, photography and so on. He'd also been squirrelling away specimens for his 'Black Museum': a Chinese torture cage seized at the docks and the skull of an eighteenth-century plague victim, along with other mementoes of his varied work. Eventually, Olive Branson's revolver would take its own place in his custom-built cabinets.

For the time being, however, all of Béroud's equipment and souvenirs were crammed into just one room, necessitating a certain amount of shimmying and squeezing to move from station to station. He was also constantly interrupted by detectives seeking his expert opinion on mysterious hairs or suspicious liquids. It was therefore a day or so after the autopsy before he could turn his attention to the clothing and samples taken from Mas de Chiscale.

The equipment he used for such purposes was mounted on a long optical bench, the sliding frame of which held a battery of lenses, lamps, clamps and stands. In the centre, angled against a giant tripod, was his treasured micro-camera. An invention of his former mentor, it was a simple arrangement – a large bellows camera attached to a powerful microscope – but it enabled Béroud to provide investigators with evidence of microscopic anomalies in the most efficient manner.

After a few absorbing hours making use of this contraption, along with his spectrograph, ultra-violet lamps and various chemicals, Béroud returned to his desk. There, he gathered his final pieces of equipment: two fountain pens (one containing red ink, one blue), a ruler, a tub of glue, some red sugar paper, a needle and a spool of cotton thread. By the time Béroud's finished reports arrived at the Palais de Justice, they were proudly draped in the colours of France and reminiscent of the homework of a particularly conscientious schoolboy. *Liberté, égalité . . . véracité!*

Unfortunately, the *véracités* contained within did little to move the investigation forward. Although he'd been able to confirm that the state of Olive's stockings proved she had not walked barefoot outside, the rest of her clothing had offered nothing of forensic interest: no suspicious stains, no microscopic damage. Nor had the sponge, thought to have been used to scrub away evidence of a crime in the bedroom, held any trace of blood.

Béroud was still awaiting Rochu's orders to analyse the blood scrapings taken from the mattress and staircase, along with the suspect's clothing, but did not hold out much hope there, either. As Dr Rey had already informed Rochu, the bullet wound would not have produced sufficient blood to account for the amount they had found – no more than a few drops, in fact, and only if the body was held at a certain angle. Nor had François Pinet sustained any injuries. Either the blood in the house was from an unrelated incident or they had the wrong suspect.

In the light of Béroud's findings, Alexandre Guibbal was contemplating his next steps. His quick identification and arrest of François Pinet had been hailed as a *coup de maître* – a masterstroke – but now he needed firm evidence to prove he had the right man.

He'd known from the start the murderer had to be someone close to Olive – or, to be more precise, to Frida, Marcel, Tony and Fly. More than one witness had mentioned the silence that followed the gunshot: it was the reason the farmers had dismissed the sound as someone shooting vermin. Yet, Guibbal had seen for himself the racket Olive's dogs made and how they'd pulled at their chains and bared their teeth when Joseph brought them out for his inspection. They were half wild. Why, therefore, had they not raised hell when their mistress was attacked, unless it was by someone they knew?

His inquiries over the weekend had established that only five people in Les Baux fitted this criterion: Joseph and Marie-Thérèse Girard, Etienne Patin, François Pinet and the Pinets' fifteen-year-old nephew, Pierre Vayssière. Not even Olive's long-standing friends could visit Mas de Chiscale without the dogs being restrained in advance.

Marie-Thérèse had been swiftly eliminated, having been seen at the hotel with her three daughters at the time of the shooting. Guibbal was also satisfied that Pierre Vayssière had been at home with his family, and Etienne Patin with his father. This had left just Joseph and François. At that point, Joseph was an unknown, although his early and vocal questioning of Fabre's suicide verdict suggested a lack of involvement. François, on the other hand, was already within Guibbal's sights for the simple reason that he'd been the last known visitor to Mas de Chiscale. Olive's pocket diary and the revelation that the pair had been in the habit of visiting hotels together had narrowed those sights even further.

After that, the pieces of the jigsaw had fallen into place with surprising ease, helped in no small part by the fortuitous discovery in François's wallet of Olive's letter stating her intention to leave him the hotel. This had led François to admit to the affair, although not to the murder.

Guibbal found him a strange young man. Unreadable, in fact. His face had betrayed no emotion in their dealings so far, and now he was refusing to talk at all. But his ready admission of the affair suggested that, if presented with the right evidence, he might be provoked into a full confession. As things stood, however, that evidence was sorely lacking. All Guibbal had, other than his gut instinct, was the secret codicil to Olive Branson's will that proved François stood to gain from her death. He had theories about how the events of that night unfolded, but first he had to prove that his chief suspect had been present at the time of the murder.

This was easier said than done. Guibbal knew François had to be lying about the length of his visit to Mas de Chiscale. He hadn't seen his lover alone in weeks, yet he claimed to have stayed no longer than the few minutes it took to unload the provisions from his car. At first, he'd also been vague about when he'd arrived back at the hotel, saying only that it had been dark and well before nine o'clock. By the time Rochu interviewed him after his arrest, and having had time to digest the evidence against him, he had settled on eight-thirty.

The farmers had all heard the gunshot later than that, although their estimations varied, too. The day after the murder, all three had placed it at around nine o'clock. A week later, Félix Tougay told Rochu that it had been around quarter to nine. When Guibbal spoke to André Ricaud, he said it had been dark and sometime between quarter to nine and nine o'clock. Vincent Aracil, on the other hand, was sure that it had been lighter and no later than eight forty-five.

Somehow, Guibbal needed to establish the exact time at which the revolver had been fired and link that to François's actual movements. In Marseille, they had the giant, resounding bells of La Major and La Bonne-Mère to keep everyone ticking along at the same pace. The city ran to a schedule: there were shipping timetables and business appointments, and therefore pocket watches and municipal clocks, all of which were regularly consulted as people were swept along by the tides of the day. In Les Baux, everything just seemed to happen when it happened, in varying degrees of darkness and light, as the sun and moon meandered across the sky.

Guibbal, however, had an idea of how he could marry the two. Just a short distance from the Flying Squad offices was arguably the ultimate timepiece, one of only twelve in France, and it governed both city and farm.

The Marseille Observatory was hidden away in the parkland behind the Palais Longchamp, which had been built on a plateau above the city seventy years earlier to celebrate the construction of a canal bringing much-needed water from the River Durance. The outflow from the canal ended at the Palais's central Château d'Eau and fed into a magnificent, multi-level fountain topped by four large bulls and statues representing the bounty the water had brought. On one side stood the city's natural history museum, on the other the Musée des Beaux-Arts.

The eight-acre site was also home to the zoological gardens, where oriental pavilions held giraffes and elephants, and lions and bears paced inside their elegant iron cages. Trams trundled up and down the Boulevard Longchamp all day, ferrying sightseers and picnickers from the crowded streets below.

The domed observatory on the far side of the park was one of the first buildings erected on the site. Its telescope had once been the largest in the world; it had detected hundreds of new objects in the night sky, including a galaxy cluster 290 million miles away. Guibbal's appointment with the astronomer René Baillaud, however, was about something closer to home.

Baillaud was renowned for inventing a precursor to radar known as the paraboloid, which had saved countless lives during the First World War. He had since turned his attentions to the field of chronometry, but was also involved in the ambitious Carte du Ciel project, an international effort to chart the entire night sky by means of photographic plates. It was this brilliant mind Guibbal intended to use to answer a simple question: at what time had it got dark in Les Baux on Friday, 26 April?

Once he was installed in Baillaud's office, the science lesson began. The astronomer consulted the observatory's records for the day in question, which showed that official sunset had been scientifically set at 7.31 p.m. But, Baillaud explained, this did not mean it was dark: sunset marked the start of civil twilight and, as Guibbal would learn, twilight only ended when the sun fell six degrees below the horizon. As it took thirty-two minutes to reach that point, night had actually fallen at 8.03 p.m.

Had Guibbal got up to leave at this point, he would have been asked to sit back down, for there was more. Nightfall did not mean it was fully dark, either. In order to calculate that, Baillaud continued, one had to consider the state of the sky. Factors such as cloud cover were meticulously noted each day by Baillaud's colleagues at the observatory, but similar records were also kept by correspondents throughout the region. Those in Saint-Rémy had reported a very cloudy sky that night – eight out of ten on the scale they used – and the clouds had been fairly high in the sky. As for the moon, although it was full, it had not risen until after ten o'clock. Taking all this into account, Baillaud was happy to conclude that, on the evening of 26 April, it had been fully dark by eight thirty at the latest.

This was all Guibbal needed. None of the farmers had been correct about the time they heard the gunshot. Whether they had been deliberately lying or simply mistaken was a question for another time. What mattered was that the shot must have been fired before eight thirty, the time François claimed to have arrived at the hotel.

*

Guibbal's chances of proving François was at Mas de Chiscale at the time of the murder had improved considerably, but that proof still had to be tight enough to stand up in a court of law, preferably with reliable witnesses to back it up. He had doubts that any of the villagers would impress a jury in the state's favour. Their attitude towards him had gone from wariness to outright contempt since the arrest, and the word *perjury* would mean nothing to them.

He was more confident about the statements he had gathered in Maussane. Baptistin Moucadel, for example, had seen François drive off at eight o'clock at the latest, and the butcher was already keenly aware of the time, having had his day disrupted by the missing meat order. The journey to Les Baux couldn't have taken François more than ten or fifteen minutes, putting his arrival at Mas de Chiscale no later than quarter past eight. Had he left after spending just a few minutes putting away the oil and milk, as he claimed, he would be in the clear. But Guibbal soon uncovered further evidence that put that version of events in doubt.

At first, Guibbal had been forced to rely on the testimony of the drinkers in the hotel bar to establish the time of François's arrival back in the village. This had only narrowed it down to somewhere between twenty past eight and nine o'clock – and that was in Baussenc time. But something else François had said during his interview had given Guibbal another lead.

It related to his journey back to the hotel after Olive had supposedly waved him off and closed the gate to her yard. François had stopped at his family's old mill by the fountain to collect a basket of laundry for his sister; on leaving the mill, he said, he'd needed to switch on his headlights. The implication was that he'd left Mas de Chiscale before it had started to get dark – and therefore before Félix Tougay and the other farmers had heard the gunshot. However, he also claimed to have passed another car in the valley, which is where his alibi began to fall apart.

François said he'd recognized the car: it was a Donnet and belonged to a travelling salesman who'd bought it from the administrator of the Tarascon poorhouse. When he'd driven past, François said, it had been parked up near the fountain with its headlamps on low, and there had been two men standing in front of it. With some effort, Guibbal managed to track down both men.

Ludovic Porte lived on a narrow street in Beaucaire, a small town opposite Tarascon on the banks of the Rhône. The twenty-six-year-old spent his days travelling around the region, selling shoes out of the back of his Donnet. When Guibbal questioned him about his movements, he confirmed he had indeed been in the Vallon de la Fontaine on the evening in question.

Porte had been joined on his travels that day by a silk merchant called Pierre Piney. Their first stop had been Mouriès, before moving on to Maussane and then to Les Baux. They'd set out their wares by the *mairie* at around five thirty and had stayed for a couple of hours before packing up and taking two aperitifs at the Hotel Monte-Carlo next door.

It had been dusk when they'd driven down into the valley for their final stop. Marguerite Patin had asked them to drop by on their way home, as she'd needed some new shoes for her children. The thirty-six-year-old widow lived in a large *mas* about a hundred metres before the crossroads by the fountain. After the three children had tried on various sandals and Madame Patin had selected a new pair of slippers for herself, she had offered the merchants a drink. They had stayed for half an hour before heading home.

Porte was certain that he had not seen François Pinet on the road that evening. He knew him by sight – they were roughly the same age – and he also knew his wreck of a Renault. 'If I'd met him, I would remember,' he told Guibbal. Nor had he heard any other cars. The valley had been pitch black and silent when he and Piney had left Marguerite Patin's house.

What Porte told Guibbal next, however, was very strange: François couldn't possibly have recognized his vehicle. It was a Donnet, that much was true, but he'd only owned it for about six weeks and hadn't been to Les Baux in that time. François would have known his previous vehicle, though. That, too, had been a Donnet, although a car rather than a van, and he had indeed purchased it from Monsieur Gras of the Tarascon poorhouse. Furthermore, François's statement that the two men had been standing in front of the vehicle by the fountain with the headlamps on low was impossible. He'd had trouble with his new electric lights: he couldn't dim them, and a problem with the wiring meant that they only worked when the engine was running.

Ludovic Porte couldn't be precise about the timing of any of this, though. He hadn't looked at his watch while in the village or the valley. All he could say was that they'd arrived back in Beaucaire at about half past nine. As the journey was about thirty minutes, they must have left around nine.

When Guibbal visited Pierre Piney at his warehouse on the Rue Aldebert in Marseille, the picture became clearer. The silk merchant remembered their visit to Les Baux well. One of his customers that day had been Marie-Thérèse Girard, who had bought two shawls for herself and a pair of blue lampshades for the hotel. He'd fitted the shades himself under her supervision. She'd also served them in the cafe before they left.

Piney had taken the wheel to drive the short distance down to the valley. He remembered it had been light enough to get by without headlights. He hadn't been able to get into Marguerite Patin's courtyard as a farm cart was blocking the gate, so he'd had to park on the side of the road, about a hundred metres before the crossroads by the fountain. The rest of his statement mirrored that of Ludovic Porte: the sandals, the slippers, the offer of a drink.

He said it had been completely dark by the time they made their way out to the van. He'd cranked the engine while Porte had sat in the driver's seat and switched on the headlights. They had then driven down to the crossroads at the fountain, where Piney had got out to guide his friend as he made a three-point turn before heading back towards the road to Tarascon. At no point had they both been standing in front of the van when the lights were illuminated.

Like Porte, Piney couldn't recall meeting any other cars in the valley. He did, however, think that they had arrived back at Beaucaire somewhat later than nine thirty, probably after ten o'clock.

Either way, it looked as though François had become entangled in his own lies. He'd clearly known that the merchants intended to visit Marguerite Patin, but not that Ludovic Porte had replaced his car with a van. Nor had he realized just how long they had stayed. If they had been in Porte's old car, quickly dropped off some shoes for the children and gone on their way, it would have been a neat little alibi: the details François had given about Porte's vehicle would have been corroborated by those who'd seen it outside the *mairie*, and his sighting would have put him on his way back to the village and well away from Mas de Chiscale before the shot had been fired. As it was, he had inadvertently placed himself in the valley at least half an hour later than he thought.

*

Meanwhile, a note from Rochu had arrived on Guibbal's desk instructing him to follow up another line of inquiry: that of a possible accomplice. This was something they had already discussed. Although it seemed that François had acted alone in the murder itself, his disposal of the body was another matter. He was no doubt capable of wrangling Olive's body onto the wall of the cistern and getting it into the water, but to do so without scraping it on the masonry or catching her clothing on the wire of the grille? That alone suggested it had been a job for at least two people.

Guibbal and Rochu were also in agreement that François wouldn't have had time to summon help straight after the murder, although he could have temporarily hidden the body and shut away the dogs. The disposal must have therefore occurred in the middle of the night, once the village was fast asleep.

Once again, Guibbal was content to rule out Joseph's involvement, for the simple fact that no murderer in their right mind would entrust such a dark secret to a man so garrulous and lacking in guile. Joseph's brother, too, had been eliminated. Guibbal's colleagues had tracked down Etienne Girard to a hospital on the outskirts of Marseille, where he was indeed undergoing a hydrotherapy cure for his nerves. When Félix Martin went to interview him, Etienne admitted that, contrary to what he'd told the butcher's boy, he'd barely known Olive. In fact, they'd only met once, at his niece Odette Girard's baptism in Les Baux that January.

He also gave a satisfactory account of his movements in the days and hours leading up to Olive's death. Numerous butchers and charcutiers had confirmed that he had been trudging around Marseille on the Friday, looking for a job. At five thirty on the Saturday morning, he had, in fact, reported for work at a delicatessen in the Belsunce district, only to find that his services were no longer required. He had then gone to the Frigo employment exchange and had secured work with Monsieur Pélissier by nine o'clock. He simply hadn't had the time or energy to travel to Les Baux to hide a body.

As François's friend Adrien Sautel and Louis Vigne also had solid alibis, that left, in Guibbal's mind, one obvious candidate – someone he already suspected of helping François with his own alibi by informing him of Porte and Piney's intention to stop in the valley on their way home. Admittedly, the salesmen had been outside the *mairie* for nearly three hours, so any number of people could have tipped François the wink, but only one knew precisely when they had left to deliver Marguerite Patin's shoes. That person also had a proven history of lying to the authorities.

The circumstances of that earlier deceit, as recounted to Guibbal by Félix Martin at the start of the inquiry, were distressing and certainly elicited a degree of sympathy for the person involved. Nevertheless, to a detective, their conduct also demonstrated a strong capacity for deception.

It all began four days before Christmas in 1916, when a group of boys, including a twelve-year-old François, made a discovery in the manure heap at the back of the Hotel Monte-Carlo. It was, they thought, a dead monkey, which they fished out for closer inspection. After a series of disturbing incidents, including a burial and exhumation, this eventually found its way to the *mairie*, where it was correctly identified as a human foetus.

The mayor duly alerted the authorities, and Louis Rey was dispatched to conduct an autopsy. Although the pathologist was unable to tell whether the three-month-old foetus had been expelled due to miscarriage or deliberate abortion, it was nevertheless decided to open an investigation into infanticide. The balance of that delicate decision had been tipped by an anonymous note sent to the Sûreté in Marseille. Pasted with individual letters cut from magazines, it read:

LOOK AT THE GIRL – BAUX HOTEL

Accordingly, Félix Martin, then a young *commissaire*, arrived with an inspector to hunt down the mother. The only girl to be found in either hotel was seventeen-year-old Marie-Thérèse Pinet. When searching her room, they found spots of blood on the bedsheet and further stains on the floor. Pierre Pinet, incredulous, insisted that these must have come from his daughter's period, but Marie-Thérèse told a different story.

She had indeed been pregnant, she confessed. The father, who she refused to name, was a young soldier she'd met in 1914 and had been secretly courting. Marriage had been discussed, but he'd died in battle that autumn, just after she realized she was carrying his child. To avoid the wrath of her parents, she'd decided to get rid of the baby. Three weeks earlier, having heard that laxatives could bring on contractions, she had snuck into a chemist while shopping in Arles with her father and bought two bottles of castor oil. She had then waited for a suitable opportunity to drink them.

That chance had not arisen until three days earlier, on the Tuesday morning. The violent pains had started the same evening and lasted nearly twenty-four hours, during which time she carried on her usual chores. Marie-Thérèse had finally delivered her son on the Wednesday evening. Later that night, she had wrapped his body in newspaper and buried him in the manure heap. Although she had burned her nightgown and most of the sheets, and thrown the empty castor oil bottles off the rocks at the top of the village, she'd had no opportunity to dispose of the final sheet before her brother and his friends made their discovery.

On hearing this tale, Félix Martin had no choice but to arrest her. She was taken to Tarascon jail while the examining magistrate considered what action to take. Not only was she a minor, but there were doubts about the details of her confession: considering the relatively advanced stage of her pregnancy, it was unlikely that she had used a simple castor-oil purge. A more probable scenario was that someone more experienced in such arts had aided her. In the new year, therefore, the magistrate sent Dr Rey to Tarascon to examine Marie-Thérèse herself for evidence.

Again, Rey was unable to reach a firm conclusion. 'I will not claim that it is impossible,' his report said of her use of castor oil, 'but simply say that, as presented, it is implausible. She must be hiding part of the truth.'

Although the question of third-party involvement was never cleared up, at the end of January Marie-Thérèse was charged with procuring an abortion and sent home to await trial. After a month in the company of the wise women of Tarascon jail, however, Marie-Thérèse came up with a new story. She hadn't been sure she was pregnant, she now said, and had only used a laxative to purge herself because she was tired – with her brothers away at war and her mother indisposed, she had been working flat out. She also claimed ignorance of castor oil's abortifacient properties, citing the most likely cause of her loss to be a log that she'd tripped over while attending to the hotel's fires.

She was a very convincing liar. By the time the case came to court in May, the jury found it easy to acquit her.

And so, as the investigation into Olive's death entered its second week and Guibbal continued to stalk Les Baux, he questioned Marie-Thérèse repeatedly, trying to catch her out in some small but incriminatory detail. At first, things seemed hopeful. Although she claimed to have no knowledge of her brother's affair or the bequest, his situation had made her more forthcoming on her own activities. She now offered, for example, an explanation for the incongruous shine on the bedroom linoleum: it was the only patch of floor in the house on which she could use her trusty

O-Cedar dust mop, and she had done so vigorously every day, the last time being the Friday morning before Olive's death. On the whole, however, her statements did not change and she denied that either she or François had been involved in any murder or cover-up.

Eventually, Guibbal had to admit defeat: the thirty-year-old Marie-Thérèse was an even tougher version of her seventeen-year-old self. In fact, he was beginning to doubt that the case would ever be cleared up at all. Having exhausted the supply of willing witnesses in Les Baux, it was hard to see what else might be forthcoming. 'We have sufficient evidence to bring Pinet before the Assize Court,' he told one reporter, 'but not enough, I think, to obtain a conviction.'[2]

When he returned to Marseille to report his findings to Rochu, however, the examining magistrate was undeterred. While admitting the investigation was in a 'stage of grave presumption', he instructed Guibbal to continue searching for some morsel of evidence, however small, that might induce François to break his silence. Rochu himself would address the lack of material proof of François's guilt by preparing a set of legal presumptions that would categorically rule out any other possibility. These would establish that Olive could not have died by suicide, that the murderer must have been someone close to her and her dogs, that she had not been assaulted or robbed, that she had no serious enemies and that only a handful of people, of whom François was one, had known where she kept the revolver that killed her. It would take time, but that was the one thing they had in abundance.

IV

Chave Prison had been cutting edge when it was built in 1857. Sitting squat and foreboding behind a high wall in Marseille's fifth arrondissement, it had been designed on the then-fashionable separate system, which kept prisoners in solitary confinement day and night so that they might reflect on their sins. An octagonal chapel occupied the centre, from which radiated four wings of thirty-six cells each, arranged over two floors. Each cell contained an iron bed, a table, a chair and a window high enough to prevent any joy seeping in from the outside world. The prisoners were ghosts to each other.

Such a set-up might have suited François. By 1929, however, any hopes of pious reflection among the inmates had long since been abandoned. As Marseille had expanded – from approximately 200,000 inhabitants in 1857 to nearly one million in the late 1920s – so had its criminal population. The single cells now held up to four prisoners each.

In a separate wing, there was also a large first-floor room where foreign vagrants, picked up daily from the docks, were corralled into a multicultural, flea-infested hell. Escaped convicts from Syria and Egypt fought with Chinese opium traffickers, Caribbean stowaways and suspected Indian bandits for space on one of the twenty or so greasy straw mattresses on the floor. Tobacco smoke filled the air, alongside the smell of unwashed bodies and the stench emanating from the small hole in one corner that served as a toilet. No guard had been known to enter that room within living memory.

By contrast, the accommodation in the infirmary below was the height of luxury. There were spare blankets for the comfortable beds; tables and chairs, spirit lamps and running water. As such, it was primarily the domain of the city's top mobsters, whose powers of persuasion could make even the most stubborn doctor recognize their need for ongoing medical care in the form of breakfast in bed, a daily newspaper and regular bridge tournaments. On one memorable occasion, its residents had even staged an operetta.[1]

François, who was neither wretched enough for the fleapit nor had the means to enter the infirmary, had been allocated to one of the small cells holding other suspected murderers, rapists and thieves. And it was there, after just eight nights with his new room-mates, that he got a taste of his potential fate.

At one o'clock that Wednesday morning, the stillness of the night was broken by the sound of hooves and cars on the streets outside: Anatole Deibler, France's chief executioner, had arrived in Marseille with his guillotine, La Veuve.* More than a dozen roadblocks were in place and the police had formed a hundred-metre cordon around the prison, but the men inside could hear every bang and scrape as the contraption was erected in front of the prison gates. Every now and again, purposeful footsteps echoed in the air as the bowler-hatted Deibler stepped forward with his flashlight and spirit level to check his assistants' progress.

Deibler's client that morning was Bonaventure Balsanti, a young Corsican who had shot and killed a Sûreté officer during a routine identity check in October 1927. Balsanti had always been something of a wildcat, yet, after attempting a final prison break a few months

---

* The Widow.

earlier, he had transformed himself into a model prisoner. It was generally accepted that he had shown genuine repentance for his crimes. His execution, therefore, was regretted in many quarters.

Joseph Rochu and Auguste Rol, who had been responsible for his prosecution, formed part of the small procession that led Balsanti out of his cell an hour before dawn. They watched as he dictated a loving letter to his aunt, heard a Mass in the prison chapel and downed three tots of rum, before Deibler ushered them outside.

'Ah, there it is,' they heard Balsanti say quietly when he saw the guillotine.

At quarter to five, the blade fell.

How this affected François, however, was impossible to tell. Reports from the prison guards suggested he had withdrawn into himself completely. Incarceration had not dented his composure; on the contrary, his internal life seemed capable of sustaining him indefinitely. During his one brief appearance in Rochu's chambers – to witness the transfer of evidence seized at Mas de Chiscale to Georges Béroud for testing – he had refused to speak beyond confirming his name and assenting to the proceedings.

He had, however, been receiving letters from his family, which, along with his replies, were intercepted by the prison governor and diverted to the Palais de Justice. François seemed aware of this, remarking in a letter to Marie-Thérèse that the post was unusually slow, before adding, 'An innocent person is subjected to even greater scrutiny. Modern justice!'

Nothing about the ongoing investigation appeared to have ruffled him, however. Writing to his niece Madeleine to wish her a happy Pentecost ten days after his arrest, François assured her, 'I'm just a resigned soul who, with tranquillity and confidence, endures the fate of his existence.'[2]

He asked Marie-Thérèse to stop writing so often, while also urging her to rein in her anger over his arrest: 'Don't bear any grudges on my behalf, because I don't . . . This is simply a crude endeavour by powerful men, who think they're smarter than the rest of us, that we must endure. With patience, the truth will emerge, as it always does.'

François continued: 'Why do people prefer the idea of murder over suicide? Especially if you consider that, in the murder theory, the body would have been transported to the cistern via the kitchen.* How would that be possible with such a narrow staircase? In fact, why take that detour when going through the studio would be more direct? Human stupidity!!'

More than anything, however, he wanted to know how the first article in the *Petit Marseillais*, the one that had first cast doubt on Sergeant Fabre's conclusions, had come about. Village gossip appeared to suggest that it had not been Arthur fforde's doing, but rather someone from Les Baux itself. One of the main suspects was Vernon Blake's wife, Marie – a.k.a. Olive's 'Madame Blot'. But on what grounds, François asked, had she been so sure it was murder? 'Supposing the investigation is justified,' he wrote, 'there could be surprises ahead.'[3]

But were these the words of an innocent man enduring his fate or those of an unrepentant murderer warning his accomplice to be prepared? François remained impossible to read.

Over the following weeks, Guibbal enjoyed a few minor victories. One of these, surprisingly, came from within Les Baux itself when a farmer came forward to say that he and his wife had heard two

---

* As the trail of blood found during the search of Mas de Chiscale led down the stairs.

vehicles, fifteen minutes apart, outside their house in the valley on the evening of Olive's death.

Louis and Marie Pascal lived next to the Pinets' derelict mill, directly opposite the fountain. Motor traffic during the day was rare; at night, it was almost unheard of. Louis believed the first vehicle must have been the travelling salesmen turning their van around before heading home. The driver of the second, however, had shut off its engine for a few minutes before starting up again and turning around at the fountain – as was François's habit when collecting laundry from the mill.

The reason for this unexpected breaking of ranks became clear when Guibbal realized to whom he was speaking: Louis Pascal had known about the salesmen's visit to the valley because their customer was his sister, who also happened to be the widow of Etienne Patin's brother. With Etienne no doubt considering himself to be in a precarious position vis-à-vis his alleged poisoning activities and long-standing feud with Olive, nudging the investigation closer towards François Pinet would be in his family's best interests.

Nevertheless, Louis Pascal's account dovetailed perfectly with those of Porte and Piney. When the salesmen had arrived at his sister's farmhouse, he said, it had been his farm cart blocking the gate, forcing them to park on the road. He'd been collecting a load of manure from her dung heap and had even exchanged a few words with them as they made their way to the door. Loading and unloading the manure had taken about half an hour, during which time it got dark. He and his wife had then sat down to supper, which was when they'd heard the vehicles. Guibbal estimated that the first one – Ludovic Porte's Donnet – had passed by at nine o'clock; the second – François's Renault – at nine fifteen. Pascal broadly agreed.

Louis Vigne, too, had things to get off his chest. The taxi driver, having discovered that his new business partner was not only implicated in the murder of his biggest client but had been lying about his financial standing, allowed any lingering notions of loyalty or discretion to melt away along with his plans for manufacturing ice. He now told Guibbal that he'd harboured suspicions about an affair between Olive and François for some time – despite François privately referring to her as 'that woman' and complaining she was 'annoying'.

Vigne also expanded on the largesse François had enjoyed at Olive's expense: the theatre trips, dinners and excursions. Their first jaunt had been two or three years ago, he said, to see a play at the Roman amphitheatre in Orange. More recently, there had been the five-day trip to Embrun to look at the Alpine hotel François had hoped to buy with Adrien Sautel. Vigne was sure Olive had intended to advance François the money for his share. He was equally certain that the purchase had not gone ahead because she had changed her mind. The official line had been that François had decided to invest his father's inheritance in the ice venture instead, but as it was now clear that the inheritance was long gone, Vigne said it was reasonable to assume François had thought Olive would lend him the money for that, too.

Whether she had felt in a position to do so, however, was debatable. Inspector Laforgue's analysis of her finances suggested she had been struggling to manage the bills for the hotel renovation, albeit due to issues of cash flow rather than of capital. Louis Vigne admitted that she'd even borrowed 2,000 francs from him at the end of March, which she had paid back the day she left for England. Had François asked for a loan, therefore, he might well have been rebuffed.

V

By 5 June, Rochu was ready to interview his prime suspect again. A month after his arrest, François was therefore escorted, unshaven and unkempt, to the Palais de Justice, where his new legal team was waiting. The lawyers were an incongruous pair: at sixty-eight, Jean Dorlhac de Borne had the sharp bearing of a circus ringmaster, complete with waxed moustache and dyed black comb-over, while his fair-haired colleague, Paul Muselli, bore his younger, pinker plumpness with angelic grace. Both, however, had known the Pinet family for years, Dorlhac de Borne having represented Marie-Thérèse during her abortion trial and Muselli being the son of Saint-Rémy's justice of the peace.

Whether it was due to their trusted counsel or the boredom of his extended incarceration, François once again found his voice. Throughout the four-and-a-half-hour interrogation, he used it to calmly profess his innocence in all matters, from murder to the idea that his relationship with Olive had been mercenary.

'She never gave me any money.'

'Yet her bank statements show she wrote you a number of cheques. You even cashed one for 1,250 francs on the twelfth of April – that is to say, just as your mistress was on her way to England.'

'She owed me that money from Christmas – for a meal she hosted at the hotel for the shepherds, and for her niece's board.

I remember it came to eight hundred and fifty francs, and she added another four hundred for all the times I'd driven her and Miss Phyllis. All the cheques were for the hotel.'

'Come now, didn't you also try to get her to buy the Hotel du Tourisme in Embrun for you in February?'

'There was never any question of that.'

'How would you have got the money, then?'

'From one of my brothers, or I'd have sold my car.'

When presented with Louis Vigne's allegation that he had found Olive irritating, he simply replied, 'Well, it wasn't fun walking around Marseille with a woman of that age.'

The exercise continued six days later, with the first of fifteen judicial *confrontations* Rochu had organized, in which François would have the opportunity to respond to selected witnesses. Those summoned to Marseille included both supporters of his innocence and those who brought it into doubt.

At the request of François's lawyers, a new witness joined the first session on 11 June. This was the road-mender André Graugnard, who believed he had spotted a third vehicle in the valley on the evening of Olive's death. Just before nightfall, he said, he had been walking home down the steep path that led from the Porte Mage to the fountain, when he'd seen a car enter the yard of Mas de Chiscale on the far side of the valley. At the time, unaware that Olive had already returned from England, he'd assumed it was Louis Vigne delivering her home. Now, he wondered if it had been someone with more nefarious intentions. Due to the distance and fading light, however, he'd been unable to tell how many people were in the car. All he could say was that it had an open top.

François, himself the owner of an open-topped car whose

movements were under scrutiny, chose not to respond. He did, however, challenge Louis Pascal when the farmer claimed his Renault had been in the valley after nine o'clock. Neither of the vehicles Pascal had heard reversing by the fountain could have been his, he argued, despite the second pausing by the mill; he had turned around at a track that led to Les Baux's new electricity transformer some hundred metres further on – and Pascal couldn't possibly have heard that from inside his house.

'Monsieur Pascal,' Rochu asked, 'are you sure that the two vehicles you heard took the turn at the fountain?'

'I think so. Both engines revved loudly, as they do when cars reverse there.'

When Marguerite Patin told Rochu that François always turned around at the fountain when collecting laundry, François disputed this, saying he only did so when he wanted to wash his car or needed to fetch water for the hotel, and preferred to use the transformer track.

He also continued to insist that he had driven past the salesmen's car on his way back to the hotel, despite both Porte and Piney saying they would have noticed. And when confronted with the fact that Ludovic Porte now owned a van, he had an answer for that, too: 'I thought it was a car. I could only see the shape of the bonnet, and the front of all Donnets look the same.'

In a later session, the drinkers from the Hotel Monte-Carlo attempted to help him by confirming his exact time of arrival. Albert Montfort remembered Marie-Thérèse had switched on the lights in the cafe while they were playing *cheville*. He estimated the lamps had been lit for about half an hour by the time he left, which was soon after François arrived.

Rochu turned to François, 'So, this witness left the cafe just after you arrived, and it had been dark for about thirty minutes – in other words, about nine o'clock. If you were telling the truth about how long you stayed at Mas de Chiscale, you would have arrived at the hotel before eight thirty, when it was still light.'

'But it *was* light when he arrived!' Montfort cried, but was silenced by Rochu.

'Well, Pinet?'

'I don't know what time it was. What can I say?'

Rochu dismissed Montfort and called nineteen-year-old Denis Chieusse, the hotel's bellboy. He was more definite. He and the others had just finished a game of *cheville*, he said, when he heard a car pull into the hotel garage. Thinking it was a guest needing his services, he'd gone outside to find François unloading his Renault. François had brought a basket of clean laundry inside, along with some shopping, and placed it on a table near the bar. Although it had been dark outside, Denis was sure it was only between twenty past and half past eight.

'You looked at the clock?'

'No, but Journet asked Brusset for the time shortly afterwards because he had to get home, and it was eight thirty.'

Yet, when the stonemason Noël Journet was called, he said he had no idea what time he had left. This was despite having previously told Guibbal it was around nine o'clock.

'But didn't Brusset check his watch for you?'

'No.'

Félix Brusset, who arrived in uniform from his military-service camp in Aubagne, did his best to clear up the confusion. Denis Chieusse was mistaken, he said: it was he who had left at eight thirty. He knew because he'd been late home and his wife had come to find him. She had let him finish the game, at which point he'd heard the cafe clock chime and had checked his watch. He had not, however, noticed François.

Again, François kept quiet. In fact, the only other witness he chose to challenge during the subsequent *confrontations* was Jean

Baltus. When the artist testified that Marie-Thérèse had said Olive needed to be buried as quickly as possible and then couldn't be disturbed for a year, he leapt to his sister's defence. 'She was only repeating what the mayor told us on the Saturday. He'd said we couldn't keep the body in the mortuary beyond Monday morning, but my sister pointed out that Miss Branson's family may not have arrived by then and suggested using our family vault.'

'What about not moving the body for a year?'

'That's just from a country saying.'

François also couldn't remember asking Baltus if there would be an autopsy. 'I mean, it's possible. But if we had to remember every little thing we said . . .'

By the time the *confrontations* ended on 3 July, François had been in legal limbo – detained but uncharged – for two months, and public opinion about the case had become increasingly divided. Press reports of his perpetual sangfroid had worked to make François a tabula rasa in the public eye, capable of taking on any qualities a chosen narrative demanded. He could be the best or the worst of Provence; a naive son of the soil or an indolent playboy; a dignified martyr or an unrepentant murderer – and he was rapidly becoming all these things and more. Rumour had it that he'd requested pen and paper from his guards one evening, and had written late into the night. A confession? A rebuttal? That was for the public to decide. By morning, it was said, the words had been torn into scraps, as monosyllabic and unreadable as their author.[1]

Theories about what had happened that night in Les Baux abounded. Some were simple: that Olive had shot herself in François's presence and he had hidden her body out of fear; or that the actual murderer had been concealed in Mas de Chiscale when François made his deliveries. Others were more complex, such as the idea that Joseph had plotted to murder Olive and frame François, so that he and Marie-Thérèse might inherit the Hotel Monte-Carlo on his execution. One letter the Sûreté received from Preston in Lancashire suggested Olive had been killed in revenge for Sir George Branson's failure to imprison an abortionist at the Manchester Assizes in 1926. Another claim was that she had been a spy.

Les Baux itself, however, remained convinced that Olive had taken her own life, a conviction that was only strengthened when the results of Dr Béroud's latest round of forensic tests were released. The clothing François had been wearing on the night of Olive's death had proved to be completely free of blood, with no signs of recent laundering. Furthermore, the blood found inside Mas de Chiscale was not even human. Marie-Thérèse had been right when she suggested that the stains had come from a dog fight – a fight, incidentally, that Olive had recorded that February:

> . . . [Fly] couldn't use his lower jaw. So Marcel finished the good work by a bad bite on the throat, a bad bite on the front of the shoulder, & the worst one across the top of the withers. Marcel himself has slightly torn ears – & is stiff – that's all. He's also deeply ashamed. Tony, I fancy, looked on – & poses now as the Good Boy. Marcel wouldn't face me when I came home – he hid right in a corner of the studio & stayed there. I shouldn't have been surprised at Tony & Fly tearing each other to pieces wholeheartedly – but Marcel has always been so kind that I've sometimes wondered whether he was as game as the others.[2]

If the blood in the house hadn't even belonged to the Anglaise, the Baussencs reasoned, where was the evidence that she had been murdered at all? As Sergeant Fabre and Dr Cot had been saying from the start, everything pointed towards suicide. That she had chosen to enact it in such a bizarre manner was put down to her eccentricity and incomprehensible English ways. Perhaps, some ventured, she had even staged her death to look like murder: a 'spite suicide', so to speak, to make François pay.

PART IV:

THE EAGLE'S NEST

1

As the last drops of spring rain were coaxed from the cisterns, and lizards began to dart among the ruins, Les Baux fell into the dusty stupor of summer. It was a season Olive had always luxuriated in.

> *I wish you were here now – exquisite weather – Blue sky, no mosquitoes – they are dead of the drought – "cigales"* working hard – just as if someone was using a Chemin de Fer** at Carita – & figs!!!! Quantities of ripe figs from the big fig tree.*¹

Her figs now lay rotting on the ground, while the birds feasted on the fruit from her cherry tree. Meanwhile, her neighbours piled their own harvests high on kitchen tables, ready to be bottled for the winter. Throughout the valley, golden apricots were doused in sweet brandy syrup, gluts of tomatoes transformed into *coulis*, and figs and plums were coaxed into sticky *confits*. Inside the shuttered Mas de Chiscale, dirty dishes still sat on the chequered tablecloth in the studio, while Saint Roch and his hound looked

---

* Cicadas, an unavoidable and noisy feature of Provence in midsummer. They were said to have been sent by God to disrupt siestas and prevent the Provençal people from becoming too idle.
** A railway train.

down on a silent kitchen, the memory of claws clattering over stone flags and hopeful noses seeking scraps fading fast.

Despite all the speculation about her death, Olive as a vibrant, living woman was becoming easier to forget. Her body had been discreetly interred, and Frida and the pups rehomed. Her only representative in Les Baux was Jacquot the parrot, now resident in the Hotel Monte-Carlo and doing his best with his pothouse manners to undo her attempts to elevate its position. Those who chose to remember their old friend, however, remembered her summer self well.

When she had first arrived in Les Baux, Olive saw it as a place for overwintering, somewhere to explore that would be good for her bones and her soul, both of which suffered in the dark and damp of the colder months. As soon as the Provençal sun started to burn, she planned to scurry back home to the lush green hills and balmy evenings of England.

For many years, summer had meant wandering in her caravan. Among her books was a small, black journal that bore testament to this love of the open road. Between its worn covers were notes of a journey she had made to the West Country in the spring of 1914. She had left her gilded van behind on that occasion and was travelling in a large canvas wagon stacked full of art equipment. At the reins was her Irish groom, John, who gently urged their half-blind horse across the South Downs and beyond.

It had been uncommonly hot that May, with the heat only occasionally broken by thunderstorms that hammered down on the canvas and left them damp, steaming and fractious. The dogs – a youthful, energetic Spring and his companion Jane – had been torn between lolling in the wagon and hopping out to chase hares. Olive, too, found it exhausting, but her journal danced with a quiet joy. Soothed by the clop of hooves on chalk and the rhythmic sway of the wagon, her customary dashes took on a less urgent tone, creating a lulling ode to the sensory pleasures of an English summer.

> *. . . the sun hot on our backs – the sky hot blue – the horse walking sedately in the shadow of the wagon – & our shadows – sharp & hard – pushing on in front of us . . . gold gorse – & white feathery dandelion heads thick along the side of the road . . . elderflower in the hedge – & honeysuckle . . . Larks, chaffinches, cuckoo – nightingales . . .*

She captured an almost dreamlike snapshot of Edwardian England's final days as they passed bell-tented yeomanry camps where it was still fun to play soldiers, great estates where the gardeners battled nothing more than feral rhododendron, and countless idyllic villages lazing in the heat.

> *Fair Oak . . . There is a dance in the village room – we hear the music & see the girls walking to it – in muslin dresses – & the young men flying by on bicycles – & after we're in bed . . . we still hear the dance music – & laughing & great stampings on the floor as they do the Lancers & other rollicking dances . . .*
>
> *West Wellow . . . The post office door open – opening into a big sitting room with the old couple at tea (shrimps) . . . 3 little boys & one little girl offer bunches of flowers – ragged robin – orchis – wild columbine . . . I give them oranges & cake.*

It was the people that really mattered to Olive: the youngsters who sat atop a wall and offered advice as they hitched the wagon; two old seafarers on the road near Bath; a friendly policeman with thoughts about bishops and suffragists; destitute ex-soldiers who unconsciously fell into step with anyone who walked beside them. As they approached Bristol, they met an old traveller who'd spent five years in charge of the wild beasts at Frank Bostock's circus before becoming a cattle drover. Owing to an outbreak of foot-and-mouth disease, he said, there was no work to be had, so he was off to make a little money haymaking – and off he had gone.

These transient encounters had once been Olive's lifeblood. But the twin miseries of war and marriage, and then the glorious pull of Provence, had put paid to those carefree journeys. Her caravan had long sat in a corner of her cousin Jim's farm, its wheels and shafts buried in weeds, sinking into permanence as a playhouse for future generations. Even her treasured visits to Hampshire for the hop-picking had fallen by the wayside as she'd become entangled in the daily life of Les Baux.

Nevertheless, summer in Provence had offered good substitutes for life on the road. With summer came *fête* season and the chance to experience Provence at play. Each week, there would be a different town to visit to watch the festivities. Instead of a gentle clop towards adventure, Olive would be whizzed in by Louis's roadster and deposited among the crowds. But she still found plenty to delight her senses and make her reach for her sketchbook.

No aspect of Provençal life escaped celebration. Les Baux even held a popular 'Blessing of the Cars' each July, in which motorists from as far afield as Nîmes and Cavaillon would form a giant queue along the road from Paradou and inch through the valley until they reached the turning for the village. There, they would find the Abbé Cheilan standing by his lemon-yellow Citroën 5CV with a statue of Saint Christopher, the patron saint of drivers, propped up in the dickey seat amid swathes of reeds and flowers. After receiving a sizzle of holy water and a medallion of the saint, the drivers would disappear into the hills for a day of Sunday motoring.

The attitude of the villagers to this annual spectacle was one of indulgence. What could they say? Their priest loved cars, from the smallest *teuf-teufs* to the roaring eight-cylinders, and, despite all the noise and the fumes, no one could argue with a blessing. As old Elisa Quenin would tell a reporter in 1933, with a smile playing on her lips, 'In years to come, perhaps we'll have to bless the aeroplanes or the machines they use to blast the quarries . . . but, who cares? We will always bless.'[2]

Olive's own tastes, however, had run towards the more traditional *fêtes votives*. From spring to autumn, each town in turn would celebrate its patron saint by decorating the streets and holding a series of entertainments, with processions, dancing and late-night banquets. For an artist with a talent for lightning sketches, the *fêtes* were a treasure trove of spectacle.

At Tarascon, for example, the parade was headed by a giant, wooden Tarasque, a fearsome beast, half hedgehog and half hippopotamus, supposedly tamed by Saint Martha. The smaller communes in the Baux valley honoured Saint Eligius, the patron saint of horses and their human companions. To Olive's delight, this meant parades of horses bedecked with ribbons and plumes, and draped in brightly embroidered caparisons reminiscent of those worn by their ancestors at medieval tournaments.

And how could she resist the carnival at Saintes-Maries-de-la-Mer, which saw Roma from all over France gather to celebrate Sara La Kâli, or Black Sara, their own patron saint? Sara, it was said, had been the first to welcome three other saints – Mary Magdalene, Mary Salome and Mary of Clopas – to the shores of Provence after their exile from the Holy Land.* The celebrations, therefore, included a riotous procession down to the beach, where men on horseback galloped Sara's statue into the sea as accordions blared and the crowds yelled, 'Vive Sainte Sara!'

Unfortunately, Olive had never had much luck at Saintes-Maries-de-la-Mer. It rained every time she went. One year, Louis drove her and Etienne and Marthe Patin to the similar, though more sedate, blessing of the three Saint Maries that followed the Roma celebrations. A gale was blowing and it was pouring with rain, so they had to watch from a sand dune as the Archbishop of Aix gave his blessing from an unlaunched boat because the sea was so rough. They'd then retreated to the car to eat gritty sandwiches before heading home.

Olive had spent a lot of her summers in Provence sheltering from the elements. If she wasn't getting soaked to the skin, she was dissolving in the heat.

> *I was simply blasted off the Camp de Marius by the sun – between sun & red hot rock is an impossible position – Hell on earth!*[3]

Nonetheless, in 1927, she announced her intention to do a series of etchings of the *fêtes*, and started collecting 'oddments' to this end. Some of the liveliest events were held in Aigues-Mortes, a medieval walled town surrounded by marshland in the Petite Camargue. That year, Olive intended to take in all the Aigues-Mortes festivities, which promised some of the magic of her circus days.

---

* Another version of the legend puts Sara La Kâli as the servant of one of the Marys.

> *I want to stay there the whole time for them, as there's a fair between the walls & the canal – & at night the lights & the reflected lights in the water are exquisite. I must work while I feel well.*[4]

In the end, she just went for the final day, when there was to be a show of water jousting on the canal, a sport that had arrived in Provence with the Ancient Greeks who settled Marseille. She'd dodged an invitation to accompany Andrée Sous and her husband, and had instead taken François – at that time, just a friend – who'd been desperate to escape Les Baux. His father had died that January and he'd been working at the hotel since Easter without a break. The arrival of his sister Marguerite and her family for a visit had all but finished him off.

The trip was a disaster.

> *Last Monday – what a day! The Fête at the Grau du Roi!!!!!!!!*
> *. . . the completest washout you can imagine.*

Their driver, one of Louis Vigne's younger employees, hadn't known the way and had overshot the town by twenty kilometres. When they finally arrived, Aigues-Mortes itself was deserted. After asking around, they were directed across the salt marshes to the town's old harbour at Le Grau-du-Roi, where the jousts were to be held at three o'clock.

> *. . . you remember that sordid village? In summer it stinks of fish & wet rubbish & it was crammed with myriads of people – people without end!!!! No chance of a table at a café! nor even a window to sit at.*
>
> *We thought the opposite bank of the canal looked emptier – but there was only one ferry. François tried to get a boat – but boats were forbidden to ferry! So we waited in a queue, packed*

> *like sardines & being pushed – cheerfully – but still!!!! I wonder the ferry didn't sink – at last when we got near it we got separated. François got taken – & I was left!! So we had to wait – one on each side! Then I got over & we – at last – found a little chink in the people – on the edge of the canal embankment.*

The air had been heavy and sticky all day, and they'd seen black rain clouds over the distant mountains during the drive from Les Baux. As they stood in the crowd, the pressure became almost unbearable.

> *... the air was simply intolerable with thunder – I began a headache – & rain fell – a few drops on & off. Miserable – everything grey & mixed up – instead of blazing sun. If there'd been sun, the "Jousts" would have been very decorative. Two heavy boats rowed by six men, a ladder on a little platform built up – & out – over the rudder.*

Here, she provided a sketch of one of the boats, which looked like a long-nosed trireme with a warrior holding a javelin aloft at the prow.

> *On the platform, the performer with a wooden shield & long blunt lance. On the rungs of the ladder – those who wait to replace him – & below, the man who steers. The boats row past each other – & as they pass, the men tilt. If they push even – nothing happens or both fall into the water. If one is stronger than the other – after an awful moment's suspense, you see the other slowly lose his balance – & fall with an almighty splash into the canal – his shield & lance floating near. His boat goes on – the next one takes his place on the platform & he swims ashore, or to the boat that collects the shield & lance.*

Usually, Olive would have delighted in the spectacle, but the oppressive weather and her growing headache had drained her of energy.

> *I felt too rotten to draw! & at the interval I told François I thought I'd better go – but we ought to see the Sous's [sic] first – as they'd asked me to lunch & I'd excused myself. At that moment, Madame Sous came along – so we had to stay. The car was the other side of the canal, so I manoeuvred over there ... said I must go. But we stopped at Aigues Mortes! I told François to go & see the sights. He said it was too hot – he'd have an apéritif – & I lay down at the Hotel St Louis. The Patronne gave me a glass of cognac – & later on we had supper – & drove back at night.*
>
> *The next day I stayed in bed – feeling completely done in! No temperature – no upsets, merely done in!! ... never again a water fête at the Grau – in thunder weather!!!!!!!*[5]

Olive did not give up, however, because with the *fêtes* came the bulls. There had been black *Raço di Biòu* cattle on the Camargue since Roman times, grazing the marshes in semi-feral herds. From the Middle Ages onwards, the young bullocks had been rounded up each summer and brought down to the towns and villages for sport.

Bullfights were a core part of the identity of Provence. As Madame Sous's husband, Jean Bouquet, had once told a visiting scholar at the Roi René, 'We have an old ballad about a Provençal sinner who slipped into heaven when St. Peter nodded [off]. How should the good God get him out? It was a matter demanding the most exquisite tact. It was done by advertising a *course des taureaux* in hell. There were no attractions in heaven comparable. Once out, the sinner never caught St. Peter napping again.'[6]

The *courses des taureaux* or *courses à la cocarde* (or simply *les cocardes*) were not bullfights in the Spanish sense, with posturing matadors and a fight to the death. Rather than baiting solid walls of snorting Iberian fury, the Provençaux took on the lean and fast *Raço di Biòu* in a contest of agility. The only blood likely to be spilled was that of the young men who had to retrieve the cockades of ribbon glued between the young bulls' horns – and, even then, the chance of mortal injury was small. The fun – for the humans, at least – came from celebrating the glory of the beast and the vigour of youth.

Boys, beasts, muscles, sweat. Unsurprisingly, Olive had been a keen spectator at the summer *cocardes*. The largest events were held in the restored Roman amphitheatre at Arles, but she preferred those in the smaller towns, where makeshift arenas were formed by rings of farm carts and she could explore behind the scenes.

Wherever they took place, the *cocardes* always followed the same pattern, with the games themselves bookended by two other events: the *abrivado*, or charging of the bulls, with local youths racing and tumbling through the streets in an attempt to beat them to the arena, and the more sedate *bandido*, where the animals were returned to their herds with appropriate ceremony.

An equal attraction for Olive were the wild, white Camargue horses ridden by the bulls' *gardiens*. An ancient breed, they were stocky and strong, with large hooves capable of traversing their marshy habitat, and long, thick tails to swipe away the flies and mosquitoes. Two years earlier, as part of the preparations for her series of *fête* etchings, she had spent a few days in the peaceful town of Châteaurenard. Before sketching the actual bullfights in the company of 'two dear old men' and their flea-ridden dog, she had sought out the farm where the horses were decorated and harnessed for the opening ceremony. It turned out to be a two-mile walk away in the blazing August sun – 'how I streamed!!!!!' – but she was delighted by what she found when she arrived.

> *The farm was beautiful – a big one, a big courtyard with plane trees like the one at Carita – long trestle tables & benches set out – & a déjeuner for the 60 young men who lead the horses. They all wore scarlet berets, scarlet sashes & white shirts & trousers & red handkerchiefs – & all the time the sixty horses were coming in & out to be harnessed – a really lovely sight.*[7]

A few days later, she was at Fos-sur-Mer for another spectacle involving bulls and wild horses: the annual *ferrade*, in which yearlings of both species were rounded up and galloped in turn to an enclosure, where they were branded with the mark of their herd or *manade*.

Olive took as her guest Madame Passa, the Saint-Rémy tobacconist from whom she had acquired Frida. Madame Passa had recently offered to look after Frida for a week while Olive and Spring undertook a round of diplomatic visits in an attempt to persuade Marthe Patin to continue her tuberculosis treatment at the sanatorium. It was a kind gesture on Madame Passa's part: the Saint-Rémy *fêtes* were in full flow, so the timing was inconvenient, and Frida had been quite a handful at the time. Olive was racking her brains for a suitable thank-you gift when the tobacconist mentioned that she'd never seen a *ferrade*.

Louis drove the women out to the Crau at eight thirty in the morning and the *ferrade* had finished by half past ten, just as the heat was becoming unbearable. After Olive had packed up her sketching kit, they took their picnic lunch to a bungalow Louis had recently had built near Fos, to sit out the hottest part of the day. When they ventured out for coffee, Madame Passa bumped into some friends and they all drove to a local farm where there was to be a *course à la cocarde* at four o'clock.

> ... *to my dismay the arena was in blazing sun – no possibility of shade nor of sitting!!! ... Monsieur Feraud the proprietor of the manade was charming – let me go up a straight ladder into a loft overlooking the arena – where I could sit in the open window door – the door beneath was locked – & I was left peaceful to myself. The bulls were started under me!*[8]

Yet, for all the joy she'd felt that summer and her plans for a series of etchings, her sketches of the *fêtes*, *ferrades* and *cocardes* never progressed to finished pieces. Her work hadn't been going well for a while, but she thought she had time.

> *Hokusai,* I think it was, when he was 100 said he was beginning to understand something of Line – & George Moore,** at about 80, said given another 10 years' work he would begin to understand something of the writing of English prose. So there's still a chance . . .*[9]

Olive's art as a whole had become curiously static in recent years. There had been a time when it was full of figures, brought to life through her deft strokes and dynamic lines. She had been Munnings' 'whizz with a pencil' and Orpen's 'excellent' anatomist; the wrestlers at the London Palladium, the Romany horses of Hampshire and the acrobats from Fossett's Circus had all tumbled

---

* Japanese artist, best known for his prints of Mount Fuji and *The Great Wave off Kanagawa*.
** Irish novelist, dramatist, poet and author of *The Confessions of a Young Man*.

onto her paper, full of life. But in the years and months leading up to her death, that vivacity had all but disappeared.

She had endured fallow periods before: during the war, when she barely picked up her pencil at all ('. . . one couldn't draw then – & I was so in despair over it that I thought I'd better chuck it for good . . .'[10]), and in the years that followed in which she came to terms with all that she had seen and all those she had lost – not just Harry La Place and her colleagues in the YMCA hut, but others such as her circus friend Ada 'Ohmy' Smith, who had been interned in Germany at the outset of the war and died in 1918. With the folly of her wartime marriage, she had thought she might never draw again, until late 1922, when – 'for no reason that I can explain' – the desire had begun to stir once more.[11]

By the time she arrived in Les Baux in 1924, she was back in the flow and ready for artistic adventure. But a part of her still seemed to crave certainty and stability. Her mind and eye found comfort in the solid, immovable rocks and ruins, which she recorded in obsessive detail. Only occasionally did she turn her attention to living subjects, such as a portrait of François in his soft leather driving helmet, or the quick caricatures of the villagers she sometimes included in her letters. The freedom and joy that had once peppered her work remained stubbornly elusive.

Two letters she had kept from her cousin William addressed her disappointment with her recent output. The first was dated 18 June 1928. William had just been to the New English Art Club (NEAC) exhibition at the New Burlington Galleries in Mayfair, where one of Olive's drawings of Les Baux was on display. She had completed the drawing perched up on Les Bringasses, an Iron Age fort to the rear of Les Baux, which overlooked the jagged walls of the castle keep. Although it captured the bleak majesty of the site, she had been unhappy with it and regretted her choice of grey paper. The reception to the exhibition as a whole had been lukewarm.

Pencil sketch of François Pinet by Olive Branson.

At that time, Olive was reaching the peak of the nervous crisis that would find her under the care of the nuns at Sault. Dr Leroy would, in fact, send her away the following week. She had not shared the full extent of her distress with her family, but William knew something was wrong and approached her with tender honesty.

I'm sure there's no need to feel sore really, for I can't help feeling that it must appeal to cultivated taste; it is delicate and seems truthful (to an ignoramus at least). But, as you say, it is not the sort of thing to catch the eye, especially on that paper. I can't pretend that I think it compares with some others of yours . . .

The catalogue calls it "Les Baux" but I did not see any houses or signs of life except three tiny figures high up on the right. The general impression (to me) is of a gaunt & desolate rock surrounded by a ruin. But I know there are people living there & olive trees & friendly things. What about a goat next time, Polly?*

... As I have often told you, anyone who could dash off such fine action-drawings as yours of me, fishing at Semer, ought to get your light out from under your bushel.[12]

William repeated his regret that she had 'retired from action-drawings' in the second letter, written that December after Olive had returned from Sault. He had been back to Mayfair to view the NEAC winter exhibition, which was featuring another two of her Baux drawings: one of the Carrière des Grands Fonds (a

Les Baux by Olive Branson (pen and ink).

* A family nickname.

vast limestone quarry in the Val d'Enfer), and the other a view of the village. Once again, he struggled to find the Olive he loved in her work. Choosing his words carefully, he said, '. . . of course there is nothing there to touch them for delicacy, but they need close study & a good light for their proper appreciation – and it was a dull afternoon when I was there.'[13]

This correspondence was added to the judicial file by Rochu, as was the letter from Olive's London art dealer informing her that she had been 'crowded out' of the Royal Academy's Summer Exhibition. The letters didn't help the case against François Pinet directly, but they did go a long way to repudiating the argument put about by François's supporters that the Royal Academy's rebuff had contributed to her 'suicide'. For one thing, she was already dead when the letter arrived in Les Baux; for another, her correspondence with William Branson suggested that, even at the height of a neurasthenic crisis, Olive had been able to assess her work and accept criticism without undue anguish.

Small details, perhaps, but Rochu was determined that every angle be thoroughly explored. Public mood around the case was volatile, and he knew that science and logic did not always hold sway.

II

In the last week of July, a letter arrived at the Palais de Justice addressed to the public prosecutor, Auguste Rol. It was from Daniel Millaud, the long-standing representative for Saint-Rémy on the General Council of Bouches-du-Rhône, and had been countersigned by the mayors of Les Baux, Maussane and Saint-Rémy. The elected officials, it transpired, had been busy conducting their own 'meticulous investigation' into Olive's death.

'Mindful of the good reputation of our region,' they wrote, 'we saw it as our duty . . . not to hinder or doubt the action of justice nor encroach upon its rights and prerogatives, but to guide our consciences and establish an opinion in the light of the facts. In short, to reveal the truth.'[1]

The resulting four-page summary was both stilted and verbose. Clearly, each man had wanted to have his say. In essence, however, it argued that there was no proof that François – or indeed anyone – was guilty of murder. In their judgement, the alleged murder and disposal of the body would have taken longer than the thirty minutes available to François: surely there must have been some preamble, a conversation of some sort? And if Olive Branson had been shot in her house, where were the signs of a struggle? Why were her clothes neatly folded on the chair?

After addressing the difficulties of getting a body into the cistern without scraping its skin and reminding the public prosecutor of Olive Branson's history of neurasthenia, the sleuths concluded 'with some certainty' that her death had been a suicide. They therefore requested that François be released pending further inquiries, if only to 'ease the family's profound sorrow and distress . . .'

Having mulled this over for a week, Auguste Rol – who had answers to most, if not all, of these points – picked up his pen. He did not reply to Millaud and the mayors, however. Instead, he wrote to Alexandre Guibbal to congratulate him on a job well done. The petition was filed away along with all the other well-intentioned yet ill-informed letters Rol had received from the public. François Pinet was going nowhere.

The petition had not been unexpected. Some weeks earlier, a letter had landed on Félix Martin's desk from Inspector Léopold Fabrega of the Marseille railway police, which left no doubt as to the mood in the Alpilles.[2]

One Monday at the beginning of June, Inspector Fabrega reported, he had been eating lunch at the Haxo restaurant near the Vieux Port when his attention was drawn to the conversation of two middle-aged women seated beside him. They were talking about the Branson case, and it soon became apparent that one of them lived next door to Joseph Girard's parents in Saint-Rémy.

This woman told her friend that everyone in the town had thought François Pinet guilty at first: he was, after all, the Anglaise's lover and had been the last person to see her alive. Yet they were now equally sure that he was innocent, in part because of the treatment he and Joseph had endured at the hands of the police. Joseph, the woman said, had told her himself that he'd been on the verge of confessing at Tarascon just so he could get some sleep. His friend, a taxi driver, had added that the Marseille police were all 'thugs'.

Instead of locking up Pinet, she declared, the police would

have done better to subject Raoul Dumas to the same treatment. Why? Because, a few days before the murder, the hotelier had warned Joseph, 'You won't be in the Anglaise's employment for much longer.'

Her conclusion was that the case was too impenetrable for the police to clear up. They simply didn't understand the Baussenc mentality. Those people wouldn't even open up to gendarmes from Arles, let alone the Marseille Sûreté.

Fabrega had provided a detailed description of the woman, from the distinctive rings on her fingers to the warts on her face, along with clues about her husband's employment. It wouldn't be hard for the Flying Squad to track her down for questioning, but there seemed little point. As far as Félix Martin was concerned, Fabrega's letter only told him what he already knew: that the people of Les Baux were angry and, if the authorities refused to believe that Olive Branson had killed herself, they would rather the blame was pinned on an outsider like Raoul Dumas.

It was Joseph Rochu who received the first indication of what had been going on in Les Baux itself. This arrived on 3 July in a lilac-lined envelope, which bore the name 'G. L. Arlaud' in flamboyant chocolate-brown lettering. The matching letterhead showed Georges Arlaud to be the owner of a small publishing house in Lyon and editor of Visions de France, a popular series of illustrated books.

Due to his work, Arlaud wrote, he was a frequent visitor to Les Baux. He had come to love the village and had therefore been shocked by what he'd seen on a recent trip: Joseph and Marie-Thérèse Girard, he claimed, had turned the Hotel Monte-Carlo into a 'centre of corruption' and were using the contents of Olive Branson's cellar to buy the silence of anyone who might be called to testify against François Pinet. He suggested the Sûreté might usefully question Vernon Blake's wife about the details.

Georges Arlaud repeated throughout his typewritten letter that, although he was a 'great friend' of the village, he had little interest in its internal affairs: 'That is none of my business.' He had only been moved to speak out after the subject of Olive Branson's murder had come up at a recent meeting of 'fairly important personages from the world of arts and letters.' The consensus among his fellow literati had been that, if no one was brought to justice, it would damage the reputation of France abroad, especially as there were other deaths of Englishwomen that remained unsolved. 'Above all,' Arlaud wrote, 'the British press must not be allowed to develop the theory that the English can be endlessly murdered in France.'[3]

Such concern was understandable. Arlaud's work, after all, was all about promoting Provence as an attractive and carefree tourist destination. What the sixty-year-old had not disclosed, however, was his close friendship with Raoul Dumas, nor the fact that he had undertaken a number of commissions on behalf of the Hotel Reine Jeanne over the years, both as photographer and publicist. Far from being a disinterested party, he was as embroiled as anyone in Les Baux's internal affairs. In Baussenc terms, he was a de facto enemy of the Pinets.

Rochu knew none of this at the time. Even if he had, allegations of witness bribery were too serious to ignore. He therefore sent Guibbal back to Les Baux to investigate and speak to Vernon Blake's wife. Guibbal must have known it would be futile, that he would be greeted with suspicion and resentment, and that the Hotel Monte-Carlo would turn into a model of benign hospitality as soon as he stepped foot in the village. He went, nonetheless.

The Baussencs gave him the welcome he expected. Even Marie Blake, an outsider from Paris with few friends in the village, was reluctant to talk to him. At first, she only offered a snippet of conversation she'd heard while walking past the Monte-Carlo two weeks earlier. It had been around ten o'clock at night, she said, and the windows of the cafe were open, so she had been able to hear quite clearly when Joseph exclaimed, 'It was Monsieur Guibbal who told me! If it's not true, then he's a liar. Either way, he and Monsieur Rochu are going to murder my brother-in-law!' She did not know, however, what he meant or to whom he had been speaking.

Guibbal asked her about another incident Georges Arlaud had mentioned, namely that one of the villagers had been heard to say, 'Think about it! François is no murderer – he's just a simple country boy – but Marie-Thérèse could have helped him.' Madame Blake confirmed that was what some people thought. She'd also heard that Marie-Thérèse had been inviting potential witnesses to her home 'to teach them good manners.'

It was all hearsay, of course, and Marie Blake refused to elaborate, so there was nothing Guibbal could do but take her statement and return to Marseille.

Two weeks later, and hot on the heels of the mayors' petition, another lilac-lined envelope arrived in Marseille, landing this time on Félix Martin's desk. It was not addressed to the chief inspector directly, but had been forwarded by the office of Bouches-du-Rhône's highest official: the prefect, Hilaire Delfini.

Written as it was in a fit of pique from the Hotel Reine Jeanne and without resource to a typewriter, the details of the letter were hard to make out in Arlaud's eccentric handwriting. It appeared, however, that word had got out in Les Baux that the publicist was responsible for Guibbal's visit, and he was now paying the price.

Arlaud had only been in the village for three days, he told the prefect, but in that time he'd been subject to numerous affronts and provocations from Joseph Girard. His complaint to the mayor had fallen on deaf ears, as had his previous appeals to the police. 'If this continues,' he raged, 'I cannot say what may happen because I will not allow myself to be insulted by a person whose only claim to fame is that he is the brother-in-law of a person who has been accused, and rightly so, of a dastardly and heinous crime.'[4]

Arlaud's letter hinted he might use his position to publish all the sordid details of the 'nice little racket' perpetrated by the Girards at a later date. In the meantime, he simply wanted to ensure that the prefect was aware of the 'inadmissible' and 'scandalous' situation in Les Baux and the failure of Delfini's underlings – the Sûreté – to put a stop to it.

There being no discernible request for action, Félix Martin stamped the letter as received and put it aside for filing. Some battles were best left unfought.

Whether Arlaud's allegations had any real substance or had been invented for the benefit of his friend Raoul Dumas, one thing the publicist said was unarguably true: that the British press had been linking Olive Branson's death to other recent murders of Englishwomen in France.

There had been three such cases in as many years. The first hit the headlines in July 1926, when Annie Gordon, a widowed teacher, had been found strangled in her villa near Antibes. Three months later, nurse May Daniels had gone missing from the quayside at Boulogne while on a day trip. Her body had been found in February 1927, decomposing in a nearby bush. Finally, in May 1928, fifty-four-year-old Florence Wilson was savagely attacked in a pine forest on her way home from the golf links at Le Touquet.

Each murder had presented specific investigative difficulties, and no culprits had ever been charged. In fact, with unfortunate timing, the examining magistrate in Le Touquet had shelved the case on Florence Wilson due to insufficient evidence on the very same day as Olive Branson's autopsy.* This prompted some British newspapers to revisit these murders en masse, evoking the image of swathes of British women lying bloodied and abandoned in the French countryside while an indifferent justice system looked on and shrugged.

Naturally, this caused some consternation in France. Certain quarters of the French press accused certain quarters of the British press of attempting to whip up anti-Gallic sentiment. The accusation was no doubt true, it being something of a traditional pastime in the muddier gutters of Fleet Street, but the idea of an angry British nation screaming for justice ignored how little such stories affected the general reader or the powers that be.

Sir Reginald Lee, the acting British consul at Marseille, for example, had been keeping an eye on events as they unfolded and forwarding any necessary documentation and letters from the public to the authorities. He had limited his personal involvement, however, to a note of thanks to Auguste Rol for his attention to the case, firmly believing that French justice should be allowed to take its course. His superiors at the Foreign Office tended to agree. Sir George Branson, who was in contact with both, had joined them in their discreet silence, patiently waiting for any developments. And, as it happened, they did not have much longer to wait.

---

* The following year, in July 1930, a local teenager would confess to Florence Wilson's murder, along with a string of other assaults, after he was identified by a woman who had been attacked near the same spot.

III

On Wednesday, 7 August – three months to the day since his arrest – François was escorted from the prison to the Palais de Justice. Marseille was steaming in the heat, its residents willing the thunderstorms that were gathering out at sea to bring some respite. After being led handcuffed down to the cool, dark basement, he found his lawyer, Paul Muselli, waiting with Rochu and Jeanpierre. The judicial investigation was now complete, Rochu explained, and François was going to hear its conclusions.

Rochu began by addressing the question of suicide. Point by point, he outlined the evidence ruling it out – from the autopsy results to the state of Olive's stockings – before turning to that in favour of murder.

'Miss Branson died at Mas de Chiscale on Friday, the twenty-sixth of April, immediately after her evening meal. The autopsy found the food had barely entered the stomach. At Mas de Carita, a hundred and twenty metres away as the crow flies, neighbours heard the shot very clearly before nightfall. Now, it has been mathematically established by the observatory of Marseille that, on that day, nightfall occurred at eight thirty in the evening. It was therefore before eight thirty that Miss Branson was killed.

'You had left Maussane at about eight o'clock. You admitted this from the start, but then you could hardly give any other time as, in the company of various people, you'd had several drinks in the local cafes. The short drive between Maussane and Miss Branson's property took a matter of minutes.

'On your arrival, the latter comes to meet you; you enter, drop off your commissions, and immediately leave. You exchange, you say, only trivial words with the woman who is your mistress, who you haven't seen in private since her return from England . . . Logic dictates that your visit was longer; Miss Branson's state of undress alone is evidence of that.

'How long did you stay? Not long, as the digestion of her meal had only just begun when she died and the shot rang out before eight thirty. But, still, you stayed long enough to have a conversation – a tête-à-tête – with her, which was probably accompanied by a request for money on your part.'

Rochu paused and looked at François. 'You see, I still want to believe that you did not kill her in cold blood. Yet who else could have murdered this woman in that short space of time, if not you?'

François did not reply.

'The dogs would have barked at the arrival of a stranger, which would have been heard at Carita even if they'd been locked up at the time – and that was not the case. Moreover, the bullet which killed Miss Branson came from her own revolver. This was kept in a drawer next to her bed – a place known only to those familiar with the house – and you can't reasonably maintain you were unaware of this.

'There is also proof that you were still at Mas de Chiscale at the time of the shooting. Your car was heard on the road at nine o'clock, when you collected the basket of linen from the mill. But you wanted to make people believe that you arrived at the Hotel Monte-Carlo earlier – at eight thirty, you claim. Various customers say they saw you enter the hotel bar at this time, but their statements are neither concordant nor precise – for good reason – and cannot override the proof unearthed by the investigation.

'You say that you turned on your headlights when leaving the mill and passed the travelling salesmen, who also had their headlights illuminated. Yet, if your meeting with Miss Branson had been as brief as you say, you would have been on that road before it was dark.'

François remained silent.

'So, it has been established – without you having volunteered it, mind – that you were the young lover of a woman of forty-four, for whom you had only a mercenary affection. You were getting "fed up" with this mistress; she was "annoying" you. You found that she preached too much about economy; her gifts were too meagre for your liking.

'At the time of the murder, you had only four or five hundred francs to your name. You had squandered your share of your father's inheritance in a month, yet you had entered into a partnership with your friend Vigne, Miss Branson's driver, to whom you would soon have to pay the sum of five thousand francs.

'You had already managed to secure the maximum profit possible from your mistress by encouraging her to bequeath you the Hotel Monte-Carlo – a property, it should be noted, that she had bought with the sole aim of pleasing you. Only her death could provide you with the funds you needed.

'I therefore charge you with the murder of Miss Branson, committed in Les Baux on the twenty-sixth of April 1929. Do you have anything to add in your defence?'

'I am innocent and stand by all my statements,' François said quietly. 'She committed suicide, just like the doctor said.'

That weekend, after reviewing Rochu's file, Auguste Rol forwarded it to the Chamber of Indictments in Aix for the final decision on whether the case would go to trial.

The battle lines had been drawn, with Old Provence up in the hills defending its eagle's nest and New Provence camped out on the plains, each side convinced they had the true facts of the case and each immoveable in their conviction as to what justice should entail. What it would not entail, however, was the guillotine. Rochu had stopped short of charging François with *assassinat* – murder with premeditation – settling instead on *homicide voluntaire*. The penalty was nonetheless a lifetime of hard labour in some distant colony.

IV

On 16 September, Alexandre Guibbal travelled to Digne for the trial of Jules Ughetto and Joseph Witkowski, the murderers of the Richaud family, whom he had tracked from Valensole to the coal mines of the Gard the previous December. It was raining, the sky heavy and grey to match the mood inside the courtroom.

No one relished hearing the details of the massacre again. Its barbarity had even Ughetto's father calling for the death penalty, which was duly handed down upon his son. As for the baby-faced Witkowski, after providing eleven other false identities, he was now claiming to be a sixteen-year-old called Stephan Mucha, who had only been fifteen at the time of the murders. As such, he could only be tried as a minor and was sentenced to twenty years in a penal colony.

Afterwards, the people of Valensole presented Guibbal with a small *objet d'art* by way of thanks. It was a rare token of gratitude for the detective, and one he knew was unlikely to be replicated in the foreseeable future. He was unaware, however, that his detractors in Les Baux were about to be given a gift of their own: the opportunity to voice their frustrations to the whole of France.

Two weeks later, seventy-seven-year-old Daniel Millaud was enjoying a quiet Sunday at home with his wife in the Monclar district of Avignon when there was a knock on the door. The smartly dressed man on the doorstep of the Villa du Printemps introduced himself to the councillor as Eugène Blanc, the new editor of the local *Radical de Vaucluse*. He said he wanted to talk about Les Baux.

The timing was fortuitous. Millaud, having had no response to his petition to the public prosecutor, was preparing to appeal on François's behalf to the prefect, Hilaire Delfini, who had ultimate responsibility for the activities of the region's police. Indeed, he had told Delfini of his intention just two days earlier at the opening meeting of the Bouches-du-Rhône General Council autumn session.[1] It had been seven weeks since the case was referred to the Chamber of Indictments, yet there had been no word of any decision.

Inviting Eugène Blanc inside, Millaud listened as the young man explained that he was a former member of the editorial staff at the *Petit Marseillais*. Although he had left the paper shortly before Les Baux hit the headlines, he had followed the story closely and occasionally met up with his former colleagues to catch up on the latest developments. One thing had been bothering him in particular: the behaviour of the British press, who had leapt upon the story as soon as the first dispatch arrived in London.

'French press agents,' Blanc would later write, 'were literally drowning under a flood of telegrams requesting new details, sometimes absurd, but always as original and fantastical as possible. Within twenty-four hours, the local correspondents were no longer enough: reporters and detectives from across the Channel came to form their own opinion.'[2]

That opinion, so rumour had it, had been formed in a nightclub in Marseille's Place de la Bourse five days before the police had even stepped foot inside Mas de Chiscale. Aided by endless sloshes of pale ale and gulps of brandy and soda, and with the Le Touquet golf-links murder at the forefront of their minds, the British journalists had decided that the only way they would allow the story to end was with a conviction for murder. It was, in Blanc's eyes, a conspiracy.

Now, with a suitable murderer awaiting trial, the British press had lost interest in the case. Their French counterparts, too, could find little new to say. But Eugène Blanc, keen to make his mark at the *Radical de Vaucluse*, had identified another angle to the story – and he saw in Daniel Millaud a useful ally.

Blanc had chosen well. Millaud, a lifelong socialist, had a long history of public service on behalf of the rural population of Provence and an entry in the Legion d'Honneur to prove it. Even as he approached his ninth decade, he showed little sign of slowing down.

The only noticeable concession Millaud and his wife, Régine, had made to their advancing years was their recent move to Avignon to be closer to their adopted daughter, Hélène. Millaud's heart, however, remained in his native Saint-Rémy, where his parents lay in the Jewish cemetery. His father had been a cloth merchant and, for many years, Daniel himself had run a drapery shop on the Rue Carnot that sold traditional Provençal dress alongside tailor-made clothing and household linens.

Millaud had first been elected as the town's representative in 1919 and his popularity had seen him sail unchallenged through every election since. During that time, in his plain-speaking manner, he had fought hard for Saint-Rémy and its outlying villages, lobbying for improved roads and public transport, better irrigation for the valleys, and anything else that might improve the well-being of its people. Once, after the minister for agriculture had told him that the population of Les Baux was too small to justify the expense of piping drinking water into the village, he'd replied, 'That's no reason to make them die of thirst.'[3] Work was now underway to pump water up from the valley with the help of the new electricity transformer.

Millaud's efforts had made him popular in Les Baux. Eugène Blanc was not aware, however, until he had been ushered into Millaud's villa and made comfortable, that his host had also been friends with the late Pierre Pinet. He had known François since he was a child and refused to believe that he was capable of murder.

'On the contrary, he is a pleasant, helpful and kind-hearted boy . . . nothing could suddenly turn him into a despicable assassin.'[4]

Not that Millaud thought Olive had been murdered at all. As his petition to Auguste Rol had demonstrated, he was firmly of the belief that she had committed suicide. He also shared Blanc's view that the whole investigation had been designed to mollify the British. 'Despite all the sympathy and the deep respect I have for our friends from across the Channel,' he said, 'my good feelings do not go so far as to grant them the freedom – and, if ordered, perhaps the life – of one of my constituents.'

'I've heard that the League of Human Rights has come out in favour of Pinet?' Blanc prompted, knowing Millaud was a long-standing and active member.*

'We did indeed address the League. The section president, however, had to admit they could do nothing to help. Although

---

* The League of Human Rights (*La Ligue des droits de l'Homme*) was founded in Paris in 1898 to defend Captain Alfred Dreyfus against his wrongful conviction for treason in what became known as the Dreyfus Affair. Following Dreyfus's pardon, the League continued to fight injustices and abuses of power on behalf of all French citizens.

our goal is to rise up against injustices and redress them where possible, Pinet's imprisonment, if it is an abuse of power, is not, strictly speaking, an injustice. We must therefore wait for events to play out and see what the court decides before acting.'

Millaud was hopeful, however, that François was heading for acquittal. 'As I have repeatedly pointed out, there is no evidence against him. All the damage that has been done has come from following mere lines of theory. But what theorizing has done, debate will undo.'

He continued, 'They're going to use the matter of timing against him. A beat of a few minutes – thirty at most – represents the famous "proof" of murder. I still contend (and all reasonable people – at least those familiar with criminal affairs – will agree with me) that, in thirty minutes, a murderer would not have time – not on your life! – to hold a conversation, carry out the fatal act, undress his victim, transport her to the cistern, arrange the famous "staging", then erase all traces of his movements and the crime from inside the house. Especially not an assassin on his first attempt!'

Millaud, by now thoroughly worked up, eased himself out of his chair and went to fetch a folder. 'I can't tell you everything,' he said, handing it to Blanc, 'but you might want to make yourself acquainted with some of this.'[5]

It was the research Millaud and the mayors had undertaken while preparing their petition to Auguste Rol. Among the various papers that caught Blanc's eye were some letters that François had written to his family from prison. One, sent to his mother on 6 June, read:

What must you think of my long silence? That I forget you? ... No, there does not pass an hour – what am I saying? – not a <u>minute</u> that my thoughts do not turn to you. Besides, what is the purpose of my living longer, if not to devote my whole existence to you? To prepare you for happy, well-earned days of peace? Sadly, current events prevent us from tasting these delicacies. But with patience, slowly but surely, we will overcome this base behaviour and truly gorge ourselves.

François had then reminded his mother of some of the small pleasures she enjoyed – her garden, her chickens, and spending time with Marie-Thérèse's baby, Odette – before adding:

Don't worry about me. I have a clear conscience; I eat, I sleep well and I wait. In my situation, that is as good as it gets.[6]

Writing to his niece Madeleine on 8 July, however, a note of bitterness and frustration had seeped through his optimism:

Who knows how many thousands of questions still need to be cleared up? With each one, I think it's over, and I'm disappointed every time . . . I can't wait for my innocence and honesty to be acknowledged. I'll have received a valuable lesson in human nature and, believe me, I'll do my best to forget this whole damned episode.[7]

No journalist had seen these letters before – and they painted a very different picture of the alleged murderer from that of the sullen, monosyllabic playboy of popular imagination.

This was Eugène Blanc's moment. He would be turning thirty the following month and, compared to most of his cohort, had little to show for his years. That, he hoped, was about to change.

The eldest son of a bank clerk turned commercial agent, Blanc grew up in the fourth arrondissement of Marseille, not far from Chave Prison. He had suffered mild problems with his nerves since childhood, when his body was ravaged by typhoid fever. Joining a heavy artillery regiment at seventeen had presumably not helped matters, nor had his decision to stay in the army after the war. But he struggled on and, in 1921, he was assigned to the colonial forces in Senegal.

It all came to a head in 1924. After two years in the trenches, two more mopping up the post-war mess, and three in the heat of West Africa, Blanc was a mental and physical wreck. One sticky night in May, he walked out of his barracks in Dakar and did not return. The army declared him a deserter.

The charge, however, was withdrawn six days later, when Blanc returned to barracks in severe distress. He was drifting in and out of a fugue state, confused about who he was and where he had been. The examining doctor, noting his previous medical history, sent him back to France on indefinite leave. Two years later, he was released from the army altogether.

At twenty-five, Blanc had found himself at a loss. He had no profession other than soldiering, and his pitiful army pension, at one tenth of the usual rate, did not stretch far. Needing work that would not be too physically taxing, he decided to try his hand at journalism. He eventually found a position with the region's oldest newspaper, the *Petit Marseillais*.

His reasons for leaving the *Petit Marseillais* three years later with no immediate prospects of other work are unclear: there appears to have been no ill will on either side. Perhaps he had come into a small inheritance, his father having died the previous year, or maybe it was a matter of political conscience: his next employer, the smaller *Radical de Vaucluse*, sat as far to the left of the political spectrum as the mighty *Petit Marseillais* sat to the right.

Either way, when Blanc arrived in Avignon in June, he was presented to the townsfolk as a current-affairs journalist with excellent references, who would be taking charge of the *Radical*'s local news coverage.[8] By the time of his visit to Daniel Millaud in September, he'd been appointed editor of the whole paper. And now, with Millaud's help, he intended to cement his position by conducting his own investigation – one that didn't ignore the concerns of the common people.

V

The next morning, Eugène Blanc set out to start his investigation in earnest. He'd hired a guide familiar with Les Baux to drive him from Avignon, and it was a beautiful day as they made their way through Rognonas, Maillane and Fontvieille, before taking the road through scrubland and olive groves towards the Vallon de la Fontaine.

Like so many in the region, Blanc's guide had been following the case with interest. 'It's been said that the starting point of the whole thing was the matter of inheritance,' he said to Blanc on the way. 'That's very possible, but the argument is misplaced. Some may have had an interest in Miss Branson's death, but it wasn't the people they say. Not Pinet and his family, but the other side.'

'The other side? You mean Miss Branson's other heirs? Her nieces?'

'That's yours to look for . . . but I didn't say heirs.'

While Blanc was mulling this over, his guide spoke again.

'There is one rather disturbing character who seems to have been the main instigator of all the fuss around her death. He lives in Les Baux and has close links to the Pinets' rivals. You know that a lengthy lawsuit has divided the hoteliers up there for some time?'

Someone with a connection to Raoul Dumas, then.

'There's a rumour that this gentleman was spurned quite severely by Miss Branson. In any case, he seemed attracted to her or someone around her – her nieces when they were visiting, perhaps? I'd also point out that this same character has always tried to bring suspicion, not on Pinet himself, but on his sister and her husband.'

At this point, the guide fell silent and would not be drawn further (or so Blanc would later claim, possibly with libel laws in mind), choosing instead to point out interesting topographical features or historical titbits as they approached Les Baux.

Their first stop in the valley was Mas de Chiscale. The steep, stony track leading to the gate had become overgrown in the five months the house had been empty, the verges that Joseph had once so assiduously weeded and trimmed having grown freely in the summer sun. Blanc, whose limited experience of rural life had never given him cause to consider the finer points of hedgerow management, found the resulting narrow path suspicious.

It was so small as to be almost a goat path, he thought. Yet, hadn't the police insisted that François Pinet had taken his Renault right up to the house? 'In places, he would have had to carry his car on his back!' he would later write. 'True, they also made him out to be strong enough to manoeuvre the dead weight of his lover without breaking a sweat, but still . . .'[1]

After battling through the undergrowth to the wooden gate, Blanc got his first view of the infamous *mas*. The triple aspect of the house brought to his mind the Holy Trinity – one house in three parts – but there his analogy and imagination failed him, so he climbed to the top terrace to seek out the spot where Olive Branson's body had been found.

The cistern was three steps from the studio door: he counted them. He was sure the reports he'd read back in May had suggested it was practically lost in the wilderness, twenty-five metres away.

Was this the wrong cistern? He cast his eyes around for another, but there was none.

A ladder rested against the wall, so he climbed up and looked down on the stone flags. In his mind's eye, the iron-framed grille at the rear had also been more substantial. Rather than the expected hazard of skin-gouging jags of thick wire, he saw the frame was inset with a neat trellis of fine filaments held in place by brass rods. It would be easy to lift a corner of one of these flimsy panels and slip into the water without injury, he noted.

Later, he would claim to have found a blanket discarded in a corner of the path below, which, when he lifted it up, held the 'sickening, heavy smell of dried blood in its folds.' He assumed, incorrectly, that it had been used to cover Olive's body after she was removed from the water. Why, therefore, hadn't it been taken into evidence? And why had the police exaggerated the difficulties she'd have had in getting into the cistern of her own accord? Moreover, why had his own colleagues – those who had seen the place with their own eyes – gone along with them? These were all rhetorical questions, of course. Eugène Blanc already believed he knew exactly why.

His next stop was a farmhouse just past Carita, where he found Madame Tougay in the yard.

'My husband isn't around. You'll have to come back.'

Blanc explained he only wanted to verify what the press had said about Félix hearing the gunshot on the night Olive had died. Jeanne Tougay confirmed it was all true: her husband and Vincent Aracil had both heard the shot at about quarter to nine, and assumed someone was shooting a badger. It had been a sharp report, clearly coming from a gun discharged in the open air and not, as the police insisted, inside Mas de Chiscale.

'And what did Monsieur Guibbal say when your husband told him this?'

'There were two of them, Guibbal and another. They kept him here in the yard for a very long time, taking turns to question him. Then, when they were leaving, Monsieur Guibbal shouted at my husband, "We'll do some tests with a revolver – then we'll see!"'

The plan, Blanc learned, had been to fire some shots inside and outside Mas de Chiscale and listen to the difference. But the experiment was never carried out.

'You should also speak to the shepherd François Griffe,' Madame Tougay said. 'You'll pass him on your way up to Les Baux.'

The elderly, bearded shepherd, dressed in his traditional smock and gaiters, was guiding his flock along the dirt road near the base of the cliff. When Blanc caught up with him, he discovered that Griffe had known Olive quite well. She'd encouraged his family to let their sheep graze down the rough grass between her olive trees and always hailed him or his son Dzanne for a chat if they were passing Mas de Chiscale. She'd been fascinated by their sheepherding customs, such as the 300-kilometre journey Dzanne made each summer to the green pastures of Bourg d'Oisans, moving the flock in the cool of the night and resting during the day.

The night the shot rang out Griffe had been in his fold in the valley. 'It's on the other side of Miss Branson's house, more than six hundred metres away,' he told Blanc, 'but I heard the bang quite clearly. Had the weapon been fired inside Mademoiselle's living quarters, I wouldn't have noticed it because there are no windows or doors at the back of her house.'

Unfortunately, he hadn't had the chance to tell the Sûreté at the start of their investigation, because, a few days after Olive's death, he had taken his flock into the hills for a month. On his return, finding François Pinet in jail and the village in uproar, he'd written to Rochu, asking to give a statement he felt was 'of great importance.' The Sûreté obviously felt differently: he'd written at the beginning of June, but Guibbal had not come to find him until July.

When the detective did turn up, Griffe had also told him that, the one time he'd seen Olive in her garden after her return from England, she had remained seated under her cherry tree instead of coming to greet him as was her habit. She had seemed so downhearted, in fact, that when he'd next seen Joseph, he'd joked, 'What have you done to your boss to make her so sad?'

After making note of this and Griffe's insistence that the revolver had been fired outside, Guibbal had once again promised to arrange the gunshot experiment. The shepherd advised him they would need to do it on a cloudy evening, at the same time as the original shot had been fired: after a lifetime of guarding against predators, he was attuned to the valley's soundscape and knew how the acoustics changed according to the time of day and the weather. Guibbal agreed, but nothing had come of it. Nothing had come of anything Griffe had said.

Up in the village, Blanc gathered more information about Olive's state of mind in the days leading up to her death. Andrée Sous told him that Olive had been to see her the day before she died. This wasn't unusual in itself, as Olive often enjoyed a chat with her and her mother. That day, however, Madame Sous had noticed that she seemed anxious and looked 'gaunt and despondent.' As Olive was such a private person, Madame Sous explained, she hadn't liked to ask what was wrong.

A few villagers also had something to say about the clothes

Olive had been wearing when she died. An unfounded – and, indeed, false – rumour had taken hold that her shirt and stockings were traditional funeral dress for the deceased in England. The villagers complained that the police had failed to pick up on this important detail.

'So, according to you,' Blanc asked one such cultural expert, 'Miss Branson deliberately dressed in this macabre way before committing suicide?'

'It's a natural assumption.'

The idea intrigued Blanc, but the only person with any in-depth knowledge of Olive's wardrobe and her usual mode of dress was nowhere to be found: neither Marie-Thérèse nor Joseph were at the Hotel Monte-Carlo. He therefore walked next door to the *mairie* to interview the mayor, Joseph Ricaud, about François.

'If you'd been told that Pinet could one day become a murderer, knowing what you know about him, would you have believed that?'

'Never! That's why I signed the petition in his favour.'

François, Mayor Ricaud explained, had always liked to have fun, but he was good at heart.

'What about his laziness?'

'He's no lazier than anyone else. As a hotelier, he did his job as he should. He did all the shopping in his car in Maussane and Saint-Rémy; he actively took care of the hotel's supplies and was always ready to be of service to anyone who asked.'

'But it's said he had expensive tastes?'

'He was always clean and well dressed for his customers. People make this out to be some excessive love of luxury, when he was only paying attention to his professional appearance. That's not to say he didn't like to show off a little, but then he was a handsome young man with cash to spare. But let's not forget that he's not a peasant; he's not a farmer who has to work the fields: he's a hotelier in constant contact with a wealthy and elegant clientele whose manners are much less crude than our own – and he comported himself accordingly.'

That day, Blanc also went looking for the friend of Raoul Dumas to whom his guide had alluded. He eventually spotted him in an alley near the Hotel Reine Jeanne. It was Vernon Blake, whose identity Blanc would later attempt to disguise under the moniker 'Monsieur B.'

'Monsieur B.' was wearing pyjamas, the sight of which reminded Blanc of a film he had been to see fourteen years earlier in Toulon. *Les Mystères de New York* featured a Chinese villain in similar clothing, and had prompted the friend accompanying him (a colonialist to her core) to declare, 'Always be wary of the Chinese. They know nothing but deceit and deception. You'll rue the day you get involved with them.'

It was apparently on the basis of this prophecy (and a curious sartorial xenophobia) that Eugène Blanc chose not to approach Blake, electing to fish for details about him in the village instead. He was rewarded with the rumour that the artist had once pursued Olive around the hills for hours 'like a faun.'[2]

There was still no sign of the Girards.

It was on Eugène Blanc's second visit to Les Baux, undertaken solo on his motorbike, that he finally managed to speak to Joseph and Marie-Thérèse. They were preparing to shutter the Hotel Monte-Carlo, as the management agreement they had made with the ffordes was about to end. Despite the unfavourable reports he'd heard, Blanc found the couple pleasant and likeable. Joseph, in particular, struck him as frank and honest.

Although they refused to say anything about François or his relationship with Olive, they were happy to talk about Olive herself, for whom they still held some affection. Marie-Thérèse offered a few glimpses into their late employer's eccentricities, such as the fact that she had powdered her hair white and wouldn't allow anyone to disturb the spiders in Mas de Chiscale. Above all, she praised Olive's kindness and expressed the pain that both she and Joseph had felt on her death.

The suicide itself had been a shock, Marie-Thérèse said, but she knew that something was wrong as soon as Olive returned from London. For a start, she arrived two days earlier than expected.

'Did she say why?'

'No, and it was very difficult for me to ask her.'

'And what was Miss Branson's state of mind?'

'I found her very preoccupied. So much so that I said to her, "Mademoiselle, you have to take life as it comes." She was almost crying when she replied, "When we can." My embarrassment and the nature of our relationship prevented me from pursuing it any further, so I said nothing and withdrew. I regret that to this day.'[3]

Joseph added that Olive had also been worried about money, giving as an example the black mare she told him to sell that week. She had been very attached to it, despite being a little disturbed by its wild energy when she was in the saddle. Knowing how much she would miss the beast, he'd tried to dissuade her, saying, 'Mademoiselle, if your mare is impatient and restless, it's because she is too well fed for her work. It will be the same with any other horse after a while.' Olive had simply said, 'I have a lot of expenses right now. Just hurry and close the sale.'[4]

Before he left, Blanc asked, 'Can you give me the name of this painter Miss Branson was seeing?' The couple seemed confused, so he elaborated: 'She often travelled to Arles, and possibly Marseille, with an artist? I've been told which hotel they stayed at in Arles.'

Both looked stunned. After gathering their thoughts, they said, 'It's surprising. Possible, if you say so, but we didn't have the slightest idea.'

Heading to interview his two final witnesses, Blanc was sure the Girards were telling the truth. If nothing else, another lover meant another suspect, a fact the couple would have leapt upon long ago in their campaign to free François. Either the painter was a fiction, or Olive Branson's facility for concealing her activities was greater than anyone had given her credit for.

Over in Saint-Rémy, Sergeant Fabre was in a circumspect mood.

'You'll understand why I can't tell you much,' he told Blanc. 'The investigation was withdrawn from me when Monsieur Guibbal arrived.'

'But, in your judgement, it was suicide?'

'Certainly. The mere sight of the corpse and its position left no room for doubt . . . Still, it was found that it could be otherwise. We shall see in court who is right and who is wrong, but at this moment I'm in a very poor position to say anything other than I stand by my conclusions.'[5]

Blanc had more luck at Pierre Cot's consulting room in Maussane. The doctor was pleased that someone from the press was finally willing to listen to what he and others had been trying to say for five months. His earlier statements, he complained, had often been truncated or completely misrepresented by Blanc's colleagues. One example he gave was a newspaper in Marseille that had claimed he refused to issue a burial permit. 'Perfectly false! How could I refuse this permit if I had already concluded that it was a suicide?'

'May I ask, doctor, what brought you to that conclusion?'

'Quite simply, the findings I made on the body . . . Miss

Branson's arms were raised – the right at about the same height as the breast, the other reaching the forehead. This left hand was clenched, as if it were still gripping the handle of the revolver. Finally, the thumb of that hand was stiffened to the position of squeezing the trigger. Suicide was obvious.'

'Yet Doctors Rey and Béroud concluded that it was murder?'

'I speak without acrimony, but they didn't see the body as I did. If I'd thought there would be disagreement, I'd have had it photographed. But how was I to know that such a drama would be made of this unfortunate suicide?'

No one, he said, had asked him about what had happened to the corpse after it was removed from the water, about how the villagers had straightened Olive's fingers and legs, and bound her arms against her chest to transport her up to the village.

'I was expecting a visit, or to be called by the investigators, but everyone neglected to hear me. I'm not offended. I just note that the process systematically excluded me from the inquiries.' He had not been summoned by Rochu until the middle of June, he said, 'and then only at the request of the defence.'

'But doesn't the autopsy report destroy your findings?'

'It may seem so on a cursory reading. Yet, although it seems to oppose my own conclusions, nothing in it invalidates them. On the contrary, it strengthens them.'

As the doctor explained, he, Rey and Béroud all agreed on the fundamental facts: that Olive had been killed by a bullet to the forehead, that there were no traces of bodily violence and that she was immersed in the water after death. 'Where my opinion differs is on the interpretation of these facts.'

Even the findings that could only be determined by autopsy had not altered the viability of his interpretation, Cot said. He had been able to estimate the angle and path the bullet had taken into Olive's brain, for example, by simply inspecting the wound.

Rey's measurements had been, for him, mere validation of his own observations.

Yet, he said, the report's subsequent conclusion that it was impossible for Olive to have shot herself at the required angle due to the limited headroom in the cistern was 'completely gratuitous', based as it was on an erroneous assumption of how Olive would have held the gun. Cot, after all, had seen her hands.

'I insist on this point. Miss Branson didn't hold her revolver as she would to shoot at a target, using her index finger to pull the trigger. She used her thumb, and it is perfectly possible to shoot oneself at a downward angle, without raising the butt of the gun – on the condition, and only on this condition, that one pulls the trigger with the thumb and nothing but the thumb.'

He also took issue with Rey and Béroud's interpretation of another of their findings. 'My colleagues concluded that death was instantaneous, so why is it so shocking that no water was found in the poor woman's lungs? ... They wanted to make it serve their thesis, in the sense that Miss Branson was deposited in the cistern after her murder, but it also serves my own. Her head did not immediately plunge into the water after being struck by the bullet: surely we can allow a second between the shot of the gun and complete immersion – even half a second would have been enough.

'No matter what is said or done,' he concluded, 'nothing will remove the certainty of suicide in this case. Of the two theories, it's also the simplest – so simple, in fact, that people don't want to believe it. Still, there are at least three of us that have faith and, when this comes to court, Justice will find us there to explain.'[6]

VI

Meanwhile, the wheels of justice had been grinding on. On 15 October, after a delay of almost two months, the three judges of the Chamber of Indictments were ready to rule on whether the case would go to trial. François was therefore taken to Aix to hear their verdict.

It was the first time François had left Chave Prison other than for visits to the Palais de Justice to appear before Rochu. During the twenty-two-mile drive to Aix, he had his first sight of the countryside for five months.

The fields were bathed in warm autumn light. The grape harvest – a poor one that year – had all but ended and the vines were turning to gold; the hay and wheat had been gathered, and new furrows ploughed. François had missed the lavender, but small glimpses of purple could still be seen in the small patches of crocuses from which farmers would soon pluck tiny stamens of saffron. As in Les Baux, they would already be gathering the walnuts and chestnuts as they fell from the trees and trying to keep up with the figs and orchard fruits by bottling what they could to last them through the winter. Above all, their thoughts would be turning to the olive harvest, which was due to begin any day.

François did not have much time to dwell on all he had missed, however. Before long, the prison transport turned up the wide avenue leading to the centre of Aix and the Palais de Justice. Inside the courtroom, the judgement was swift. The panel had decided to commit him to trial, and a date was set for the new year: 17 January, three days before his twenty-sixth birthday.

As the trial was to be held in Aix, François was not returned to Marseille, but taken instead to the prison behind the courthouse. Built on the foundations of the medieval home of the counts of Provence, this had as much cheer as their old dungeons. The heavily barred windows in the external corridors were set so high as to deny any view of the outside world, while those in the cells overlooked a bleak internal courtyard. In dormitories of up to ten rattling bunks, the prisoners ate, slept and counted the characterless days until they were called for trial. François silently took his place among them and waited.

In Avignon, meanwhile, Eugène Blanc had been tapping away at his typewriter, moulding his observations of François's plight into a work of literary obfuscation: just as Olive had loved the exclamation mark and the dash, Blanc favoured the question mark and ellipsis. Using the conceit of film-making to frame his thoughts, he posed as a cinematographer snipping and rearranging scraps of celluloid to present an alternative view of the case and its evolution. He documented the numerous conversations he'd had in Les Baux and elsewhere, alluding to witness statements that had been curiously truncated by the authorities and hinting at allegations of police brutality.

He presented François as a martyr to Franco-British relations, whose arrest had been 'purely arbitrary', as evidenced by the prolonged investigation and the 'patent hesitancy' of the Chamber of Indictments to send the case to trial.[1] He reminded his readers that even Alexandre Guibbal had been against the idea of murder at one time: the detective had said as much to Arthur fforde and also allegedly urged a reporter to do something to ease the unwarranted speculation: 'Can't you retract? Backtrack a bit?'[2]

However, Blanc asserted, someone on high had decided that a murderer was required, if only to appease the British, and from that point on, any talk of suicide was forbidden. If the word of one villager was to be believed, even the forensic scientists had been made to toe the line: Les Baux's gravedigger had told him he'd seen the doctors arguing over this very point after the autopsy – Béroud clearly troubled – before Rey noticed and gestured for his colleague to shut up.

With the aid of his interview with Dr Cot, Blanc dismissed the autopsy report as a work of medico-legal deceit, leaving him free to speculate on what really happened. The murder theory, he said, was so full of holes as to be impossible. Not even the police had been able to give a definitive account of how they thought François had carried out Olive's 'assassination.'

In the generally accepted version, however, François had dropped off the provisions and then entered the studio, where Olive was finishing her meal. He asked her for money, and she refused. So, in a paroxysm of fury, he went into the bedroom, took her revolver from the drawer, loaded two bullets into the chamber, returned to the studio and shot her at close range. Here, Blanc highlighted the first stumbling block, a fact which he lamented had been largely overlooked.

> Miss Branson! This distinguished name readily evokes in many minds one of those little English puppets which bring such joy and delight to our eyes on the stage . . . And yet we must face the facts . . . I saw a photograph of her stroking her mare, and Miss Branson had the effect of what is commonly called a 'dragon' – if not in terms of corpulence, at least in those of height.[3]

As this 'dragon' was significantly taller than François, Blanc pointed out, she must have remained seated while he held the gun to her forehead, in order to explain the downward trajectory of the bullet. But would she really have just waited patiently for death, making no move to defend herself? And where was the blood? Blanc refused to believe Dr Rey's assertion that the bullet wound had not caused profuse bleeding, especially as it had started to flow again after sixteen hours in the water.

François, it was said, then partially undressed his lifeless victim – including removing her garter belt but leaving her stockings – and folded her clothes neatly on the back of the bedroom chair before carrying her body to the cistern. Blanc also considered an alternative theory: that Olive had undressed herself when her lover first arrived. But, if she had seduction on her mind, why would she have taken the time to fold her clothes, yet leave the dogs' hair-strewn blankets covering the bed?

As to François's subsequent disposal of the body, much had already been said about the difficulties he would have encountered getting it into the cistern without leaving any marks. Blanc now expanded on this with the body's position in the water. Because of the way the grille opened, he asserted, had Olive been dropped into the water and left, she would have been found parallel to the wall of the studio; instead, she was ninety degrees clockwise. Moreover, her arms would have gone limp while she was carried, yet they were found raised in front of her body, with her hand clenched as if gripping a revolver.

Blanc maintained François would therefore have had to strip off and climb into the water himself to rearrange her body to look like suicide. All this would have taken time and would have needed to be done while the body was still warm. Yet, the indictment gave him thirty or forty minutes at most to accomplish both the murder and this staging.

He found the suicide, on the other hand, easy to reconstruct. Furthermore, he said, he had found the missing key that unlocked the whole tragedy. At first, he had believed that something had happened during Olive's final trip to London to upset her or that her money troubles were more severe than thought – but the key had been in Provence all along.

It took the form of two letters that had been torn up and thrown away by a nameless young woman. The scraps of paper were found by the woman's aunt, who pieced them back together. They were letters from François. The pair were in love, but François had evidently been dragging his feet on his promise to 'drop the old woman.' After a bit of detective work, the aunt had therefore taken matters into her own hands and arranged for these 'testimonies of disaffection and ingratitude' to be shown to Olive on her return from England.[4]

Blanc did not say whether he had seen the letters himself; nor did he give any clue as to his source, other than to say he had been tipped off by a colleague in Marseille. But, for him, their existence made everything slide into place.

Olive, he suggested, had been heartbroken and deeply wounded by what she read – and her sadness only increased as the week progressed and François made no attempt to see her. When he arrived with her shopping on the Friday evening, unable to avoid her any longer, she had hoped to talk, to resolve their relationship one way or another. But he brushed her off, perhaps saying he was busy and still had more errands to run. After watching him drive away, she had returned inside.

'It is almost night. . . the time of sorrow and disquiet for poets and those whose feelings run deep; the time of black thoughts when one is alone.' Having set the stage for his imagining of what happened next, Blanc continued:

Feeling weak in the face of life, Miss Branson finds another kind of strength. She undresses, folds her clothes on a chair, and proceeds to clothe herself in the funereal garb of her country. She takes the revolver and cocks it. All she has to do is shoot. But she hesitates. What if it doesn't kill her? Having resolved to die, she wants to be sure. She therefore decides to make death doubly certain. The cistern is only three steps from the door . . .[5]

Olive, he made clear, was 'temperamental and impulsive, like many artists'; she was 'whimsical', yet kept her innermost feelings to herself.[6] And if the clothes in which she had chosen to meet her Maker – just a shirt and a pair of stockings – seemed absurd to his readers, he assured them that he had known enough Englishwomen to put any doubts to rest. 'From what I have observed of their often naive sentimentalism, Miss Branson putting on her nation's attire of the dead to commit suicide does not surprise me.'[7] Nor did the state of her stockings. The length of time she had lain submerged in the cistern, he asserted with all the confidence of a bachelor, was sufficient to wash them clean – if, that is, Dr Béroud had even analysed the correct pair at all.

Suicide was, as Dr Cot had said, the simplest explanation.

Why, then, had there been such an insistence on Olive's death being a murder? In part, Blanc said, it was due to the rigidity of British morals: 'English mores do not admit the right to suicide as easily as our own. Wilfully killing oneself still appears to be a source of scandal among our neighbours across the Channel.'[8] It followed that Olive's wealthy family, wishing to avoid such stigma, had used their connections to cast doubt on Sergeant Fabre's initial conclusions.

At the same time, he claimed, there had been a bad actor within Les Baux itself, 'a character who appears to be the "mysterious soul" that one finds in any murky affair.'[9] From the outset, this man had carefully implanted the idea of murder, first in the mind of Arthur fforde and then in the press. Blanc left it for his readers to speculate as to the man's identity and motive. Earlier in the manuscript, however, he had already mentioned the various goings-on in Les Baux.

'One cannot without embarrassment define Les Baux as a village,' he had written. 'It is, in fact, more of a termite mound . . . More so than anywhere else, the disagreements that exist between families tend to develop and persist.'[10] He had also highlighted the rivalry between the two hotels and devoted a small section to the pyjamaed 'Monsieur B.', a.k.a. Vernon Blake.

He now revealed that this 'mysterious soul' had once been suspected in Les Baux of being the murderer himself, an impression that still lingered in the minds of many. 'If I didn't know that murder was impossible,' Blanc wrote, 'I, too, would lean in this direction, and would have good reasons for doing so.'[11]

With press and diplomatic pressure building in the days following Olive's death, he argued, the Sûreté had been ordered to find a culprit – any culprit. Yet, Blanc implied, in sending their best man they had gone some way to mitigating this abuse of power. Alexandre Guibbal, tasked with finding a culprit for what he knew to be a non-existent murder, had been able to use his substantial intellect to find one that not only satisfied the press, but would suffer the least long-term harm: the young and introverted François Pinet. 'Was it not better, in this case, that the person arrested had every chance of being later acquitted by the Court of Assizes?' Blanc asked.[12]

All the clues were there: Guibbal's sudden change of heart about the likelihood of suicide, the tortuous investigation that had failed to produce a single piece of prima facie evidence, and the widespread disbelief that François was capable of violence.

Not even Olive's family seemed to think he was guilty: while compiling his findings, Blanc learned that Arthur fforde had recently extended the agreement with the Girards to manage the Hotel Monte-Carlo. Why would the Englishman do that if he thought they had even the smallest connection to his cousin's murder?

No, Blanc concluded, François had been caught up in an elaborate game of appeasement, with Guibbal gambling on the fact that the courts would redress the wrongs he had been forced to commit.

As his manuscript had long outgrown the space afforded by the *Radical*'s columns, Eugène Blanc contacted César Sarnette, a publisher in nearby Cavaillon, to arrange the typesetting and printing of a stand-alone work that he hoped would shake the world, or at least a small corner of it.

Le Drame des Baux et son Mystère appeared in bookshops and on news-stands in early December. Subtitled *L'hotelier Pinet a-t-il vraiment tué Miss Branson?* – 'Did Pinet the hotelier really kill Miss Branson?' – the ninety-page paperback was clad in rough yellow paper and cost just three and a half francs. It was an immediate hit and soon required a second printing to keep up with demand.

PART V:

A L'ASARD BAUTEZAR!

I

In December, with the olive harvest complete and the nights drawing in, Les Baux started to retreat back into itself. The weeks leading up to Christmas were always a magical time. With the tourist buses mothballed for the winter, the Baussencs had their bleak citadel to themselves. As *Les Tablettes d'Avignon* put it, 'It seems that in the deserted streets, under the light of the moon, the icy spectres of the lords of yesteryear return.'[1] Outhouses stocked full of firewood and pantries replete with the fruits of summer made the long winter nights a time of simple pleasures and gentle fireside pursuits.

In his house by the Porte d'Eyguières, Vernon Blake was busy correcting the proofs of his latest oeuvre, *Nor Rhône Nor Reason: Being Digressions Concerning Literature, Art, & Manners* – the book which Olive had feared would seek retribution against her and her fellow artists.

As it happened, Blake had barely mentioned them. His disdain instead was directed towards the native population. As the precis of chapter twelve, in which Blake took on 'the character of the Midi', concluded: 'Let no man, after having read this chapter, accuse The Author of being in League with the Provençal to entice the Stranger within his Gates.'[2]

And no man could. He described one Baussenc family (easily identifiable, on account of adjacent detail) as 'recognized thieves who seek to terrorize the village, who are in constant dispute with the gendarmes and regularly condemned to prison or to fines.' But this, apparently, was par for the course in Blake's Provence, whose population was infected with a 'peculiar malignity' and a 'love of doing evil for its own sake'.[3] Without the endless lawsuits and denunciations to the authorities, he said, 'the South would die of weariness.'[4]

The people, he wrote, were both violent and cowardly, full of empty Catholic piety, and displayed a 'deeply ingrained hatred of the northerner be he French or English, or indeed anything but Provençal.'[5] Provence itself was 'a land of old romance and modern nullity',[6] an intellectual wasteland: the poetry – including that of the Nobel Prize winner Frédéric Mistral – was mediocre and much of the art displayed a 'terrible Provençal lack of restraint and taste.'[7] Where others saw exuberance, he saw 'insupportable vulgarity and noisy pretension.'[8] He was, he made clear, a Parisian at heart.

Now, having read Eugène Blanc's pamphlet, Blake added a lengthy footnote by way of response. The pamphlet had, he said:

> ... demonstrated, more or less perfectly, that Miss Branson committed suicide. But in order to make assurance doubly sure, it is also asserted that there is no serious doubt concerning the fact that I murdered her. This somewhat confuses the argument, but that is of little importance. I also learn that, intent on rape, I pursued Miss Branson for hours over the hills. (As a matter of fact I had always avoided her!)
>
> The author of the book tells us that he came to the village of Les Baux with the intention of interviewing me on the matter, but meeting me by chance, my view filled him with such indescribable loathing that he was unable to speak to me, and went away without carrying out his investigation. It appears that I

was clad in pyjamas – a word in your ear: I have never possessed pyjamas in my life!

In spite of the fact that this book has been on sale, at the time of writing, for a month, I am still at liberty. The authorities are, from long experience, acquainted with southern ways. Yet all blame should not be attached to the ingenious southerner. Mr. Fforde [sic], who is British, takes no steps whatever to relieve me of the onus of this libel . . . on account of the behaviour of his relatives, cousin and daughter.* An amiable world.[9]

On Christmas Eve, Les Baux burst briefly and exuberantly into life. The village's famous midnight Mass drew crowds from all over Provence. Places in the church itself were always in high demand, but people also came to see the torch-lit *pastrage* in which the chestnut-cloaked shepherds processed through the streets to the joyful sound of fifes, pipes and tambourines. As their forebears had done in centuries past, they led a ram pulling a little two-wheeled cart, his harness bedecked with stars. Under the cart's ribboned canopy lay a newborn lamb, their offering to the infant Jesus. Once inside the church, they would join the choir in a Provençal recitative of the nativity, during which only the angel Gabriel was permitted to sing in French.

Cars and buses had been streaming down the road from Saint-Rémy for hours and parking wherever they could find space. The hotels were full to bursting, as was Charles Cornille's cafe. François's absence was no doubt a topic of conversation among the locals, Olive's less so, but nothing could put a dampener on a centuries-old

---

* Some of the less savoury rumours circulating after Olive's death said that she had been prostituting Kay and Phyll among high-class clients in Marseille, or that one or both had been conducting a parallel affair with François.

tradition involving drink, God and carefully coiffured sheep. Even the Archbishop had failed, having tried to cancel the festivities on account of a small riot that had occurred outside the church the previous year. Widespread protest had forced him to back down, on the understanding that it wouldn't happen again.

The riot had been just the sort of drama Olive relished, and she had excitedly relayed the tale to May fforde afterwards. The trouble had begun, she said, when the Abbé Cheilan introduced a ticketing system because of the growing popularity of the midnight Mass. His aim was to give the Baussencs a chance to secure their seats before he opened sales up to outsiders. And it had worked: he'd issued tickets for every place in the church, including every inch of standing room. His error, however, was in deciding to forgo the customary opening of the large oak doors just before the Mass began, leaving those freezing outside unable to even listen to the service.

> . . . *the huge crowd outside tried to smash in the door – I don't know where the police were – anyhow they wisely kept out of the way – as they wouldn't have liked using their revolvers on the crowd – if they had, the crowd would have dropped them over the ramparts – & that would have been that!*[10]

Unfortunately, Olive hadn't witnessed the commotion in person. Although she'd secured her ticket in plenty of time, her seat in the stone-built gallery went instead to a grateful Phyll, who had arrived in Les Baux seeking to escape the dreary British winter. After walking her god-daughter up to the church and handing her over to Gazin, a hefty stonemason from Maussane – 'a dear & the sort of cheery young man no one dares to take liberties with' – Olive had sought refuge from the cold in the Hotel Monte-Carlo.

François was there, preparing for the *Réveillon* she was hosting after the service. This midnight supper was a Christmas Eve tradition, and, throughout the village, tables were being pushed together and spare chairs found to accommodate extended family groups. *Oulos* had been bubbling away above kitchen hearths all day, the best wines had been brought up from the cellars and *lei tretze dessèrts*, the thirteen sweetmeats representing Christ and his twelve apostles, laid out. As the new owner of the Monte-Carlo, Olive had invited a small group of guests to join her and Phyll in the *petite salle*: Monsieur and Madame Sous, Gazin the stonemason, and the Brun family, who owned a lime plant near Marseille and were friends with Andrée Sous. The Girards and Pinets were celebrating in the adjacent *grande salle*.

News of the affray at the church trickled in with their guests. No one had been seriously hurt and Madame Sous was in her element, dragging up old gossip about Cheilan and disturbances of yore. As Olive reported to May, the party was 'a <u>great</u> success.'[11]

> *Phyll & I really had the time of our lives. She looked lovely in the dark stiff silk & the pale green shawl. I was carefully powdered – silver-grey & dark brown in grey cord – & masses of furs & shawls, as it was bitterly cold and I was Patronne of the Monte-Carlo!!!! having bought it & <u>paid</u> for it!*
>
> *. . . After the Réveillon – about 4 a.m. – François drove Phyll & me back here (I pay for the petrol when I use his car for joyriding) – & we slept most of Xmas Day.*[12]

Of course, something else had happened that evening, which she did not disclose. At some point – while the Mass was underway in the church or after she got home – Olive had picked up her pen and written the codicil to her French will that, depending upon who you asked, had either sealed her fate or condemned an innocent man to prison.

Would foreknowledge have given her pause? Perhaps. But Christmas in Les Baux had always brought out her generosity. She revelled in the ancient traditions as well as creating a few of her own.

One of her new customs involved the schoolchildren. The village school was housed in an old Renaissance mansion next to the church, which retained fragments of frescoes on the walls and a pietà above the door. A few days before Christmas, Madame Raynaud, the schoolmistress, would line up the children and walk them along the ramparts to the Hotel Monte-Carlo, where a gift from Olive awaited each one. Some years, depending on her health, she had sent Joseph with two haversacks of toys to act as her Père Noël. In 1928, however, she had ridden up to the hotel on her new mare and handed them out personally.

On Boxing Day, Olive hosted an 'International Ball' at Mas de Chiscale, for which she and Phyll had spent the day decorating the old disused kitchen for dancing and clearing space in the studio for a candlelit supper.

> *François did all the catering at Arles & the cooking at the Hotel, & after we had a supper for 18 in the studio: François in charge of the meat – & wine, Monsieur Brun. As salad maker (it was a cold supper) Gazin, & young Charles Corneille from Tarascon to lay the table – the very greatest success. Phyll looked lovely – in the pale taffeta. We got to bed at 5 . . .*[13]

A few days later, Louis drove Olive, Phyll and François to Marseille – 'the greatest lark' – to stay overnight at the Hotel Beauvau and shop for New Year's gifts in the city's department stores. Four had gone and five came back, Olive having been unable to resist Jacquot the parrot.

Then, on New Year's Eve, Phyll, François and Madeleine went

to a dance held by the Eccentric Club at the Café Malarte in Arles. Olive had stayed at home with Jacquot and the dogs, resting before her final contribution to the village festivities the next day.

The New Year's *déjeuner* for the shepherds had been held at the Hotel Monte-Carlo for as long as anyone could remember, and was the highlight of their year. As the new *patronne*, Olive was hosting it for the first time and was anxious that it passed muster. She had already been let down by the Abbé Cheilan two days before the event by way of a letter informing her that he would be unable to lead the blessings. Furious, she had resisted the urge to ride over to Paradou to confront him at the presbytery; instead, she took some unspecified revenge which, as she cryptically told May, had been 'better than that.'[14]

On New Year's Day, however, she and Phyll had woken up to find fat flakes of snow tumbling from a leaden sky. At eleven o'clock, a howling mistral arrived, turning what had been a gentle snowfall into a violent blizzard. Marcel, Tony and Fly went berserk, never having experienced weather like it in their short, Provençal lives. With the lunch guests due at midday, Olive and Phyll wrestled the pups into the house with Frida before struggling up to the hotel. 'We had to get up to the village – & we got! But it was <u>awful</u>.'[15]

François had prepared a lavish feast, which both he and Olive expected would go to waste on account of the weather. The shepherds, however, were hardy folk and had been determined to enjoy their annual gathering. Only two hadn't shown: '. . . one Shepherdess, who had been sitting up all night nursing old Père Armand, who is dying – & old Denis Poulinet, the poet from Maussane . . . sent a wire saying the snow prevented him bicycling.'[16]

In the end, twenty-four sat down to lunch – 'the greatest lark' – while the blizzard raged outside. After coffee, everyone –

'almost' – sang traditional songs, taking it in turns to perform solos ('delightful'). Olive had welcomed in the new year as though in a fairy tale: with music and laughter in front of a roaring fire, her young lover nearby, and the ancient citadel blanketed by sparkling, white snow.

The fantasy hadn't lasted long, however. No more than a few hours, in fact. At half past three, just as she and Phyll had stepped outside to trudge back to the valley to attend to the dogs, they heard an engine struggling up through the Porte Mage. It was a small bus from Avignon that had set off, as it did every Tuesday, at eight o'clock that morning. The driver, having inched his way along his usual route through increasingly heavy snow, pulled up outside the hotel and announced he could go no further. While he squeezed his bus into the Monte-Carlo's covered garage, Olive helped four of the stranded passengers into the already full hotel. The remainder went to the Reine Jeanne.

The snow continued to fall for days, lying ten inches deep and confining the valley dwellers to their homes until the thaw arrived a week later. It was a welcome rest after the busy Christmas season. It seemed some of Olive's neighbours, however, had spent their unexpected isolation mulling over past grudges, because with the thaw came her run-in with Etienne Patin that prompted her to summon the gendarmes about the threat to her dogs. The hunters had returned, too, bouncing their bullets off the rocks above her garden and leading her to send Phyll up to the *mairie* to beg for assistance.

Then Kay had arrived in need of nurturing, and the hotel renovation had got underway, with all the administrative and financial stress that brought. Although the strain was relieved by the company of her god-daughters, their trip to the Alps, a sortie to Marseille with François and a party for his twenty-fifth birthday, Olive barely had a moment to herself until her visit to

London at the end of April. And within six days of her return, she was dead.

Now, as the Baussencs saw in another new year and a new decade, the events of that tragic night were once again at the forefront of their minds. Just before Christmas, the bailiff Léon Jeymet had placed fifteen envelopes in his bag, left his bicorne hat and sword hanging in his office in Saint-Rémy, and set off for Les Baux. Each envelope contained a subpoena signed by Auguste Rol, the public prosecutor, summoning the recipient to Aix for the trial of François César Pinet on Friday, 17 and Saturday, 18 January.

It hadn't been hard for the bailiff to track down the witnesses in the Vallon de la Fontaine. Recent rains had made the fields sodden and unworkable, and daily frosts had brought a halt to the pruning of the vines. Accordingly, Jeymet found almost everyone at home. The farmers Tougay, Aracil, Ricaud and Pascal, as well as the shepherd Griffe, were all hunkered down in the valley. The only chimney not puffing out signs of cheerful domesticity was that of the shuttered Mas de Chiscale. For those who were out working, such as Etienne Patin and the road-mender André Graugnard, Jeymet handed over the wax-sealed envelope to a family member.

Raoul Dumas had been easily located up at the Hotel Reine Jeanne, overseeing arrangements for the impending influx of visitors for the midnight Mass, and the Girards were similarly hard at work at the Monte-Carlo. In Maussane, he'd found the butcher Baptistin Moucadel at his shop.

Jeymet's home town had given him the most trouble. There were only two witnesses from Saint-Rémy on his list, but neither was at home. Louis Vigne was out with his taxi, so his mother-in-law took the envelope. Jean Baltus, on the other hand, was nowhere to be found. Asking around, Jeymet discovered that the artist had left for Paris five or six days earlier and no one knew when he would return. He therefore handed the summons to the mayor, on the understanding that it would find its way to Baltus by whatever means.

The proximity of the trial had not gone unnoticed in Avignon, either. In the second week of January, the town's post office took charge of forty-four small parcels for distribution throughout the region. At first glance, the unsuspecting recipients had been seemingly chosen at random. In Marseille, one arrived at a pharmacy near the Vieux Port, one at a patisserie, one at the private residence of an agronomist not far from the Gare Saint-Charles, and another found its way into the greasy hands of a mechanic in the sixth arrondissement. An insurance broker in Arles took possession of one, while another had to await the return of a fishing trawler and her skipper on the quayside at Cassis. A few went to pensioners – a former railwayman, a retired colonel – one to an arbitrator, another to a young industrialist. One made its way through rows of vines to a country house in Lambesc; yet more went to farms and smallholdings in Bouc, Boulbon, Meyreuil and Rognonas.

Tearing back the wrapping, each addressee discovered a slim book, its yellow cover bearing the title *Le Drame des Baux et son Mystère*. They all knew exactly why they had received this anonymous gift. It was for the same reason that the threatening letters had started to arrive.

The recipients had two things in common. Firstly, they were all men. Secondly, their names had just been published as jurors for the forthcoming session of the Aix Court of Assizes. Only twelve would be selected for the Branson case, scheduled for the end of the first week, but neither the sender of the parcels, nor the writers of the more sinister notes, could predict which twelve.

The court would be overseeing ten trials that month: one each for sexual assault, armed robbery and handling stolen goods, and seven for varying degrees of murder. The schedule allowed one day for each case, apart from that of François Pinet, for which an extra day had been set aside in anticipation of the fight ahead. The selected jurors would only be confirmed at the beginning of each trial.

The author of the yellow booklet had previously made clear his views on the jury system. Writing in the *Radical de Vaucluse* in October, Eugène Blanc had quoted an aphorism by the nineteenth-century statesman Jules Favre, before rejecting it as idealistic and outdated. 'The jury is the invisible soul of the nation, lighting up justice with its rays, only to return to the crowd and get lost in it,' Favre had said. 'Theoretically, yes,' Blanc responded. In an ideal world, he wrote, the eclectic nature of juries meant that a balance of intellect and experience could be achieved; they were not always 'twelve idiots'. But the cleverest prospective jurors – those most capable of weighing up complex arguments – either knew how to recuse themselves or were recused by whichever of the prosecution or defence had the weaker case, meaning that in reality the quality of the jury pool was diminished.[17]

He went on to discuss the flawed practice of each juror's individual vote being made public, which opened the door for decisions to be influenced by fear of reprisal or, conversely, by the prospect of gangland protection. It was clear that, in Blanc's mind at least, the modern juror needed a little help in reaching the correct verdict. Fortunately for him, postage was cheap.*

---

* Although Blanc was widely believed to be behind this attempt to influence the jury in François Pinet's trial, it was never proved and he faced no official sanction.

II

On the morning of Friday, 17 January 1930, a stream of passengers left the railway station in Aix-en-Provence and scurried up the Avenue Victor Hugo and the Cours Mirabeau towards the Palais de Justice. Provence's learned old capital – the 'Athens of France' – was clad in bright, winter splendour. The pollarded trees designed to give shade from the fierce heat of summer were bare, their spindly branches reaching up to the sky like bony hands in supplication, a silent Greek chorus lining the route. Every kiosk along the way displayed rows of small yellow books, whose red lettering posed the question on everyone's lips: *Did François Pinet really kill Miss Branson?*

Journalists from all over France, along with their English counterparts, were already installed in the city's cheaper hotels, having visited Les Baux over the previous days in search of local colour. This had not been hard to conjure up. Rarely did a case encompass so many of the seven deadly sins. Pride, greed, lust, envy, gluttony, wrath and sloth: each was present to a greater or lesser degree in the Baux affair. Now, with notebooks in hand, they stalked Aix's steamed-up cafes, where invisible scales of justice jostled for space among the coffee cups and winter coats as people weighed the facts of the case as they believed them to be.

The spectators had begun to arrive in the Place de Verdun before dawn. It was a chilly morning and all the tickets for the public benches had long since gone, but still they came – from Aix itself, but also from Marseille, Avignon, Arles and everywhere in between – to join the throng gathering outside the courthouse. The authorities had anticipated the crowds. Gendarmes on horseback were scattered throughout the square, while a cordon of Senegalese soldiers guarded the entrance, their bayonets gleaming in the low winter sun.

There was a bristle of excitement as two dusty charabancs pulled up in a cloud of exhaust and offloaded a gaggle of passengers, who were swiftly herded into a cafe to have breakfast. Was that *them*? The witnesses from Les Baux?

Everyone in the crowd knew Les Baux. Who hadn't, at one time or another, visited that strange little citadel perched atop its desolate rock? Who hadn't wandered the ruins of the old castle, peered into the stone graves of the Gallo-Roman cemetery, and half-listened as tour guides spoke of princes and poets whose names they hadn't heard since their schooldays?

But had they seen the other village, the one that belonged to the living? Well, they saw it now. That other Les Baux had been prised open, painfully and publicly. Ancient feuds and family secrets had been laid bare and, for every established fact, there were a dozen rumours. Everyone had an opinion – and not just about the innocence or otherwise of François Pinet, but about the behaviour of the villagers, the gendarmes, the police, the doctors, the politicians – and, of course, Olive Branson herself.

At quarter to nine, the soldiers guarding the entrance moved aside and the giant doors to the courthouse swung open. The crowd surged into the building, where they found ropes strung between the great columns of the central hall to create a path to the courtroom, and gendarmes stationed at intervals to filter the ticket holders from the hopeful.

With sunlight streaming through the large windows, the richly panelled courtroom echoed with voices as the public and press benches filled up. At the far end, a long mahogany dais draped in red velvet awaited the three judges. To the right was the empty jury box; to the left, the long wooden dock. The benches in the well of the court were already bustling with activity as the court officials took their places. François's lawyers, led by Jean Dorlhac de Borne, were spreading out their papers on the bench below the dock. To the spectators, the mood of the sixty-nine-year-old already seemed as black as both his robe and the dye on the sparse comb-over that sat beneath his ceremonial toque.

A clatter of feet on iron stairs announced the arrival of the prisoner from the cells below. All eyes turned to the dock as the kepis of two gendarmes rose into view, followed by François's bare head. Although he had elected to meet his fate in a dark lounge suit, white silk shirt and blue bow tie, nothing could disguise the toll eight months of incarceration had taken on his body. His skin was pale, there were dark shadows beneath his eyes, and his jacket hung loosely from his reduced frame. Nevertheless, the only sign that betrayed his nerves was a slight tremble in his jaw.

As François surveyed the room and leaned over the dock to murmur something to Dorlhac de Borne, he was met by a fusillade of pops and flashes from the press cameras. Neither this nor the noisy chatter from the gallery showed any signs of abating until an angry voice rang out from the front of the court.

'Cease fire!'

The cameras fell silent and an obedient hush descended over the room as the owner of this voice – a tall, scarlet-robed and thunder-faced figure – adjusted his gown and took his seat on the dais beside his two fellow judges. President Lafont's temper, along with his perpetually dishevelled grey beard, was legendary among court aficionados. After waiting for the elderly advocate general to settle at the adjacent desk, he nodded for the proceedings to begin.

The men from the jury pool who had not been selected for the previous day's trial were brought in. As the lots were drawn, jurors were rejected or selected by the two sides until thirty-two had been whittled down to twelve: five farmers, an administrator, a shop assistant, a landowner, a building contractor, a baker, a manufacturer of bronzes, and the owner of a chain of home decor shops. After each swearing to evaluate the case 'without hatred or fear', they took their places in the jury box directly opposite François.

A folder had been placed on each of their seats containing a plan of Mas de Chiscale, a map of the valley, and ten annotated photographs of the house and garden taken on the day of the autopsy and search. As they leafed through the documents, Lafont gave them a precis of the case.

'You will appreciate, gentlemen, the unusual nature of the place in which Miss Branson lived and met her death. Here was a woman of evident culture and means, who for years lived utterly alone in a place known for its strange and forbidding air. There are probably few more beautiful spots in Provence. Yet, at the same time, there are few that would be likely to have such a depressing effect on the nerves of a highly strung person.'

He then summarized the circumstances in which Olive's body had been found and the events that had led to François's arrest, before turning his attention to the young man himself.

'Stand up!'

François rose calmly.

François Pinet and Jean Dorlhac de Borne in court.

Reading from his notes, Lafont began, 'Your name is François Pinet; you were born in Les Baux on the twentieth of January 1904. In forty-eight hours, you will turn twenty-six. You have been detained since the seventh of May 1929. You have no prior criminal record. From a family point of view, you are the youngest of five children. Until the age of thirteen, you attended the municipal school in your village and then you worked alongside your father and learned the trade of a baker. After completing your military service, you returned to Les Baux, where you worked at your family's hotel. In the meantime, in 1928, your father died, and you took over the hotel's management.'

François remained motionless as the president continued, 'Miss Branson, the one the prosecution will call your victim, came to settle in Les Baux and ended up buying the hotel and some adjoining land for the sum of 75,000 francs. This sale was necessary to pay your father's death duties. She gave you 11,000 francs, the sum representing your share. Correct?'

'Yes.' It was the first time François had spoken. His voice was weak.

'Did you receive these funds at the beginning of 1929?'

'I really couldn't say.'

Lafont paused and looked at François. 'You're a very closed off young man, aren't you? Some say you're rather sly, but no one seems to know much about you.'

Silence.

Lafont moved on. 'Miss Branson had an annual income of six hundred pounds, or about 75,000 francs. In fact, she had to be wealthy to maintain a driver and car, didn't she? She also had in her service your sister and brother-in-law, whom she paid 1,200 francs every month.'

Without any transition, the president asked, 'Pinet, were you Miss Branson's lover?'

François, surprised, glanced at Dorlhac de Borne before giving a brief nod.

'And you were also one of her heirs?'

'Yes.'

'On the twenty-seventh of April 1929, the corpse of Miss Branson was discovered at the bottom of the cistern of Mas de Chiscale in Les Baux. The authorities, both legal and medical, concluded that it was suicide. But later observations steered justice towards the idea of murder, completely ruling out the theory of suicide. The question then was who could have committed the crime? Who could have benefited from Miss Branson's death? It was discovered that you were the legatee of the hotel and that your financial situation was difficult. On that basis, you were apprehended and arrested. What is your defence?'

It was a few seconds before Pinet answered. 'She killed herself.'

'It is therefore incumbent upon the prosecution to demonstrate otherwise.'

Lafont proceeded to give an overview of the evidence gathered during the investigation, from the results of the autopsy to the difficulties Olive would have encountered if she had indeed shot herself in the cistern. When he came to the bloodstains found in the house, the president paused. 'Well! What seemed at first to be a charge against a dog had to be dropped.'

Amid a smattering of laughter, Dorlhac de Borne shot from his seat. 'If the investigators had followed their own logic, they would have dropped the whole thing!'

Lafont silenced him and turned again to François.

'So, Pinet, explain yourself. Tell the gentlemen of the jury why you think it was suicide.'

François hesitated before looking over at the jury. 'How could I have killed a woman who was taller than me, in the way suggested? I didn't even know where she kept her revolver.'

At this, the jury's attention turned to the dais, caught by a flash of red robes as the gaunt figure of Boissier, the advocate general, unfolded itself. 'But you were her lover,' Boissier said. 'You must have known it was in her nightstand?'

Dorlhac de Borne was on his feet again. 'It is possible, you know, to frequent a woman's bedroom without making an inventory of her drawers!'

Loud guffaws from the public benches drowned out Boissier's response. Lafont called the court to order and gestured for the two men to sit down, returning his gaze to François.

'Well, what else do you want me to say?' François said.

'The prosecution says that only murder is possible and you maintain that only suicide is possible. So . . . ?'

'My lawyers will explain that themselves.'

'You were in debt; you had only four hundred francs to your name.'

'That's not true. I had more money.'

'Where?'

François shrugged. 'At home. And I could have borrowed some or called in some debts.'

'On the other hand, you were a beneficiary of Miss Branson's will. Tell the jurors what she had left you.'

'The hotel. But it wasn't the legacy it's made out to be. I'd never have been able to afford the death duties taxes to take ownership.'

Lafont carried on. 'The will in your favour was drawn up on the twenty-fourth of December 1928. This document was seized on the sixth of May by Monsieur Guibbal. It was only then that you made your affair with the victim known. Why?'

'I didn't think it was relevant, and I have since regretted saying anything at all. Why are you asking me all this?'

'You also had a letter which revealed the feelings of Miss Branson towards you. She called you "my dear François" and told you she was going to include you in her will. But she also specified that she hoped to become "a good old girl of ninety", so she wasn't thinking of suicide, was she?'

François did not reply.

'When the body was discovered, people noticed you were worried.'

'I wasn't worried at all.'

'You asked if an autopsy would be conducted.'

At this, François reverted to silence, which he largely maintained as Lafont continued his analysis of the indictment. In the past, Lafont's lengthy and unyielding style of questioning had elicited unexpected courtroom confessions, but François seemed indifferent to any of the accusations put to him. He leaned placidly against the dock as Dorlhac de Borne raged on his behalf and Boissier sniped back, each intervention inviting louder and louder eruptions from the public benches.

After an hour and a half, with the courtroom descending into ever-increasing anarchy, Lafont ordered a short break to prepare for the first witnesses.

When the hearing resumed at twenty-five past eleven, it was to a stern warning from the president that no further outbursts would be tolerated. The first witness, the debonair Dr Béroud, was therefore able to offer his detailed testimony in peace.

After deftly navigating around the matter of the non-human bloodstains, Béroud directed the court's attention to the condition in which Olive had been found. 'Miss Branson wasn't wearing any shoes, and to get from her studio to the cistern, she would have had to walk over sharp gravel. Yet, I could find no signs of damage to the soles of her stockings. It's—'

Before he could state that she must have been carried, however, Béroud was interrupted by the sixth juror, who was holding aloft the plan of the house he and his fellow jury members had been given.

'But, according to this, it's also possible to get to the cistern by a concrete path.'

The route indicated began at the kitchen door and was much longer and more circuitous than that from the studio, but Béroud had to agree that, yes, it was possible, if unlikely.

He moved on to his and Dr Rey's observations from the autopsy and, specifically, the absence of water in Olive's lungs. This, he explained to the jury, indicated that she had been dead before being submerged.

'What if a person who has just killed herself falls into the water?' asked another juror. 'Does water go into the lungs then?'

L-R Advocate General Boissier, Dr Georges Béroud, President Lafont (in hat).

'No,' Béroud admitted, before explaining why his own experiments in the cistern had excluded that possibility: had Olive shot herself, she would have had to crouch down and duck her head under the water to allow enough room to hold the revolver to her forehead. In such a situation, he would have expected her lungs to have taken in water with her last breath.

By the end of his testimony, Béroud had made it clear he strongly favoured the hypothesis of murder. Yet, when Dorlhac de Borne asked, 'Are you absolutely certain that suicide was impossible?' his loyalty to scientific proof would only allow him to reply, 'There is no absolute certainty in this case.'

Louis Rey was called next. The pathologist gave his evidence wearing a thick overcoat and holding his hat in his hands, his bulky form looming over the bar as he gently led the jury through the findings from the autopsy.

He explained how the trajectory of the bullet, which had penetrated the skull at an angle of forty-five degrees, excluded suicide. Lifting one hand to his forehead with fingers outstretched to mimic a gun, he demonstrated that it was impossible to shoot oneself at that angle by pulling the trigger with the fingers. The only way Olive could have managed it was if she had used her thumb. But, he continued, unlike the fingers, the thumb did not move on a vertical plane; it rotated slightly, which would have resulted in a skewed shot. And this had not been the case: the path of the bullet that he and Dr Béroud had observed during the autopsy suggested that the revolver had remained perfectly still against her forehead.

The site of the wound was also suspicious, he said. 'When people commit suicide, they generally shoot themselves in the mouth or the temple. Statistics show that only thirteen per cent of gunshot suicides are to the forehead.'

The finding that had struck him most, however, was the presence of the chewed piece of fruit at the top of her oesophagus: she had only just swallowed when the bullet entered her brain and all motor function stopped. Death, Dr Rey concluded, had come unexpectedly.

Putting all his findings together, he was confident that Olive had been seated and eating when someone standing in front of her held the revolver to her head. She had barely had time to finish her mouthful before they pulled the trigger. There would have been minimal blood loss, he added, due to the lack of exit wound.

Rey's quiet testimony appeared to have impressed the court. It had not, however, convinced his old friend Pierre Cot, who took the stand after him.

Dr Pierre Cot giving his testimony.

'It was suicide,' Dr Cot began. 'I found Miss Branson lying with her left arm raised towards her head. She was left-handed and her fingers were folded over her thumb, indicating her final gesture: that of squeezing the trigger.'

No one mentioned the similar gesture of reaching up to grab the barrel of a revolver pointed at one's head, but the statement that Olive had been left-handed did cause a brief objection from the advocate general: hadn't she even said in her letter to François – a letter that had been read out to the court earlier that morning – that she was writing in pencil 'because my right arm hurts'?

'Left-handed or not,' the doctor replied, 'it was with her left thumb that she pulled the trigger. I found the revolver two feet from her head, exactly where it would have fallen as it slipped out of her left hand.'

'And you're relying solely on that fact to declare that Miss Branson took her own life?' asked President Lafont.

'That and the rest of my findings.'

To the court's surprise, the doctor produced a small Browning pistol from his pocket and pressed it against his own forehead at forty-five degrees. He pulled the trigger first with his left thumb and then with his right. Each time, the gun remained steady.

'See? It's quite easy.'

The Browning was lighter, and a good two-and-a-half inches shorter, than Olive's Orbea Hermanos, which sat on the dais in front of President Lafont, but the demonstration had the required effect. The atmosphere in the room shifted. After a brief, pounding silence, the jurors turned to each other and began to mutter in low voices. Whispers scuttled back and forth along the public benches, while Dr Cot stood triumphant.

In an attempt to regain balance, Lafont asked Dr Rey to join his old friend at the bar. It was a pointless confrontation. The two men were snippily courteous with each other, with Dr Cot reminding his 'dear colleague' that he had not seen the body until it was removed from the coffin a full six days after his own observations, and Dr Rey reminding his 'dear colleague' about the rotation of the thumb, the food in her oesophagus and the fact that, all things considered, it would have been an extraordinary way for someone to kill herself.

'Extraordinary, but not impossible,' Dr Cot retorted. 'As of yet, my dear colleague, there is no agreed code of suicide. Why, there are people who choose to slit their throats and then climb six flights of stairs to throw themselves out of a window!'

Lafont soon gave up his attempt to reconcile the doctors' opinions and called an adjournment for lunch.

*

Two hours later, after everyone had elbowed their way back into the court, a large item covered in sackcloth was carried into the centre of the room, clanging as it was set down. When the sackcloth was removed, it was revealed to be a portion of the iron grille from the cistern, which had arrived by train from the evidence store in Marseille. François shifted his chair against the wooden panelling at the rear of the dock, set back from his four guards.

Dr Edgar Leroy was the first to take the stand. He had tried to excuse himself from appearing, January being a busy time on account of winter illnesses. But, despite his offer of a written statement, Lafont had insisted on questioning him in person. Now, he kept his answers brief.

He described the neurasthenia Olive had battled the summer before her death, for which he had prescribed a month's rest cure at Sault followed by a long sojourn with her family back in England. She had returned to Provence full of life, he said, only to gradually become more depressed as the winter took hold. One of her primary concerns had been her standing in the village and whether it corresponded to the amount of good she had done. She seemed to feel a lack of gratitude.

Dorlhac de Borne, sitting directly opposite the jury box, had selected an outsized red carpenter's pencil as that day's writing implement and was making copious notes. The giant pencil, however, stopped moving at Lafont's next question.

'Yet, you do not believe her death was due to suicide?'

'I did at first, but after conducting my own experiments in the cistern, I concluded it would have been extremely difficult for her to have done so in the manner suggested.' Gesturing to the iron grille, Leroy explained, 'I'm roughly the same size as Miss Branson and found it impossible to climb inside without ripping my undershirt. Nor could I recreate the necessary actions in the cramped space.'

'But would you say it was impossible?' This came from one of the jurors.

The pencil hovered in anticipation.

'Difficult, but not impossible.'

When Guibbal took the stand, he too tried to convince the jury that suicide should be ruled out.

'I ask you, gentlemen, why any woman, whether sane or mad, would climb the wall of that cistern to commit suicide? Can you imagine a woman who is eating a hearty meal, who has three lamb chops and asparagus, plus cheese and fruit, laid out in front of her, who has ordered fifty litres of oil and a large crate of milk – can you see her suddenly deciding, after Pinet's visit, to kill herself in such an extraordinary way?'

The barrage of questions that followed, however, suggested that perhaps they could. The spectre of Eugène Blanc's pamphlet hung over the jury box, giving Guibbal the opportunity to correct some misapprehensions about the case that had gained strength since its publication. In response to one query, for example, he said: 'It has indeed been claimed that, on a whim, Miss Branson elected to kill herself in the ancient funerary dress of such-and-such an English county. But, gentlemen, I have made inquiries in the most authoritative British circles and no one has any idea what that might mean.'

Guibbal also managed to explain his findings that proved François had been at Mas de Chiscale at the time the shot was fired: his trip to the Marseille Observatory, followed by the firm testimony of the travelling salesmen and the Pascal siblings that put François's car in the valley after nine o'clock. But the jurors kept coming back to the mechanics of suicide versus murder.

'You have to see the cistern,' Guibbal kept saying. 'If you haven't seen the cistern, you can't understand anything about this case. Once you've seen it, the idea of suicide is absurd and the case for murder is beyond doubt.'

But the jury would not be seeing the cistern. A visit to Les Baux had been mooted when planning the trial but rejected for lack of time. Guibbal, therefore, tried to put his point across in other ways. Describing the interior of the tank, he said, 'It measures one metre twenty deep—'

A mistake. Juror Six, a young building contractor from Marseille, pointing to the plan in his dossier, said, 'This says it's one metre thirty-five.'

Guibbal could only reassert that, given the dimensions of the cistern and the findings of the autopsy, suicide was materially impossible. Besides, why would someone choose to use a firearm in a water tank, where the cartridges might get wet and not fire? Even the idea that Olive had climbed into the cistern without scraping her skin was implausible.

Sensing Guibbal was on the back foot, Dorlhac de Borne stepped in. 'Tell me, how is it implausible to descend into the cistern without scratching one's skin when it's feasible to dispose of a corpse without damaging it?'

'Because Miss Branson wouldn't have taken the precautions taken by the murderer.'

'So as not to hurt her, you mean?'

This brought laughter from the public benches, at which Lafont thundered that he would not tolerate any further outbursts.

Dorlhac de Borne pushed on. 'Isn't it true that you thought it was suicide at first, but told Monsieur fforde that you'd go "looking for a hair in an egg", as we say in France?'

Guibbal smiled. 'I apologize for that expression; you certainly wouldn't find it in the writings of Paul Valéry,[*] although

---

[*] A noted essayist, philosopher and Symbolist poet.

Monsieur fforde said they have it in England, too. But, when I said that, I hadn't seen the cistern. We only had the report of the gendarmes.'

Turning to the jury, Dorlhac de Borne remarked, 'I suggest instead that Monsieur Guibbal was making it up as he went along. He imagined he was writing some cheap detective serial.'

Continuing his theme of Guibbal's shortcomings as an investigator, the lawyer turned back to Guibbal and asked, 'Did you not grill my client and his brother-in-law Monsieur Girard for nearly twelve hours straight, without rest or respite? Is that not akin to moral torture?'

'I know it's the fashion these days to accuse the police of third-degree methods, but Miss Branson had been murdered. I was only doing my duty.'

There was a loud hiss from the audience.

'Did you not also urge my client to confess,' the lawyer continued, 'under the pretext that Girard had already "nibbled the bait", as they say?'

'A ruse, you mean?' Guibbal smiled. 'It's possible. Police the world over sometimes find that sort of thing necessary in the interests of society. Don't lawyers have theirs?'

'I forbid you to say that!' Dorlhac de Borne's black eyebrows shot up. 'Answer my question! Did you or did you not tell my client that Girard had implicated him in the murder, while also telling Girard that Pinet had confessed?'

At this, the advocate general got up from his seat. 'I find your line of questioning insidious. How dare you ask a policeman to divulge professional secrets?'

Boissier's intervention prompted another from Lafont, and soon they were all arguing at the top of their voices over whether such questions were within the remit of the defence. By the time the din had abated, however, Guibbal had made up his own mind.

'I admit I used various tricks to get to the truth,' he said, 'but I can't say I tried that one.'

It was at this moment that Dorlhac de Borne's hitherto silent colleague, Paul Muselli, spoke up.

'Monsieur Guibbal, in your soul and conscience, do you truly believe that François Pinet is guilty?'

'He's certainly no stranger to this crime.'

'Yet, all we've heard are theories. We're waiting for proof.'

'It's all in my report.'

The advocate general was now waving that report from the dais. 'It is not for Monsieur Guibbal to prove anything! That's my job. But my arguments are based on his findings and you will hear them tomorrow!'

The mood in the court was still fractious when Inspector Laforgue stepped up to the bar. After describing how he and Guibbal had homed in on François as a suspect, he was asked by Lafont, 'And didn't you also establish that his sister – Miss Branson's housekeeper – had appeared before the assizes on charges of infanticide?'

Laforgue had barely opened his mouth to answer when Dorlhac de Borne leapt in. 'This is unspeakable! I had the honour of defending this woman. She is an honest mother of three – and she was acquitted!'

Boissier retorted, 'Still, we need to know the environment in which we are operating.'

The matter, however, was dropped.

Sergeant Fabre was next. He approached his testimony with gravity, focusing on the discovery of Olive's body and the position of her corpse and revolver in the cistern. The only personal opinion he allowed himself was that she had always seemed eccentric and fanciful in his dealings with her.

In answer to questions from the jury, he said François's attitude had been unremarkable and that he'd understood that his visit to Olive's solicitor – presented by the prosecution as evidence of his eagerness to inherit the hotel – was simply to find the address of her relatives in London to inform them of her disappearance.

'I simply can't accept the theory of murder,' he concluded.

'You only say that because your findings were incomplete and now you don't want to admit you were wrong,' scoffed the advocate general.

Fabre's bulbous nose twitched slightly, but he kept his composure as Dorlhac de Borne intervened on his behalf: 'You are insulting the gendarmerie! This man has served loyally for twenty-seven years, and this is his reward?'

Fabre himself said, 'I swear on my conscience, the more I think about it, the less I can believe it was murder.'

Fabre's evidence had buoyed the defence, and François sat up a little straighter as Joseph was called to the stand. Lafont explained to the jury that the Girards were appearing at his discretion, but were not under oath, and their testimony should not be taken as evidence.

And so, Joseph began. Laboriously and monotonously, he inched his way through the day he found Olive's body. As he took detour after detour, the air seemed to seep from the room and the jurors began to nod off. Neither Dorlhac de Borne nor Boissier dared intervene for fear of prolonging the agony. After twenty minutes, however, Lafont could contain himself no longer.

'Hurry up and get to the cistern!'

'Oh, I'm still a *long* way from the cistern.'

'Just get on with it!'

But Joseph had lost his flow. His comic spluttering prompted a roar of laughter from the back of the room, and Lafont, at the end of his tether, ordered the guards to clear the public benches. Reluctantly, the spectators filed out into the corridor, eyeing the soldiers' bayonets as they passed. Within minutes, however, they had returned through another door and retaken their seats. If anything, the courtroom seemed more crowded than before. Lafont closed his eyes and gestured for Joseph to continue.

Some time later, when Joseph had come to the end of his statement, the president broke the torpor.

'What you have not mentioned is that, at the time of your discovery, you thought suicide was impossible.'

'I was in a state, back then.'

Boissier stood up and pointed to the grille. 'On the third of May, you said to the police you'd have to be an acrobat to get through that opening. Three days later, you were still adamant that Miss Branson could not have entered the cistern alive. Of course, your brother-in-law had not been arrested then, and you had not read a certain small pamphlet. Yet, now, you've changed your mind. I'm sure the gentlemen of the jury will take note.'

When Marie-Thérèse joined her husband at the stand, her words were as cautious as his had been long-winded. Pressed by Boissier on her interviews with Guibbal and Rochu, she said she couldn't remember anything she'd said. In the course of her description of Olive's domestic arrangements, she did, however, intimate that Olive had entertained other men at Mas de Chiscale.

Boissier confronted her on this point. 'Are you trying to say that someone other than your brother visited Miss Branson on the night of her death?'

Silence.

'Who else could go near the dogs without them barking?'

'Lots of people.'

'Name them: you, your husband, Pinet – and then who?'

'A host of others!'

When the advocate general redirected his question at Joseph, Marie-Thérèse started to scream François's innocence at the top of her lungs, jolting the sleeping jurors awake and drowning out anything her husband might have been trying to say.

The next witness was a young priest from Sorgues, which momentarily caused some confusion as people tried to remember how a man of the cloth fitted into the story. The Abbé Louis Blanc, however, turned out to be a childhood friend of François, and he had been called by the defence as a character witness.

Despite having turned up late, he soon charmed both the jury and President Lafont. Stepping up to the bar in his black cassock and soft leather motorcycle helmet, the diminutive priest reminisced sweetly about growing up in Les Baux. He and François had taken their first communion together, he said, and later shared barracks during their military service, but had since lost touch. One journalist reported a solitary tear rolling down François's cheek as his old friend described the boy he had once been.

As to the matter at hand, the Abbé Blanc couldn't imagine his friend descending into a fit of murderous violence. 'He's too laid back, too lymphatic. Miss Branson must have killed herself.'

'But are you aware of what's in the indictment?' Lafont asked.

'*Monsieur le président*,' replied the Abbé, smiling and blushing slightly, 'questions of money and passion are hardly my responsibility.'

Félix Tougay, André Ricaud, Vincent Aracil and François Griffe the shepherd were no more enlightening when they testified about hearing the gunshot. All four insisted that it had been almost dark and between quarter to nine and nine o'clock, and refused to accept the Marseille Observatory's view that it had been dark by eight thirty. Dorlhac de Borne also called André Graugnard to recount his tale of seeing a distant, open-topped car enter the yard of Mas de Chiscale just before nightfall.

And, with that, the hearing was suspended at six o'clock. It had been a long day, and one that had done little to settle any of the matters under debate.

III

By the time the trial resumed on Saturday morning, the crowds outside the courthouse had swelled to alarming proportions. Fearing a riot when the verdict was delivered, the authorities had doubled the number of troops guarding the entrance.

What that verdict would be, however, was impossible to forecast. The press were divided. Public sympathy, if the outbursts inside the court were anything to go by, lay on the side of the accused. Yet, the jurors had proved uncommonly dedicated to their duties and had been questioning both sides in equal measure. The case was an enigma. For every argument against François Pinet, there seemed to be another in his favour, and some of the testimonies they had heard so far had been in direct contradiction to one another.

Someone had to be lying, but who? Was it the Baussencs, living up to their reputation of aggressive parochialism? Or the police, acting on the orders, it was said, of shadowy figures high up in government? The trial was halfway through and it still wasn't clear if a murder had been committed at all, let alone if François Pinet was culpable.

When the doors to the courtroom were opened at eight o'clock, François was already seated in the dock, seemingly refreshed by his night's sleep. His eyes darted around the room, taking everything in. Fifteen minutes later, President Lafont arrived with a determination to increase the pace of the proceedings. As he explained, there were still twenty-four witnesses to go, as well as a repeat appearance by Dr Rey at the request of the jury. He would therefore clear the public benches – definitively this time – if there was so much as a hint of disruptive behaviour.

The first hour was taken up with a parade of witnesses who did little to clear up the jury's confusion over François's whereabouts at the time the shot was fired. The Monte-Carlo's bellboy swore François had parked his car in the hotel garage at eight thirty, just as it got dark. Others claimed to have seen him in the bar ten or fifteen minutes later, when it was still light. A few blurted out quick words of support as they were ushered away. 'He's a lovely boy, you know!' 'Everyone is for him!'

The travelling salesmen whom François claimed to have seen standing in front of the headlights of their car confirmed it had still been light when they drove down to the valley to see Marguerite Patin and her children. If François had seen their headlights, Ludovic Porte said, it had to have been after they left at nine o'clock, although they had not seen him pass.

The advocate general's satisfaction at this statement was tempered somewhat when Marguerite Patin herself took the stand. At first, she spoke so softly that no one could make out what she was saying. After multiple attempts to get her to speak up, however, it transpired that she couldn't remember when Porte and Piney had arrived or how long they had stayed, but she thought it had still been light.

With the jury becoming visibly confused, Boissier confidently announced that the next witness would bring the necessary clarity and prove exactly what time François had left Mas de Chiscale. But when Louis Pascal took the stand, it seemed he, too, was suffering from amnesia. Having previously said that he'd heard both the merchants' van and François's car, at nine o'clock and nine-fifteen respectively, now he would only say that two vehicles had passed his house while he was having his supper with his wife and he had no idea of the hour.

'Well, what time do you usually eat?' The president was losing patience.

'It depends.' The farmer shrugged.

The defence followed this minor victory with a series of witnesses from Les Baux, who each added a brushstroke to Dorlhac de Borne's portrait of Olive as an unstable eccentric. Etienne Patin cheerfully told the court about the time she had confided in him about feeling suicidal; Andrée Sous confirmed that Olive appeared to have had something 'weighing on her mind' the day before her death.

Regarding her disputed left-handedness, Madeleine Vayssière spoke of accompanying Olive on sketching trips around Les Baux. 'She drew as well with her left hand as with her right,' she said. 'In fact, I once saw her draw her dog entirely with her left.' This hitherto unnoticed ambidexterity was confirmed by Paul Isnard, the ill-tempered decorator whom Olive had hired to repaint the hotel.

Next came an estate agent from Tarascon to attest to François's moral and financial character. Introducing himself as a friend of François's father, Jean Rouget made it clear that he had nothing but respect for his late friend's son. He had always been happy to lend him money when things got tight – for car repairs, for example, or for the hotel – which François had always faithfully returned.

'Wasn't one of those loans for a large sum?' President Lafont asked.

'Yes. Five thousand francs – and he paid it back.'

'And didn't Pinet approach you again two days after Miss Branson's death?'

Rouget admitted that François had appeared at his office on the Monday morning, seeking eight to ten thousand francs to cover his share of the ice factory. After going through the proposal, however, Rouget had deemed the venture not in François's best interests and refused the loan. François, however, had seemed unconcerned.

'Did you discuss anything else?'

'He told me Miss Branson had killed herself.'

'Did you ask if there would be an autopsy?'

'Yes, and he said there was no need.'

'And how did Pinet seem to you?'

'I'd say he was more cheerful than usual.'

Before the jury could consider this last remark, Muselli cried, 'Which proves he hadn't just committed a murder!'

There was a ripple of excitement when the prosecution announced the next witness. Rumour in Aix had it that this was Eugène Blanc's mysterious 'Monsieur B.', the louche, pyjamaed artist who had allegedly chased Olive around the hills like a faun. They were soon disabused of that notion when the prim figure of Jean Baltus stepped up to the stand, looking as likely to wear pyjamas in public as he was to indulge in unnecessarily vigorous exercise. His testimony nevertheless caused a stir.

Clearly nervous, he spoke in agitated bursts about his long friendship with Olive and the enthusiasm with which she had spoken about her future in her beloved Provence. He'd found the news of her apparent suicide incomprehensible.

'Miss Branson was so attached to life that she had an almost excessive concern for her health. She would tremble at a draught,' he said. 'I thought that perhaps she might have left a letter among her papers to enlighten us, but we only found postcards that had not been sent, and there was a book open on the table—'

'A book, you say?' Lafont interrupted. 'What title, please?'

'It was an English novel – *The Silver Spoon*.'

'What is it about?'

'I have no idea. I haven't read it.'

Lafont thought he detected a note of impertinence in Baltus's tone.

'When I ask you a question, you will answer politely, monsieur.'

Baltus stammered an apology.

'Well, go on! Tell us what else struck you that afternoon.'

'The cistern. That wall is two metres high. Even I couldn't climb it without difficulty, and I pride myself on a certain agility.'

He went on to describe how Olive's body had seemed to him frozen in a gesture of defence, and how he'd been shocked by the speed at which Dr Cot had reached his conclusions: 'I said to myself, "They're very quick to bury people round here!"'

This observation, he continued, had prompted him to take matters into his own hands. 'As a friend of England, I made myself its honorary representative.'

Howls of laughter filled the room at the pomposity of this statement.

'*Monsieur le juge* . . .' Baltus appealed to the dais.

'That's *monsieur le président*, if you don't mind!' Lafont's rebuke was sharp, but so was his call for order.

When the din had subsided, he asked what action Baltus had taken in his self-appointed role.

'I sent a telegram to Miss Branson's cousin in London.'

'Ah, yes. Monsieur fforde, who arrived two days later. And what was his view?'

'That suicide was impossible. He said, "I'm going to consult forensic doctors in Marseille; I don't trust the opinion of that little country doctor who is barely capable of treating a common cold."'

At this, Dr Cot had to be restrained by his wife from launching himself at the artist.

'And did you see the Pinet family?'

'Yes. Pinet was as calm as you see him here. Not much in favour of an autopsy, mind. His sister, Madame Girard, was also very keen to bury Miss Branson as soon as possible. She even offered the use of their family vault, which I found very obliging.'

It was now Dorlhac de Borne who objected to Baltus's tone. This, in turn, invited the wrath of the advocate general, and the lawyers were soon lost in another heated argument. Lafont, who had been fiddling with Olive's revolver on the dais, stood up, yelling and gesticulating wildly for them to calm down, unaware that he was brandishing a weapon in his own courtroom.

Once order had been restored and the gun moved out of reach of Lafont's absent-minded fingers, the court's attention returned to Baltus, who was standing in shock at the bar.

'Did you know about Miss Branson's relationship with the accused?'

'Absolutely not,' Baltus replied after regaining his composure. 'It never even occurred to me that a woman of her refinement and delicacy would entertain such a thing.'

He gave a small, nervous smile, which soon disappeared as the jury bombarded him with questions. They wanted to know about Olive's dogs ('Very dangerous'), what he and Olive had talked about ('Local news, mostly') and whether she was left-handed ('She was no more left-handed than she was neurasthenic . . .').

'I have always believed,' he said finally, 'that death didn't even exist for a person like Miss Branson.'

'Well,' said Dorlhac de Borne, 'life can sometimes make one stumble.'

As England's friend slipped away from the stand, he passed the lumbering Louis Vigne, who, after swearing the oath, spoke of his own history with Olive. She had always been an enthusiastic day-tripper, he said, organizing her outings with scrupulous attention to detail. As a result, she could be quite strident when giving him instructions.

'How much did your services cost her a year?' Lafont asked.

'Oh, God . . . thirty or thirty-five thousand francs?'

'And did Pinet always accompany her?'

'More often than not – him or his family.'

When asked whether he'd known about the affair, Louis admitted that he'd had his suspicions.

'And who paid when they dined out?'

'Miss Branson, of course.'

'Never Pinet?'

At this, François, who had been silent the entire day, stood up. Of all the points raised so far, he had decided that this was one he wished to clarify.

'Actually, I always paid the bill,' he said.

'With your own money?'

'Well, no. Miss Branson would slip that to me when she went to powder her nose.'

'And you gave her the change?'

'Oh, it was never more than ten or fifteen francs.' François shrugged.

Lafont narrowed his eyes. 'You take it very lightly. You could have paid for yourself, especially when you were running the hotel on her behalf.'

Dorlhac de Borne answered for his client. 'But did Miss Branson ever ask him to?'

Lafont raised a stern finger and returned to Louis. 'Monsieur Vigne, did Pinet not say to you, "That woman annoys me"?'

'Yes, but he was laughing as he said it.'

Georges Arlaud, bald and resplendent in baggy plus fours, was introduced by the prosecution as a publicity agent for Les Baux, and immediately launched into a paean to the beauty of the landscape surrounding the village and the damage the case had done to its reputation and that of the excellent Hotel Reine Jeanne. He had just begun to tell the court of a recent attempt to set fire to that hotel when he was interrupted by Dorlhac de Borne.

'Monsieur Arlaud, are you an enemy of the Pinets?'

'No.'

'Yet you have written several times to the public prosecutor against them. I have the letters here.'

Without giving Arlaud the chance to disclose the allegations of bribery contained within, the lawyer then asked about his work as a publicity agent. Arlaud explained that he was a promoter of Provençal tourism and put himself at the service of agencies and hotelkeepers.

'But how, precisely, do you undertake this promotion?'

'I give illustrated talks and publish brochures.'

The lawyer had already started to rummage in his attaché case. 'And these?'

Arlaud was silent as Dorlhac de Borne held up four large photographs for the court to see. They did indeed show the beauty of the Provençal landscape, although this was somewhat overshadowed by other attractions draped over the rocks of the Val d'Enfer, offering olive branches up to the heavens.

'Don't you also publish, as "publicity",' the lawyer continued, 'pictures of naked women under the almond trees?'

Georges Arlaud tried to protest that the nudes represented only a portion of his artistic output, and that he was a respected landscape photographer who had worked throughout France, Tunisia and Morocco, but Dorlhac de Borne dismissed his claims. 'As someone from the area said to me, "It's not art that man produces, it's filth!"'

Several jurors, naturally, asked to assess this for themselves. Amid raucous laughter from the public benches, Lafont called for the photographs to be brought to the dais. After inspecting each one, he remarked that, as far as publicity went, their main message seemed to be that not only did the women of Provence exist largely in a state of nudity, but they were also fat. This caused a further eruption, which he dealt with by ordering a short break so the jury could form their own opinion.

When the court returned, however, Arlaud was nowhere to be found, having made a hasty exit. Instead, Dr Rey was recalled to the stand at the request of the jury. Juror Six, it transpired, had been considering the doctor's evidence and had a question about the morsel of food trapped in Olive's oesophagus.

Although new to forensic science, the young building contractor proved as adept at cross-examination as any jurist. 'You stated this "bolus" was evidence that Miss Branson died while swallowing a mouthful of food,' he said. 'But could it not have come the other way, travelling up from her stomach?'

'It would be strange, but not impossible,' Rey replied.

'And could a reflex have stopped the bolus *before* she died? Through a contraction of the oesophagus, for example?'

'Again, not impossible, but the rest of my—'

'Could nausea cause such a contraction? From taking in water, say?'

'Yes, but Miss Branson had not swallowed any water.'

'Or a strong emotion?'

Boissier leapt in. 'As in a person about to be murdered!'

'Or a woman holding a revolver to her head, preparing to kill herself,' retorted Dorlhac de Borne.

'What, in between two bites of banana?'

The lawyers glared at each other.

Rey ignored them both and replied to the juror: 'A very strong emotion, yes. But—'

A wave of sensation swept over the court at this admission, drowning out Rey's protest that other forensic evidence proved Olive had been dead by the time she entered the cistern.

The juror had no more questions.

As the lunch hour slowly approached, Lafont became ever more ill-tempered. He turned first on Dorlhac de Borne and Boissier as they sniped at each other during Raoul Dumas's inconsequential testimony about the hotel feud, and then on the witnesses themselves.

Dominique Muselli, the justice of the peace for Saint-Rémy (and father of the deputy defence counsel), received a dressing down for his 'exceedingly nonchalant' handling of the initial investigation, but it was Daniel Millaud who suffered the most. When the elderly politician took the stand, his physical frailty was evident in the tremble in his hands. His oratorical skills, however, seemed as sharp as ever as he began an impassioned defence of François.

He'd barely got started before Lafont cut him off. 'You're not here to make a speech.'

'But we carried out our own investigation!'

'That is of no value,' the advocate general cut in.

But Millaud was determined to carry on. 'Had it been murder,' he continued, 'there would have been signs, there would have been blood—'

'Enough! Go and sit down.' The president's tone was brutal.

Indignant, Millaud started shouting, 'Murder is a material impossibility! All of Les Baux supports him!'

'Go!'

As he was escorted out of the room, Millaud made one last protest. 'We're not even allowed to explain? Disgusting!'

Lafont's attention, however, had been redirected towards the public benches, where the soft, comic wail of a mouth organ had been detected during their exchange. No one would own up, but there was no time for a mass eviction because, in line with Lafont's own wishes for a fast-moving trial, the next defence witness was already making his way to the front of the court.

It wasn't entirely clear why Eugène Blanc had been summoned, other than to face the wrath of the president and advocate general. A self-appointed sleuth, he had nothing to add to the evidence other than his own conclusions, which Paul Muselli nonetheless encouraged him to repeat.

When he had finished, the advocate general held up a copy of the yellow booklet. 'Gentlemen of the jury,' Boissier said, 'every one of you has had a copy of this sent to you – no doubt free of charge.' He read out a few extracts relating to the motivations of Guibbal and Rochu for 'persecuting' François, which he deemed particularly egregious. President Lafont agreed it was a scurrilous piece of work.

'Monsieur Blanc, you are a disgrace to your country,' Boissier spat. 'When one writes such things against the judiciary and the police, one does not appear at the witness stand.'

'On the contrary,' Dorlhac de Borne argued, 'it shows true courage. Besides, he was only echoing what Monsieur Millaud had said in the chamber of the General Council.'

At the mention of Millaud, Dorlhac de Borne and Boissier went into battle once more over the way Boissier had dismissed the esteemed politician. It was therefore a relief when Lafont called the morning's final witness: an engineer who led the jury through a dull but uncontroversial explanation of the cistern's construction.

THE BRANSON MYSTERY.

MORE LIVELY PASSAGES IN COURT.

An "Offhand" Witness Censured.

PAMPHLET ATTACK ON THE POLICE.

INCREASED PUBLIC EXCITEMENT.

After a two-and-a-half-hour break, during which the restaurants and doughnut sellers in the Place de Verdun did good trade, it was time for the closing statements. The advocate general was the first to take the floor. Pacing the narrow platform in front of the dais, Boissier addressed the jury in his strong Marseille accent.

'Gentlemen of the jury, remain deaf to all noises from outside. There has been much speculation about Miss Branson's death, but none of it must find an echo here. This is a serious and deeply delicate matter. You are here to judge a man with all the strength and energy you can muster, and I ask that you fulfil your mission with the same conscientiousness as I am fulfilling mine.

'The judicial conscience of the examining magistrate charged with investigating the crime of Les Baux made it his duty to bring this man before you. Yes, criminal cases involve hard and cruel truths, but I am convinced you will examine with equanimity the one laid before you in this tragedy.'

Boissier's bony finger suddenly shot out towards François, as his voice boomed through the court: 'I accuse this man of coldly murdering Miss Branson on the twenty-sixth of April last, having already bled her purse dry!'

Boissier let the startled court, which was still digesting its lunch, recover from his theatrical outburst before stepping down into the centre of the room to continue in a more sedate manner. François, he said, was an idler and spendthrift. He had made no effort to engage in lasting work since finishing his military service in 1925, relying instead on loans and inheritances to fund his lifestyle. The arrival of a wealthy Englishwoman in Les Baux had opened up another income stream. In the two years before her death, Boissier reminded the jury, François had cashed cheques from Olive worth over 6,000 francs, not to mention extracting the promise of the hotel, while grousing about her 'irritating' ways behind her back.

Olive, he continued, had come to Provence to forge her ideal life and 'forget the London fog.' She was a generous, educated and cultured woman. Yes, she had lived under the guard of four enormous dogs, she dressed in a 'bohemian' manner and kept her studio and bedroom – her innermost sanctums – in a state of cluttered chaos, all of which had led to unwarranted speculation about her sanity. The Baussencs thought Miss Branson eccentric, Boissier suggested, 'because they didn't understand her need for solitude and art.'

Addressing François, he said, 'For her, you were a ray of sunshine; she loved you deeply and sincerely. You could have ignored it, but instead you turned it into a tragedy. You murdered the woman who adored you just because you needed money. It was an odious crime.'

François's face was a mask as the advocate general turned back to the jury. 'Miss Branson was killed at her home just before eight thirty on Friday the twenty-sixth of April last year. It wasn't suicide, as Doctor Cot believes. Although an excellent general practitioner, he has no experience in forensic medicine. You should therefore rely only on the opinion of the two experts, Doctors Béroud and Rey, who know it was murder.'

Boissier reiterated the evidence from the autopsy, as well as indications from the testimonies of Cot and Fabre that proved his point. The weight of that evidence aside, he said, the idea that a woman would have gone into her garden and clambered up a high wall and through a small hatch to commit suicide was beyond belief. And, if the jury accepted – as it should – that she had been murdered, they also had to accept that only one person could have been responsible. 'People talk about the "Mystery of Les Baux",' he said, 'but there is no mystery here.'

By the time Boissier neared the end of his speech, the light outside the courtroom windows was beginning to fade. He had been talking for nearly two hours. With radiators puffing out winter warmth to an overcrowded room, he had long abandoned his black velvet toque and repeatedly removed his glasses to wipe them on his scarlet robes as sweat dripped from his gaunt brow. He had shouted, pleaded, reasoned and cajoled, and now he summoned the energy for one last righteous blast.

'So now, Pinet, no more lies! There is still time to confess. You were a good man until the evening of the twenty-sixth of April, and a confession will count in your favour upon sentencing. So,

I urge you to find the strength and courage to tell the truth. Confess! Confess!'

François did not move.

The advocate general let out a deep breath and returned to his seat, where Lafont gave him a melancholy smile.

It was quarter to five when Dorlhac de Borne rose on behalf of the defence. All his previous displays of fury were put aside as, over the course of another two hours of skilful and uninterrupted oratory, he entreated the jury to acquit his client.

'I hope God will reveal the truth,' he began in a warm and sonorous voice. 'Gentlemen, those words are not mine, but of one of Miss Branson's relatives, who is convinced she took her own life.' Olive, he said, was a complex character: athletic and adventurous, but also romantic and whimsical. She knew how to box and had once travelled with the circus – even performing one night, it was said, as an Amazon. And it was these qualities that had drawn her, six years earlier, to the 'wild and picturesque' Les Baux – a place like no other in the Midi.

But what had drawn her to François Pinet? It was, Dorlhac de Borne said, 'to fill a void in her heart' following her divorce. As the Baussenc witnesses had made clear, François was a tranquil soul, and he had shown her kindness at a difficult time. He was also young, and Olive had developed a strong attachment to him as she sensed her own youth slipping away. She had showered him with gifts, trying to buy his affection, but the more she spoiled him, the more she changed him.

At this, several heads on the public benches nodded sagely.

Wasn't Pinet's eventual withdrawal inevitable? Dorlhac de Borne continued. The young man's usual high moral standards had been warped – temporarily – by her largesse, and he had succumbed to her advances. But it could never have lasted: any attraction he may have felt for her could never have matched her hunger for his youth and vitality.

Dorlhac de Borne then turned to the days leading up to Olive's death. She was already downhearted, he said, having found her lover distant and indifferent on her return from London. And then? He waved a piece of paper at the court. It was the letter from Olive's art dealer informing her of the rejection by the Royal Academy, which he claimed she had received on the morning of her death.*

'And this is the crux, the sensitive point of the case,' he said. 'She felt doubly wounded, both in her pride as a woman and as an artist.' Although Olive had seemed bold and fearless, he reminded the jury, she was still a woman, and thereby at the mercy of female psychology. She was sentimental and prone to neurasthenia, and had only returned from an extended rest cure six months earlier.

With mournful eloquence, he described how her final day had passed in listlessness and silence. She had sat in her garden alone, had eaten alone. The novel she was reading was joyless and dispiriting, leaving her to ruminate on the cruel disappointments life had brought. And then, the final straw, which stripped away her one remaining illusion, that of being cherished: 'Pinet arrives. He unloads his car and does not stop. He leaves without a word, without a greeting. She has nothing left to live for.'

His imagining of her subsequent actions echoed that in Eugène Blanc's pamphlet, from its emotive delivery to the theory that she had killed herself in the cistern to be 'doubly sure' that she would succeed. And, like Blanc, he skipped over how she got to the top of the cistern, focusing instead on Dr Cot's theory of her final moments.

---

* It had, in fact, arrived the following week.

'Here she is, in front of the grille,' Dorlhac de Borne said. 'She slips inside, holds the mesh above her head with her right hand. With her left, she presses the revolver barrel between her eyes and fires with her thumb. She collapses and drops the weapon, where it is later found by her side.'

Miss Branson may not have left a note, he continued, but she had prepared for death. After François's departure, she had taken off her jewellery and dressed in a simple costume, in accordance with English funerary custom. This was not only a sign that she had taken her own life, he argued, but also proof that the prosecution's case was deeply flawed.

'Can't you see that, if Pinet had killed her for financial gain, he would have collected all these jewels and taken the seven hundred francs left in her bag?'

And how could François have killed Olive in the house? he asked. Where was the blood – other than dogs' blood, that is? And, if he had carried her to the cistern afterwards, wouldn't that also have left a trail which her dogs would have followed, alerting the searchers to the body? Even Dr Béroud, he reminded the jury, had admitted that he could not be absolutely certain Olive had been murdered.

The prosecution's case, he said, depended on supposition – supposition that there had been a murder, followed by supposition that François was the perpetrator. But the defence had actual evidence to the contrary. Producing another letter, he explained that it had been written by Olive in June 1928, and said she was 'tired of life.' Furthermore, hadn't she confessed prior suicidal thoughts to Etienne Patin, and hadn't Dr Leroy reported that her despair had begun to return in the new year?

Dorlhac de Borne's tone became increasingly sharp as he dissected Guibbal's report and pointed out all the instances in which suicide could offer an alternative explanation to murder.

He was, he said, astonished that Guibbal – the 'ace' of the Marseille Sûreté – had dismissed the possibility in all his dealings with François.

'Miss Branson killed herself, and everything proves it!' he cried. 'One cannot – one must not – look elsewhere for the cause of her death. Gentlemen of the jury, you must acquit!'

The courtroom was silent as Dorlhac de Borne returned to his seat and Muselli took his place.

'My colleague and friend,' the fair-haired lawyer said, 'you have amply demonstrated that we are not dealing with a murder, so I will say no more on that subject.' Instead, he gestured to the dock, where François had been weeping quietly ever since Dorlhac de Borne had evoked Olive's final hours.

François, he suggested to the jury, was easily misunderstood. He was a mild-mannered country boy, but his unusual reserve had led the Marseille police to misinterpret his behaviour both before and after the tragedy. Yes, he had been briefly led astray by the attentions of a wealthy, older woman, and had appeared to some to be unaffected by her death, but, as his fellow villagers had attested, he was constitutionally incapable of the vile crime of which he was accused.

'Gentlemen,' Muselli asked, 'dare you send an innocent man to a penal colony for a lifetime of forced labour? Do you want the responsibility of a miscarriage of justice that would trouble you forever? If, as I firmly believe, you know in your souls that it would be a grave error, I beg you to acquit!'

At twenty past eight, the jury left to start their deliberations and François was escorted back to the prison. Just fifteen minutes later, however, as the spectators were stretching their legs outside in the darkness, word got round that the jurors were ready to deliver their verdict. Everyone rushed back inside to retake their seats.

The dock remained empty, but Lafont was already addressing the foreman.

'Have you made your decision?'

'Yes.'

'Is François César Pinet guilty of murdering Edith May Olive Branson at Les Baux on the twenty-sixth of April 1929?'

The court held its breath.

'No.'

François's supporters leapt cheering from their seats and waved their handkerchiefs in the air. Lafont pleaded for calm and told the gendarmes to fetch François.

When François re-entered the dock, he was visibly stunned by the celebratory atmosphere. Muselli smiled at him and nodded. The verdict had been unanimous. François reached down to grab his lawyer's hand and kissed it, tears streaming down his pale face, as the cheers got even louder.

Lafont called for silence.

'Pinet, you are free to go.'

With barely disguised contempt, the president gathered up his papers, his hat and – in his turmoil – Olive's revolver, and made for the door. The soldiers below tried in vain to stop the stampede towards the dock. A group of men were attempting to drag François over the railing to hoist him onto their shoulders, while women showered him with kisses. The gendarmes in the dock batted them away. 'We're not at the theatre! He can only leave via the prison.'

As François was led back down the iron stairs to the tunnel leading to the prison, the crowds raced out into the night air and across the Place de Verdun to await his release.

There, journalists swarmed the Pinet family, who stood beside a waiting car, its headlights illuminating the prison walls. Marie-Thérèse sobbed loudly next to Joseph, as her eldest brother, Pierre, spoke for them all.

'Leave my poor brother alone. We're just simple people, and he has suffered enough.'

'But what's he going to do now?'

'I'd like him to work with me in Marseille. But first, we're going to Arles to see our mother.'

'What about the hotel?'

'The hotel is closed. He still inherits it, of course, but that's beside the point. We'd have to find the money for the death duties – if he even wants it.'

When the large wooden door of the prison swung open to more cheers, François's family shepherded him into the car and sped off towards Arles – and freedom.

IV

In truth, François Pinet would never be completely free. Throughout the remainder of his ninety-five years – through two marriages and endless hours behind the bar of his cafe in Arles – there would always be doubt. The trial had settled nothing but his fate.

There would be no appeal. The French authorities accepted the verdict with resignation, as did those keeping a watchful eye from the British Foreign Office.* But all credit, it was agreed, should be accorded the judicial system for the way it had conducted itself in the face of the lengthy propaganda campaign that sought to undermine it.

But had justice been served? Not for Olive. Stripping away all the speculation about her state of mind, one thing is clear: she did not commit suicide. The forensics are compelling on this point, from the mouthful of banana she had just swallowed to the path of the bullet as it entered her brain. The latter's downward trajectory would have been impossible for her to achieve with her long-barrelled Orbea Hermanos, unless she had used her thumb to pull the trigger. Yet she could not have used her thumb – left or right, it does not matter – as its natural rotation

---

* The Bransons had made no public comment since the day of François's arrest, and Arthur fforde had elected not to attend the trial, despite being called as a witness.

would have caused the revolver to twist slightly to one side, resulting in a skewed shot – which was not the case.

Someone, therefore, had got away with murder. But was that person François? Without doubt, Guibbal had been right to arrest him: François had been the last known person to speak to Olive, they had been conducting a secret affair and he was set to inherit the Hotel Monte-Carlo. Yet, as the investigation progressed, the case against him proved increasingly weak. All three points of the detection triad – motive, means, opportunity – were lacking in some respect.

Take, for example, his alleged motive: money. He needed 5,000 francs for the ice business, but why, if he was so desperate, had he not sought a loan from his father's friend, Jean Rouget, *before* resorting to murder? And why leave all Olive's cash and jewellery behind?

Even if he had been ignoring his immediate needs and looking instead to the future, murdering Olive while his financial situation was so poor made no sense. Having recently worked through the settlement of his father's estate, François knew how probate worked. Yes, Olive had left him the hotel, a generous bequest in principle, but – as he himself pointed out – in his current circumstances, he could not have afforded the death duties to take it up.

Problematic, too, is Rochu's theory that François, being accustomed to easy access to her purse, had seen red when Olive refused him money. For a start, Olive was highly attuned to anyone taking advantage of her and there was no sign François had ever done so – no sign, even, that she had given him money at all. All the cheques that Rochu proposed were gifts appear to correspond to the amounts that she fastidiously recorded in her pocket diary as dining expenses racked up at the Hotel Monte-Carlo or for petrol he had used on her behalf.

Furthermore, François never did anything in the heat of the moment. Everything his fellow villagers said about him being too laid back for violence is borne out by Olive's letters. She portrayed him as a kind and gentle young man – and she had known him better than most (as even Joseph had admitted to her once, when he'd wanted to know why François wasn't speaking to him). On the few occasions when François had been angry – mostly at his family – she had shown him to be a sulker rather than a lasher-outer. His emotions went inwards.

This introversion did him no favours during the investigation, however. Guibbal and his colleagues saw him as sly and uncooperative; the press latched on to his unusually calm demeanour and flat expression. They found his behaviour suspicious: why was he cleaning out the hotel garage while the search for his lover was underway, for example? Nobody could work him out. He wasn't crippled by shyness – he did, after all, have a track record with the ladies – nor did his attention to sartorial detail suggest he was lacking in confidence. He was just *odd*.

Today, all this might invite speculation that François lay somewhere on the autistic spectrum. And, while acknowledging the folly of amateur diagnoses – especially those undertaken on the deceased with limited evidence – there are some signs that this may have been the case. Two instances of him missing social cues – a common autistic trait – stand out in particular: his inappropriately timed question about whether there would be an autopsy, and his unnecessary and matter-of-fact confession to Félix Martin that he had not enjoyed sex with Olive, seemingly unaware that it did not help his case. As he said himself, Olive had often criticized him for not noticing things.

This leads to the question of the nature of their relationship, which was widely portrayed to be mercenary on François's part and desperate on Olive's. They clearly irritated one another on occasion – he being unobservant and she very talkative – yet they were also good friends. They had known each other for at least two years before embarking on their affair – if one can call an arrangement so apparently lacking in passion an affair. Rather, they appear to have been 'friends with benefits', as we would say today: two misfits who had come to an understanding based on mutual need and affection. Their sporadic outings to Marseille had given them both a chance to escape the Baux microscope while enjoying diversions not available locally – which, for Olive at least, included sex.

Still, if François wasn't the murderer, who was? Guibbal's notebooks have not survived beyond a few torn-out pages, and the judicial file only contains material directly relating to the case against François. At this distance of time, therefore, we can only speculate – but let's try.

Who had motive, means and opportunity? Guibbal had whittled down his list of suspects on the grounds that Olive's dogs had not barked when the gunshot was heard – a classic Sherlock Holmes clue that suggested the killer was well known to them. Yet should we accept this? François makes no mention of Frida or the pups' whereabouts during his visit, and they were not seen until Joseph's arrival the next morning. If we allow ourselves to speculate freely, who is to say the murderer did not dope them with a juicy steak prior to the assassination? This lengthens the list of potential suspects considerably.

That said, there is one person who could have got past the dogs, drugged or not: the alleged dog poisoner, Etienne Patin. There is no proof that he really was with his father at the time of the shooting. Five minutes earlier, however, he had been talking to Félix Tougay outside Carita, and it would have taken less than a minute to dash the hundred or so metres to Mas de Chiscale. But then, one has to ask, why choose that precise time, just as all the farmers were coming back from the fields, when he could have taken his revenge at any point?

Not Etienne Patin, then. Another of Olive's known enemies? Was her elderly neighbour, François Moucadel, driven to murder over a few scrubby olive trees and some long-departed shepherds? It seems unlikely. Raoul Dumas had a better motive but also a firm alibi, having been serving tables at the Hotel Reine Jeanne. Vernon Blake's movements, on the other hand, are unknown, and he certainly had the intellectual capacity to plot a murder, and, indeed, to manipulate subsequent events to cast suspicion on François. But his weapon of choice was the pen, not a revolver, and he had already elected not to use this against Olive, despite his threats.

Of course, there were also numerous guests staying at the two hotels, any of whom could have been silently harbouring a grudge against Olive. Rochu had cast his net wide on this account, and asked Scotland Yard, the Swiss police and the Sûreté in Paris to interview those who had returned home. Not all the responses have survived, but the names of the guests have – and none appears to have had any connection to Olive, her friends, or her family.

That leaves one shadowy figure, whose presence in the valley that night had no explanation: the mystery driver allegedly seen by André Graugnard entering Mas de Chiscale just before nightfall. Yes, the car could have been a fabrication; yes, it could have been François returning shortly after his departure to do away with his friend for reasons unknown. But what about Olive's alleged second lover, the artist supposedly unearthed by Eugène Blanc, whom no one – including May fforde – had ever heard of? Did he own a car? Did he have a temper? Had he found out about Olive's relationship with François . . . ?

As the *Petit Journal* wrote in 1930, 'The cistern has still not revealed its secrets.'¹ And, nearly a century later, we can say with some certainty that it never will.

Yet, despite the lack of answers, the tragic events of 26 April 1929 and all that followed offer a unique glimpse into the dying days of Old Provence, while also affording the pleasure of meeting Olive Branson – a complex and spirited character, who, for her artistic talent alone, deserves to be better known. Too many female artists of her generation have been forgotten by the art world: having been marginalized in life, few found champions to preserve their legacy after death. And so it was with Olive.

The last piece she ever sold was a large drawing of Les Baux (see p. 253), which was purchased two weeks before her death by Sir Cyril Butler, one of London's foremost collectors of contemporary art. When it was displayed alongside another of her drawings in 1946, the critic of *The Scotsman* singled them out as being 'of quite outstanding accomplishment' and mused about the artist:

> . . . a certain Olive Branson, doubtless one of those brilliant Slade girl-students who were at once the pride and the sorrow of Professor Tonks's life. Pride, because, highly educable as girls are, they displayed such remarkable gifts; sorrow, because too soon they fell out of the race, because too soon their creative impulse died; or more likely, found other channels of expression.[2]

But Olive had grappled with her creative impulse to the end, fighting against all that society expected of her. It had delivered her freedom, friendship and adventure; it was what took her, ultimately, to Provence. There, she had found inspiration in Les

Baux's strange beauty and rich culture, as well as the solitude she needed to work. She'd become captivated by its people with their strong, inter-familial bonds and quiet defiance, not to mention their willingness to engage in an energizing scrap.

> *Why wilt respectably, when you can have a good dust up from time to time to keep your circulation going?*[3]

Les Baux, however, was never the same after the trial. With the Hotel Monte-Carlo shuttered, the heart of the community was gone. François settled in Arles; Marie-Thérèse and Joseph also left for a number of years. The resentment, however, remained, as evidenced by some graffiti recently discovered during a survey of a disused quarry in the Val d'Enfer. Dated four days after François's acquittal and signed by a waitress from a local cafe, it reads: 'Miss Branson is a big filthy whore, a dirty slut.'

Nearby is a more respectful tribute to Vernon Blake, who died three months later. Despite his robust rebuttal in *Nor Rhône Nor Reason*, the stress of Eugène Blanc's allegations had laid him low, both physically and mentally. After developing pneumonia, he had been transferred to a nursing home in Avignon, where he died at the age of fifty-four. Before his decline, however, he had begun proceedings against Blanc for libel. That June, Blanc was ordered to pay the artist's estate 5,000 francs in damages. He retired from journalism the following year.

The feud between the hotels was settled when Raoul Dumas absorbed the Hotel Monte-Carlo into the Reine Jeanne. But few victories last forever: the Reine Jeanne has since been usurped by the five-star Baumanière resort in the Vallon de la Fontaine, a luxurious refuge for world leaders and celebrities.

Today, although the fêtes and traditions continue for ever greater crowds, very few of the old Baussenc families remain.

Many of the ruined houses have been restored, and the worn paths re-cobbled to withstand the feet of the 1.5 million tourists who visit the castle each year. Gift shops and galleries abound, while the limestone quarries host immersive art exhibitions.

Amid the throng, it can be difficult to picture the old Les Baux. But, on a quiet evening as the sun goes down, one can still catch a glimpse of that lost world. In the dappled light of the clifftop cemetery, the names on the vaults and gravestones record its last inhabitants: Tougay, Graugnard, Quenin, Vayssière, Griffe, Pascal, Patin, Pinet . . .

Olive's grave stands at the very edge of the cliff, looking out over the valley and across the plain. It is a simple tomb of golden stone, and the headstone reads:

Edith May
OLIVE BRANSON
('O.B.')
1885–1929

The stonemason got her birth year wrong. She was born in 1884.
What a life!!!!
But she would have loved the view.

The End.

Appendix: Olive Branson – Known Exhibited Works

Abbreviations

AAA	Allied Artists' Association
CAS	Calderon Art Society
ISSPG	International Society of Sculptors, Painters and Gravers
NBA	North British Academy
NEAC	New English Art Club
RA	Royal Academy of Arts
RGI	Royal Glasgow Institute of the Fine Arts
RHA	Royal Hibernian Academy of Arts
RSA	Royal Scottish Academy
SAF	Société des Artistes Français
SWA	Society of Women Artists

Year	Exhibition	Work
1908 (Winter)	SWA	*Herbert Ashby's Daisy* *Study of a man* x 2
1908 (Summer)	AAA	*'Short', a portrait* *Head of an Old Horse* *Untitled sketch* *Henry Smith of London* *Untitled pencil sketch*
1909 (Winter)	SWA	*The Charcoal Burners' Camp*
1909 (Summer)	AAA	*Smiler, the Cripple*

		The Flower Stall outside St Sulpice, Paris
		Victor Bourrer, Acrobat
1910 (Spring)	RSA	The Farm Stable
1910 (Summer)	RA	Interior of a Ruined Mill
1910 (Summer)	AAA	Romany Hop-Pickers
		The Bather
		The New Stacks
1911 (Spring)	RSA	Miss Freedom James
1911 (Spring)	RHA	Freedom – Janus
		Joey Buckland
		Wishanger
1911 (Summer)	CAS	The Doorkeepers of the Wild Beast Show
		Miss Ada Ohmy's Ring Horse
		Joey Buckland
		Travellers Hop-picking
		Alfie, the Ring Horse
1911 (Summer)	AAA	Miss Ada Ohmy's Ring Horse
		Travellers Hop-picking
		'Alfie': a portrait
1912 (Spring)	RHA	Alfie the Ring Horse
1912 (Spring)	SAF	Le Bois
1912 (Summer)	RA	The Wood, Wishanger
1912 (Summer)	CAS	Various circus drawings and etchings
1912 (Summer)	AAA	The Ring Horse Tent
		The Circus Band
		The Circus Tent
1912 (Autumn)	NBA	Unknown colour prints

Appendix: Olive Branson – Known Exhibited Works

1913 (Summer)	AAA		*Behind the World's Fair, Islington*
			'Topsy', sketch of elephant for colour print
			Giro San on the Rope, sketch for colour print
1914 (Autumn)	ISSPG		Unknown etchings
1919 (Summer)	NEAC		*Havre*
			Mrs Comfort Stevens
1923 (Summer)	NEAC		*The Chateau, Les Baux*
			St Rémy, Provence
1924 (Summer)	NEAC		*Vallée de la Fontaine*
1925 (Summer)	NEAC		*La Ville des Baux*
			The Gate, Les Baux
1925 (Autumn)	RGI		*Les Baux, Provence*
1926 (Summer)	NEAC		*Mas de Chevrier, Les Baux*
1926 (Summer)	RA		*Midsummer, Provence*
1926 (Autumn)	RGI		*Mas de Chevrier, Les Baux*
1927 (Winter)	NEAC		*Le Camp de Marius, Les Baux*
			Les Baux, Vue des Bringasses
1927 (Summer)	RA		*Le Cimetière Gallo-Romain, Les Baux*
1928 (Winter)	NEAC		*Les Baux*
			La Carrière des Grands Fonds, Les Baux
1928 (Autumn)	NEAC		*Les Baux, seen from Les Bringasses*
1929 (Spring)	NEAC		*The Town, Les Baux*

Acknowledgements

Thanks, as ever, to my agent Tim Bates at PFD and to George Morley and her team at Picador. It's a pleasure and a privilege to work with you. I am also grateful to Tim Binding, whose encyclopaedic knowledge of true crime was my gateway to Les Baux.

My largest debt of gratitude, however, is reserved for the Branson, fforde and McCrum families. Without your collective rummaging to unearth Olive's papers and other family ephemera, this book would not exist. Thank you all, especially Vanessa Branson, William fforde, Diana Briggs, Caroline Long and Tony Branson.

I am also deeply grateful to those in France who patiently answered my questions and shared their knowledge with me. Particular thanks go to Jean N'gonga of the Archives des Bouches-du-Rhône, to Cyril Dumas, curator of Les Baux, and to France de La Rocque of the Association des Amis de Jean Baltus. *Merci à tous*.

Back in Britain, a big thank you to Steve Griffiths for sharing his extensive research on Vernon Blake, to James Hannah for being an excellent sounding board, to Phil Stapleton for his insightful feedback, to Kate Innes for her underrated maths skills, and to Johnnie Stephens and Linda Francis for their help with tricky translations.

As this book was written under somewhat challenging personal circumstances, I'd also like to extend heartfelt thanks to Dr Emma Ping and Dr Stephen Lonsdale, to specialist nurse Pete Downer, and to neurologist John Bowen and his colleagues at the Royal Shrewsbury Hospital. Long live the NHS!

Long live, too, my wonderful husband Jim and all my family and friends. To echo Olive Branson: I often wish I hadn't been born a misfit, but you never make me feel like one.

Sources

Private Papers

Olive Branson's letters and papers are held in a private collection, as are the diaries of Mary Branson. The diaries of Jean Baltus have been preserved by the Association des Amis de Jean Baltus. The author is indebted to the custodians of all these for granting rare access.

Libraries and Archives

The judicial and police records relating to Olive Branson's death can be found at the Archives départementales des Bouches-du-Rhône in Marseille. The archives' online records (archives13.fr), including census and property data, were also indispensable in building a picture of Les Baux in the 1920s.

Further background information was gleaned from Gallica, the online repository of Bibliothèque nationale de France (gallica.bnf.fr), the genealogy site Geneanet (geneanet.org) and the Mémoire des Hommes archive from the Ministère des Armées, (www.memoiredeshommes.sga.defense.gouv.fr).

The British Foreign Office files relating to the case, though sparse, are housed at the National Archives, Kew.

Newspapers and Journals

The majority of French titles were accessed via the BNF's excellent RetroNews (retronews.fr). Other resources included Criminocorpus

(criminocorpus.org) and the digital collections of the Bibliothèque Méjanes at Aix (citedulivre-aix.com).

British newspapers were accessed via the British Library and the British Newspaper Archive (britishnewspaperarchive.co.uk), while art journals held at the National Art Library in the V & A were a rich resource for matters relating to the careers of both Olive Branson and Vernon Blake.

Bibliography

Agard, Walter R., 'Charloun of Paradou', *The North American Review* 226, no. 2 (1928): pp. 224–31.

Anon., ('J.C.'), 'Souvenirs d'un Gardien de Prison', *Police Magazine*, vol. 150 (1933): pp. 6–7.

Baring, Maurice, *The Puppet Show of Memory* (London: William Heinemann, 1922).

Baxter, Kay (née fforde), *Eighty Odd Years* (privately published, 1993).

Blake, Vernon, 'The Thrall of Rome', *Artwork*, vol. II, issue 7 (1926): p. 172.

Blake, Vernon, *Nor Rhone Nor Reason: Being Digressions Concerning Literature, Art, & Manners* (privately published, 1930).

Blanc, Eugène, *Le Drame des Baux et son Mystère* (Cavaillon: Imprimerie Mistral, 1929).

Branson, Olive (writing as Sarah Girdlestone), 'The Castle in Spain', *The Tramp* (1910): pp. 247–50.

Cavalier, Odile, *Rythmes, Lignes et Couleur: Oeuvres inédites de Vernon Blake* (Avignon: Musée Calvet, 2021).

Cheilan, C., *La Messe de Minuit des Baux: L'offrande des Bergers* (privately published, 1929).

Conseil général du département des Bouches-du-Rhône, *Rapports et délibérations: Deuxième Session Ordinaire 1929: Procès-Verbaux des Délibérations* (Marseille: 1929).

Forrest, Archibald Stevenson, *A Tour Through Old Provence* (London: Stanley Paul, 1911).

Griffiths, Steve, *Vernon Blake (1875–1930): Gearing Pioneer, Painter, Philosopher, Polymath*, Veteran-Cycle Club Cycling History

No. 3 (Brighton: John Pinkerton Memorial Publishing Fund, 2012).

Guibbal, Alexandre, 'Le Quintuple Assassinat de Valensole', *Revue internationale de criminologie et de police technique* VII, no. 1 (1953), pp. 1–19.

Hare, Augustus, *South-Eastern France* (London: George Allen, 1890).

Holroyd, Michael, *Augustus John: The New Biography* (London: Vintage, 1997).

Klotz, Roger, 'Un Élu Juif de Saint-Rémy-de-Provence: Daniel Millaud (1852–1940)', *Revue des Études juives* 165, no. 1–2 (2006): pp. 251–64.

Martel, Philippe, *Les Félibres et Leur Temps: Renaissance d'Oc et Opinion (1850–1914)* (Bordeaux: Presses Universitaires de Bordeaux, 2010).

Mistral, Frédéric, *Miréio / Mireille* (Paris: Charpentier Libraire-Éditeur, 1860).

Mistral, Frédéric, *Memoirs of Mistral*, translated by Constance E. Maud (London: Edward Arnold, 1907).

Munnings, Sir Alfred, *An Artist's Life* (London: Museum Press, 1950).

Thorpe, Sir Edward, *The Seine: From Havre to Paris (With Illustrations By Olive Branson)* (London: Macmillan, 1913).

Woolf, Virginia, 'Old Bloomsbury', in *Moments of Being: Autobiographical Writings*, edited by Jeanne Schulkind (London: Pimlico, 2002).

Notes

PART I

I

1 Walter R. Agard, 'Charloun of Paradou', *The North American Review* 226, no. 2 (1928), p. 225.

II

1 Rolland, Joseph, 'La vie dans les ruines des Baux', *Les Tablettes d'Avignon et de Provence*, 17 October 1926, pp. 2–3.

III

1 *Le Matin*, 18 January 1930, p. 4; *Le Radical de Vaucluse*, 18 January 1930, p. 5.

IV

1 See, for example, W. Egerton Powell, 'Personality in Art (Recent Art Exhibitions)', *Artwork*, Issue 8 (December 1926 – February 1927), pp. 206–7.

V

1 Maurice Baring, *The Puppet Show of Memory* (London: William Heinemann, 1922), p. 1.
2 Kay Baxter (née fforde), *Eighty Odd Years* (privately published, 1993), p. 3.
3 Sir Alfred Munnings, *An Artist's Life* (London: Museum Press, 1950), p. 287.
4 Virginia Woolf, 'Old Bloomsbury', in *Moments of Being*, ed. Jeanne Schulkind (London: Pimlico, 2002), p. 48.

5 Chelsea Art School advertisement in *The Art Journal* (1904), p. 69. For further information on the school, see Michael Holroyd's excellent biography of Augustus John.
6 Mary Branson's diary, 8 March 1906.
7 Letter from Charley Orro to OB, 27 April 1911.
8 Letter from OB to Kay fforde, 30 March 1925.
9 Letter from OB to Kay fforde, 13 August 1927.
10 Letter from AJ Munnings to OB, undated, but *c.* 1910.
11 Letter from 'Idalia', 53 Brighton Square, Rathgar, Nr Dublin, to OB, *c.* 1903–4.

VI

1 Augustus J. C. Hare, *South-Eastern France* (London: George Allen, 1890), p. 409.
2 Letter from OB to Kay fforde, 13 September 1926.
3 'Une Lettre de M. Escoffier', *Les Tablettes d'Avignon et de Provence*, 10 March 1928, p. 5.
4 Frédéric Mistral, *Memoirs of Mistral*, trans. Constance E. Maud (London: Edward Arnold, 1907), p. 166.
5 Philippe Martel, *Les félibres et leur temps: renaissance d'oc et opinion (1850–1914)* (Bordeaux: Presses Universitaires de Bordeaux, 2010), p. 178.
6 Mistral, *Memoirs*, p. 1.
7 Frédéric Mistral, *Miréio* (Avignon: J. Roumanille, 1860), Canto III.
8 *Le Croix de Provence*, 5 May 1929, p. 3.

VII

1 Letter from OB to Kay fforde, February 1924.

PART II

I

1 Letter from Arthur Brownlow fforde to OB, 20 May 1910.
2 Letter from OB to May fforde, 14 January 1928.

3   Letter from Kay fforde to her parents, 11 April 1926.
4   Letter from Kay fforde to her brother, Arthur Frederick Brownlow fforde, undated.
5   Letter from OB to Kay fforde, 30 March 1925.
6   Letter from OB to Phyll fforde, 6 April 1929.
7   Kay Baxter (née fforde), *Eighty Odd Years* (privately published, 1993), pp. 52–3.
8   Letter from OB to May fforde, 6 March 1929.
9   *L'Humanité*, 18 January 1930, p. 2.
10 Letter from OB to May fforde, 15 March 1928.
11 Letter from OB to May fforde, 6 March 1929.
12 Letter from OB to May fforde, 22 February 1928.
13 Baxter, *Eighty Odd Years*, p. 52.
14 *Le Petit Marseillais*, 30 April 1929, p. 1.

II

1   *Le Petit Provençal*, 17 December 1927, p. 3; 6 February 1929, p. 3.
2   Alexandre Guibbal, 'Le Quintuple Assassinat de Valensole', *Revue internationale de criminologie et de police technique*, vol. VII, no. 1, janvier–mars 1953, p. 11.
3   Guibbal, p. 11.
4   Guibbal, pp. 7–9.
5   Letter from OB to May fforde, 21 April 1929.
6   Archibald Stevenson Forrest, *A Tour Through Old Provence*, Stanley Paul, 1911, p. 130.
7   Forrest, p. 130.
8   Letter from OB to May fforde, 2 January 1929.

IV

1   *Le Petit Provençal*, 4 January 1929, p. 3.
2   Letter from OB to May fforde, 18 October 1926.
3   Letter from OB to Kay fforde, 18 November 1925.
4   Letter from OB to Kay fforde, 13 September 1926.

5   Letters from OB to May fforde, 9 July 1927; 18 February 1928.
6   Letter from OB to May fforde, 2 January 1929.
7   Letter from OB to May fforde, 22 February 1928.
8   Letter from OB to May fforde, 2 January 1929.
9   Letter from OB to Kay fforde, 30 March 1925.
10 Letter from OB to May fforde, 21 October 1926.
11 Letter from OB to May fforde, July 1927.
12 Letter from OB to May fforde, 2 January 1929.
13 For more information on Vernon Blake, see Steve Griffith's *Vernon Blake (1875–1930): Gearing Pioneer, Painter, Philosopher, Polymath* (John Pinkerton Memorial Publishing Fund, 2012), and Odile Cavalier's *Rythmes, Lignes et Couleur: Oeuvres inédites de Vernon Blake* (Avignon: Musée Calvet, 2021).
14 Vernon Blake, 'The Thrall of Rome', *Artwork*, vol. 2, issue 7, summer 1926, p. 172.
15 Letter from OB to May fforde, 22 February 1928.
16 Letter from OB to May fforde, 22 February 1928.
17 Letter from OB to May fforde, 22 February 1928.

V

1   *Daily News*, 6 May 1929, p. 10.
2   Letter from OB to May fforde, January 1928.
3   *Manchester Guardian*, 11 May 1929, p. 1.
4   *Daily News*, 1 May 1929, p. 9.
5   *Evening Standard*, 2 May 1929, p. 17.
6   *Daily News*, 3 May 1929, p. 7.
7   *London Gazette*, Second Supplement, 24 May 1918, p. 6175.
8   *Evening Standard*, 4 May 1929, p. 11
9   *Daily News*, 6 May 1929, p. 9.
10 OB diary, 1 November 1922.
11 *Daily Express*, 6 May 1929, p. 1.

VII

1. *Petit Marseillais*, 22 March 1929, p. 6.

PART III

I

1. Letter from OB to Kay fforde, undated.
2. Letter from OB to May fforde, 15 October 1926.
3. Letter from OB to Kay fforde, 13 September 1926.
4. Letter from OB to May fforde, 6 March 1929.
5. *Daily News*, 16 May 1929, p. 7.
6. Letter from OB to May fforde, 18 February 1928.
7. Letter from OB to May fforde, 15 March 1928.
8. Partial letter from OB to unknown, January 1928.
9. Letter from OB to May fforde, 14 January 1928.
10. Letter from OB to May fforde, 18 February 1928.

II

1. Letter from OB to Sir George Branson, 4 January 1929.
2. Louis Forest, 'Propos d'un Parisien: "Honnestes Dames"', *Le Matin*, 9 May 1929, p. 1.
3. *Daily News*, 7 May 1929, p. 9.
4. *Weekly Dispatch*, 12 May 1929, p. 9.
5. 'Miss April Day's Dark Career', *John Bull*, 29 March 1930, p. 9.
6. *Daily News*, 8 May 1929, p. 10.
7. *The Era*, 31 August 1895, p. 23.
8. Letter from Arthur Ransome to OB, 25 July 1908.
9. Letter from Edith Wolfe to OB, 9 November 1908.
10. Letters to OB from Sir George Branson and May fforde, 6 December 1908.
11. Olive Branson (writing as Sarah Girdlestone), 'The Castle in Spain', *The Tramp*, May 1910, pp. 247–50.

III

1. Georges Béroud, curriculum vitae, 1927.
2. *Daily News*, 17 May 1929, p. 7.

IV

1. J.C., 'Souvenirs d'un gardien de prison', *Police Magazine*, vol. 150, 8 October 1933, pp. 6–7.
2. Letter from François Pinet to Madeleine Vayssière, 20 May 1929, quoted in Eugène Blanc, *Le Drame des Baux et son Mystère* (Cavaillon: Imprimerie Mistral, 1929), p. 34.
3. Letter from François Pinet to Marie-Thérèse Girard, 26 May 1929.

IV

1. *Auckland Star*, 20 July 1929.
2. Letter from OB to May fforde, 4 February 1929.

PART IV

I

1. Partial letter from OB to Kay fforde, undated.
2. *L'Intransigeant*, 24 July 1933, p. 3.
3. Letter from OB to Kay fforde, 13 September 1926.
4. Letter from OB to May fforde, 9 July 1927.
5. Letter from OB to May fforde, 20 August 1927.
6. Walter R. Agard, 'Charloun of Paradou', *The North American Review* 226, no. 2 (1928), p. 227.
7. Letter from OB to May fforde, 8 August 1927.
8. Letter from OB to May fforde, 11 August 1927.
9. Letter from OB to Kay fforde, 30 March 1925.
10. Letter from OB to Kay fforde, 30 March 1925.
11. Letter from OB to Kay fforde, 30 March 1925.
12. Letter from William Branson to OB, 18 June 1928.
13. Letter from William Branson to OB, 17 December 1928.

II

1. Letter to Auguste Rol from Daniel Millaud, Alfred Maury, Michel Durand and Joseph Ricaud, 23 July 1929.
2. Letter from Léopold Fabrega to Félix Martin, 3 June 1929.
3. Letter from Georges Arlaud to Joseph Rochu, 2 July 1929.
4. Letter from Georges Arlaud to Hilaire Delfini, prefect of Bouches-du-Rhône, 19 July 1929.

IV

1. Conseil général du département des Bouches-du-Rhône, *Rapports et délibérations: Deuxième Session Ordinaire 1929: Procès-Verbaux des Délibérations*, p. 26.
2. Eugène Blanc, *Le Drame des Baux et son Mystère* (Cavaillon: Imprimerie Mistral, 1929), p. 15.
3. *Délibérations du Conseil Général des Bouches-du-Rhône*, quoted in Roger Klotz, 'Un Élu Juif de Saint-Rémy-de-Provence: Daniel Millaud (1852–1940)', *Revue des Études juives*, 165 (1–2), January–June 2006, pp. 251–64.
4. Blanc, p. 32.
5. Blanc, pp. 31–4.
6. Blanc, pp. 34–5.
7. Blanc, p. 35.
8. *Les Tablettes d'Avignon et de Provence*, 15 June 1929, p. 15.

V

1. Blanc, *Le Drame des Baux et Son Mystère* (Cavaillon: Imprimerie Mistral, 1929), pp. 39–40.
2. Blanc, p. 52.
3. Blanc, p. 59.
4. Blanc, p. 69.
5. Blanc, p. 57.
6. Blanc, pp. 66–7.

VI

1. Blanc, *Le Drame des Baux et Son Mystère* (Cavaillon: Imprimerie Mistral, 1929), p. 9.
2. Blanc, p. 74.
3. Blanc, p. 48.
4. Blanc, p. 84.
5. Blanc, pp. 85–6.
6. Blanc, p. 69 and p. 48.
7. Blanc, p. 23.
8. Blanc, p. 87.
9. Blanc, pp. 87–8.
10. Blanc, p. 37.
11. Blanc, p. 88.
12. Blanc, p. 89.

PART V

I

1. Joseph Rolland, 'La vie dans les ruines des Baux', *Les Tablettes d'Avignon et de Provence*, 17 October 1926, p. 2.
2. Vernon Blake, *Nor Rhone Nor Reason: Being Digressions Concerning Literature, Art, & Manners* (privately published, 1930), p. 166.
3. Blake, p. 169.
4. Blake, p. 170.
5. Blake, p. 169.
6. Blake, p. 8.
7. Blake, pp. 201–2.
8. Blake, p. 223.
9. Blake, p. 170.
10. Letter from OB to May fforde, 2 January 1929.
11. Letter from OB to May fforde, 2 January 1929.
12. Letter from OB to May fforde, 2 January 1929.

13 Letter from OB to May fforde, 2 January 1929.
14 Letter from OB to May fforde, 2 January 1929.
15 Letter from OB to May fforde, 2 January 1929.
16 Letter from OB to May fforde, 2 January 1929.
17 *Le Radical de Vaucluse*, 4 October 1929, p. 2.

IV

1 *Le Petit Journal*, 19 January 1930, p. 1.
2 *The Scotsman*, 25 February 1946, p. 4.
3 Letter from OB to May fforde, 14 January 1928.

Picture Acknowledgements

13 Photograph of Les Baux in 1929: by courtesy of the author.
18 Cover of *Détective* magazine, 16 May 1929: Bibliothèque des Littératures Policières, Ville de Paris.
19 Police photograph of Mas de Chiscale, May 1929 (exterior): Archives départementales des Bouches-du-Rhône.
31 Olive Branson's identity card: Archives départementales des Bouches-du-Rhône.
39 Photograph of Jean Baltus: Association des amis de Jean Baltus, Wikicommons.
46 Photographs of Olive Branson with her dolls and cousin William: from a private collection.
46 Photograph of Olive Branson with her family: from a private collection.
53 Pencil sketch of circus performers by Olive Branson (original in colour): by courtesy of the author.
54 Photograph of Olive Branson at the Calderon Summer School: from a private collection.
63 Photograph of the Hotel Monte-Carlo: Topfoto.
65 Photograph of Madame Pinet, François Pinet and Madeleine Vayssière: Shutterstock.
93 *Le Petit Marseillais*, 30 April 1929: Archives départementales des Bouches-du-Rhône.
106 Pen and wash drawing of a sleeping greyhound by Olive Branson (original in colour): The Maas Gallery.
114 Photograph of Dr Georges Béroud and Alexandre Guibbal at the cistern: Shutterstock.
112 Police photograph of Mas de Chiscale (bedroom): Archives départementales des Bouches-du-Rhône.

113 Police photograph of Mas de Chiscale (studio): Archives départementales des Bouches-du-Rhône.
114 Police photograph of Mas de Chiscale (kitchen): Archives départementales des Bouches-du-Rhône.
147 *Daily Sketch*, 6 May 1929: Cambridge University Library.
150 *Evening Standard*, 4 May 1929: Cambridge University Library.
159 Photograph of Alexandre Guibbal, François Pinet, Inspector Antonin Laforgue at Mas de Chiscale: Topfoto.
196 Photograph of Jack Gorman, Olive Branson and Spring with her caravan: from a private collection.
203 Sketch by Olive Branson from *The Tramp*: Cambridge University Library.
252 Pencil sketch of François Pinet by Olive Branson: Topfoto.
253 Pen and ink drawing of Les Baux by Olive Branson: by courtesy of Ewbank's Auction House
310 Photograph of François Pinet and Jean Dorlhac de Borne in court, Aix-en-Provence, January 1930: Shutterstock.
315 Photograph of Advocate General Boissier, Dr Georges Béroud and President Lafont in court, Aix-en-Provence, January 1930: Shutterstock.
317 Photograph of Dr Pierre Cot in court, Aix-en-Provence, January 1930: Shutterstock.
339 *Lancashire Daily Post*, 18 January 1930.